D1034567

DISCARDED

Poets & People

Poets & People

by Charles Norman

The Bobbs-Merrill Company, Inc.
Indianapolis / New York

COLLEGE OF THE SEQUOIAS
LIBRARY

The Bobbs-Merrill Company, Inc.
Indianapolis • New York

Copyright © 1972 by Charles Norman
All rights reserved
Library of Congress Catalogue Card Number 71-161251
Manufactured in the United States of America

Some brief excerpts from this book have appeared in the *Literary Review* and *Texas Quarterly*.

Lines from *The Rivals* reprinted with permission of The Macmillan Company from *Collected Poems* by James Stephens. Copyright 1915 by The Macmillan Company, renewed 1943 by James Stephens.

Lines from *To an Isle in the Water* reprinted with permission of The Macmillan Company from *Collected Poems* by William Butler Yeats. Copyright 1906 by The Macmillan Company, renewed 1934 by William Butler Yeats.

Feather by Francesco Bianco copyright 1957 by Fairleigh Dickinson University, copyright 1966 by Francesco M. Bianco.

No. 28 of *73 Poems* copyright 1963 by Marion Morehouse Cummings. Reprinted from *73 Poems* by E. E. Cummings by permission of Harcourt Brace Jovanovich, Inc.

To R. L. De Wilton

List of Illustrations

Foreword

I went to live in Greenwich Village in the summer of 1924. Washington Square was leafy and serene, and not unlike its description by Henry James in the novel of that name. There was sky instead of skyline, and the eighteenth and nineteenth centuries still lingered in adjacent streets.

The house where I first lived is still standing, on Waverly Place. One of my brothers deposited me in front of it with this advice: "Don't write letters to women, and don't have anything to do with a woman in the same house." His wise look went with him as he drove away, leaving me on the sidewalk with a suitcase and a bundle of books. I forgot the second part of his advice that night, and failed to observe the first in the not distant future. But at the moment he left me I was full of high resolves and rejoiced exceedingly over my spiritual state. I was young, I was a poet, I was in Greenwich Village.

In addition, I had a patron. He was James Buell Munn, a dean at New York University, chairman of its entrance board, and afterwards head of the Department of English at Harvard, his alma mater. I remember him with gratitude.

Dr. Munn, of course, had cautioned me against expecting quick or sudden fame. "There is no spectacular element in your writing to catch the public's fancy," he told me; "if there were, perhaps I should not be interested." The reader will understand when I say I did not believe this; I was sure that Fame, even then, waited to enfold me in her strong wings. But perhaps Fame is masculine; in which case I can do without the enfolding.

Here, I think I can honestly say that the only poet I ever envied was Countée Cullen, who had been my schoolmate. One day, when I praised his work, he told me there was nothing of his already published that he could not have improved if he had wanted to. I received an impression of immense talent which I would be unable to overtake or match. He said it without vanity, without self-consciousness, in his soft, sincere, melodious voice. He excelled me in other things—he was Phi Beta Kappa.

I left the reader on Waverly Place. Upstairs, at no. 146, there was a two-room apartment which I had rented. The furniture was of mixed periods—basement and auction. A table in the middle of the living room was draped with a fringed shawl. A lamp in a corner dripped beads. There were two mismatched chairs—one, of wicker that had sagged, gripped me like a vise; the other showed springs and stuffing under a bedraggled flounce. The white-haired landlady told me there were other things in the cellar, should I need them; she also told me that her husband, who had left her, wrote poetry. She showed me his book. Its title was *Nightshade*.

Next to my apartment was a hall bedroom. As I re-arranged the furniture, I heard through the wall the music of a guitar. The guitar player was a woman; her door was open, and I saw her several times. It began with greetings and ended in conversation on her couch—there was no other place to sit. She offered to play for me. Her music had charms. I cannot honestly say she was mysterious or ravishing. She was a healthy, not very subtle single woman, perhaps a divorced one. She put the guitar aside and closed the door. About a week later she moved. I regret to say I was relieved. I had thought of moving myself.

I never moved with the frequency of some of my friends.

Over the years, however, I lived on many Village streets. I give some of their names here because they were useful to me in writing this book and may be evocative for certain readers: Gay Street, Grove Street, Patchin Place, Bedford Street, Perry Street, West 11th, and East 11th.

Before I began to write I was faced with a choice between autobiography and reminiscence. The former would have included the latter, but a certain rigidity of structure seemed inevitable. I chose reminiscence as being more interesting as well as more malleable, but have been unable to avoid some autobiographical details. Perhaps it will be said there are not enough of them. But this is not an autobiography. I cheerfully leave household chronicles to others and predict that the supply will continue to be plentiful.

As one must begin somewhere, I have chosen to begin with the signal year, 1925, when I was twenty-one years old. The pattern of my life seems well established in that year. It has been observed that patterns are established much earlier, and as a concession I have given the essential background, which is that of a young man with a certain occupation, in a certain place at a certain time. There are no flashbacks—a device I find unimaginative and tedious—in my narrative. I occasionally indulge in a prolepsis, or leap forward.

As the reader may be surprised over my reactions when seemingly small sums came my way, something should be said here about the money of the twenties. My rent, for example, was forty dollars a month; complete luncheons— soup, roast beef, potato and carrots, pie and coffee—could be had for thirty-five cents, and dinners for fifty or sixty-five cents, except in the more elegant Village speakeasies where the food was better and dinner cost a dollar. And you could go abroad, on a great liner, for a hundred dollars.

I can recall my first bottle of bootleg liquor. A painter I knew, perhaps De Hirsh Margules, instructed me in the ritual I was to follow to make my purchase. I went to an Italian grocer's near Sheridan Square, whispered my friend's name, wrote my own in a ledger under many others, and saw the proprietor open a trapdoor and disappear. He emerged with a bottle; I paid him and started back, already intoxicated, perhaps over my daring deed. I have never since, in fact, experienced so complete an inebriation as when I floated along those Village streets that day, the uncorked bottle cradled in my arm. It was a bottle of muscatel.

As for my daily routine, my existence was really an idyllic one. I used to sit, after breakfast, on a bench under the towering English elm in Washington Square, at the junction of Waverly and MacDougal, thinking of lines for the narrative poem I was writing, or of nothing. In that whole region there was only one building higher than five stories, and that was the main building of New York University on the corner of Waverly and University Place. The park stretched empty and silent to its four corners. The record of my other activities will be found in the pages that follow.

I cannot say I have reached any profound conclusions. Yet this book contains a multitude of experiences. Have I learned anything? Yes—the only poets and people to distrust are those with answers. I also distrust certain types of intellectuals who, whenever they get hold of a literary publication, promptly turn it into a political one. Why? Because they have answers.

I have tried not to be a bore. If, in some places, readers find me unbearably conceited, in others they will see unmistakable signs of idiocy to fortify their self-esteem. It balances out.

Poets & People

Chapter One

1

Hervey Allen was a big, blond man who was to become especially known for one of the three novels which astonished an earlier generation by their size. The other two were *Look Homeward, Angel,* which preceded *Anthony Adverse,* and *Gone With the Wind,* which followed it. Two of these books I have never read.

At the time I met Allen, he was at work on a biography of Poe. He lived on Riverside Drive in an apartment thronged with massive furniture and books. My first evening there was memorable. I rode uptown on a double-decker bus through the nightfall city strung with lamps. The ride up Fifth Avenue, through West 57th Street, and along the Drive was swift and accompanied by a swishing sound, as of a liner at sea. The fare was a dime, collected not by the driver but by a conductor.

Another guest was present when I arrived. He was Du-

Bose Heyward, whom I had not met before. I knew, however, that he was a poet. His first book, *Carolina Chansons: Legends of the Low Country,* had been a joint production with Allen, and he had followed it with a collection of his own, *Skylines and Horizons.* He was a slender, neatly dressed man with thin wrists and ankles—shy, polite, and strangely intense; in the dim-lit room where we sat and talked he seemed to glow like a filament. Allen was more assured than either of his guests. Harper had recently published his *Earth Moods and Other Poems;* he exhibited a copy with indignation, bidding us examine the paper, and complaining that it would not last fifty years. I heard him with admiration and awe.

Over dinner, in an aside, he asked me if I belonged to the Poetry Society of America. The question surprised me. It had never occurred to me that I could join. When I replied that I did not he merely said, "Should. Do you lots of good," and addressed himself once more to Heyward.

After dinner, Allen told us something about the important work in progress, which he was to call *Israfel.* He had received from his typist that day a new batch of typed material, and now proposed to read some of it aloud. Heyward and I were eager to listen. Heyward, of course, was his friend; I found it flattering—Allen, after all, was an established author, and I was being treated as an equal. I believe it is the only time I have enjoyed listening to another writer read. Two recollections remain. One was Allen's comment on a famous stanza:

> Lo! in yon brilliant window-niche
> > How statue-like I see thee stand!
> > The agate lamp within thy hand,
> Ah! Psyche, from the regions which
> > Are Holy Land!

He was certain that Poe, arriving one day at dusk at the house of Mrs. Helen Stannard in Richmond, had seen her from the doorway raising the lighted lamp to place in the window niche. It seemed plausible.

In addition to writing the life of Poe, Allen was assembling the illustrations. One of those he now passed around. It was a photograph of a painting. When Heyward and I had looked at it, Allen asked: "Do you see anything strange in that portrait?" I looked again. I could think of nothing. Heyward said: "The eyes."

"That's it! that's just it!" exclaimed Allen. He was full of excitement. "The portrait is of Virginia Clemm Poe. She was dead when it was painted. Poe would not allow her to be buried without having a portrait of her. Her eyes had to be propped open."

Mr. Heyward left early, perhaps around ten o'clock. As soon as the door had closed behind him, Allen beckoned me. He led me to a high cupboard, from the top of which he took down a slender book. Handing it over, he exclaimed: "I hope to God it goes!" It was an advance copy of *Porgy,* published a month or two later.

Not long after the dinner, I received an invitation to attend the next meeting of the Poetry Society of America. The paper was of a dazzling whiteness, the welcoming sentences felicitous and friendly. I was sure that my star was in the ascendant, that all good things would flow from my belonging to so august a body and attending its deliberations with a host of celebrities. I went.

2

The Poetry Society met once a month at the National Arts Club on Gramercy Park. In a room which seemed vast as a ballroom several hundred men and women sat in long rows on folding wooden chairs. Above the murmur of their voices hovered a silent storm of tulle and net veils and scarves. A famous poet was to read that evening, and three-fourths of the members and their friends were in evening dress. I was not. I found a seat somewhere in the middle behind a poet I knew, who was as tweedy as myself. His name was Clement Wood. He was vain, something of a bully, and feared. I asked him once how he had hit on *Eagle Sonnets,* a title much admired, and much envied, and he explained that the typesetter on the *Nation* had misread the word "Eight"; when Wood saw it in proof, he had thought it too good to change.

Down front, facing the audience, seated or standing, were several well-known poets, among them two women, one of them shyly peering at the throng from her hive of hair, the beautiful Elinor Wylie, and Leonora Speyer—tall, imperious, flushed, in a low-cut gown, bare shoulders powdered and scarved—who gazed at the nameless horde through a lorgnette.

The president of the Poetry Society was Charles Hanson Towne, who now appeared on the platform above the cluster of poets. His step was buoyant, his bearing distinguished. He wore tails. He arrested the polite scatter of applause with a practiced, deprecating hand, and proceeded to introduce the guest of the evening, the Irish poet James Stephens, author of *The Crock of Gold*. Mr. Towne withdrew.

Mr. Stephens was one of the smallest men I have ever seen, with a large, completely bald head, so that to my enchanted eyes he looked precisely like one of the leprechauns about whom he wrote. He read in a high, singsong voice, and everything he read sounded like a dirge or a chant, his body swaying, his eyes closed. Of the poems he read that evening one of them stayed with me through the years; it was called *The Rivals*.

> I heard a bird at dawn
> Singing sweetly on a tree

is the way it began, and it ends,

> I was singing all the time,
> Just as prettily as he,

which was easy to believe, seeing him there, swaying and singing, every word clear through the singsong melody. The applause was loud and long. Mr. Stephens left, and Mr. Towne reappeared. I had started to get up, thinking it was all over, but sank back into my seat. There was more poetry to come, though not from Mr. Stephens. The next order of business, Mr. Towne said, would be the reading of poems submitted by members. Another lady with a lorgnette, the official reader, stood up in full view.

The poems by members were submitted unsigned, with an envelope within an envelope containing the author's name. From the several score of poems submitted each month, a committee selected some ten or twenty for reading and discussion. Raising the lorgnette to her eyes, then withdrawing it about two inches, the lady with the lorgnette read, with professional competence, a succession of poems, many of them in free verse, since that was the vogue, and after each reading the floor was thrown open for discussion. Several poets commented. A clergyman asked, with a clerical quaver, "Why, oh why, can we not have poems written as they were thirty years ago?" Mr. Towne recognized the next speaker, and the clergyman received an answer.

Turning my head with the others, I saw, near the door, a gaunt figure in a shabby brown suit, clasping to his breast a soiled manila envelope. He stood there, patient and contemptuous, his thin face framed by yellow hair, until the squirming and whispering ceased, then asked slowly, with a clicking sound after every other word: "Will some of these infinitesimally small human atoms please desist?" Hisses flowed toward him like a horizontal rain. Many of those present had heard similar utterances before. He sat down, grinning with satisfaction, his grin revealing large, discolored teeth between which he now stuck an empty corncob pipe, making loud, sucking noises of utter gratification.

His name was Maxwell Bodenheim. He was the author

of a famous book of poems, *Minna and Myself,* with an introduction by Louis Untermeyer. I had met him once. His wife, Minna, introduced us in Joseph Kling's International Book & Art Shop, on Christopher Street, where I had met her; she was skinny, but forceful. Meeting her again, I was reproached for "not having shown enough respect to America's greatest poet." But what more I could have done than say "Hello" and "Pleased to meet you" I do not know; shyness kept me from saying more, and my own estimate of his abilities was, in any case, different. My second meeting with him was disastrous.

There was relief when the reading was resumed. This time the poem was in rhyme; it was, in fact, a sonnet. It told of two pioneers, a man and a woman, presumably husband and wife, who had reached a far frontier. The man was working in the field, the woman stood in the doorway of their cabin listening, said the last line, "To the illimitable sound of wheat." The applause was greatest for this poem; the poetess who had written it—Gwendolen Haste—beamed, with good reason.

In front of me, Clement Wood had been busily making notes on a pad on his knee. He now raised his hand and got the floor.

"This is a better poem than we have been used to hearing," he began. There were nods of approval. "However," he went on, and now his voice took on that booming, bullying quality which had struck terror in many a poetic bosom in the past, "there is a basic flaw which I must point out." There were looks of consternation. What could it be? "Wheat," he said, "takes"—here, he glanced at his notes—"months, sometimes years, of tilling the ground, sowing, waiting for the ripening grain. If the two persons in the sonnet are actually pioneers on a far frontier, the woman could not have been listening to the sound of wheat."

He glanced modestly around, and sat down.

I raised my hand, Mr. Towne recognized me, and I stood up. Almost immediately I wished I had not. My heart was beating at an unaccustomed rate, and my knees were wobbly.

"I think," I said, "Mr. Wood is mistaken." He turned to glare up at me. "A far frontier is the last place one has arrived at, and one may be there many years. It would still be a far frontier."

I sat down, and Mr. Wood jumped up. His face was flushed, and he was obviously angry. His voice boomed forth.

"Mr. Chairman," boomed that voice, edged now with anger and hurt pride, "according to parliamentary procedure the name of the previous speaker is never mentioned. He is referred to as the previous speaker."

To the man next to me, who flinched from my utterance, I whispered: "What an ass!" But it did not come out as a whisper. It was heard by all. There was pandemonium. All over that vast chamber there was a bobbing of heads, a flutter of scarves, and startled faces peering at me. Mrs. Speyer had been one of the first to react; for hardly were the words out when she had leapt from her chair and rushed to the edge of the platform to inform Mr. Towne, who peered down anxiously.

"Did you hear what he said? Did you hear what he said?" she exclaimed. "He called him an ass!"

I myself was unable to move, and could scarcely breathe.

Mr. Towne held up his hand for silence. Members sank back into their seats. A great stillness reigned. I was red-haired, and conspicuous.

"Young man," Mr. Towne began, addressing me. "If we are to proceed, I am afraid you will have to apologize to Mr. Wood."

He spoke with admirable restraint, which I regret to say I entirely lacked. I stood up again, but had to hold on to the back of Mr. Wood's chair.

"Mr. Chairman," I said. "I came here thinking this was a place where people were interested in poetry. Far from apologizing to anyone, I prefer to resign."

"Resignation accepted," said Mr. Towne, more hastily

than I thought warranted, and banged his gavel with un-wonted force. The lady with the lorgnette stood up to read again. I wanted to leave, but found it simpler to sit still. My knees.

Hervey Allen was not present at this meeting. If he ever heard of the incident he kept it to himself. I have never been back.

Mr. Wood went on to write on many subjects, not all of them dealing with poetry, history or philosophy; he also wrote about the pleasures of flagellation, and was rumored to keep a whipping establishment. One night, not long after the Poetry Society meeting, while wandering around in Greenwich Village, dateless and idle as could be, I came to his house. On an impulse, greatly desiring company, I rang his bell. He came to the door, which he barely opened, and seeing who it was, shut it again quickly. A party was in progress.

As for Bodenheim, I rather admired his independence, considering how much it cost him, for he wrote better than the poets he excoriated, although some of them had better manners. I was walking with a friend one day when I saw him approaching and raised my hat. His greeting was a grin. She said, "Why do you say hello to that bastard? I loathe him." I tried to defend him. After all, I told her, he had writ-ten some good things, and allowance must be made for that; he could not be all bad. Several days later I was in the Wash-ington Square Book Shop, on 8th Street, when Bodenheim came in. He was sucking on his empty corncob pipe, but took it out of his mouth to address me.

"How come," he said, in that slow, clicking, deliberate, half-grinning, half-contemptuous way he had, "I saw you with one of my former mistresses the other day?"

Rage seized me. I doubled up my fists. I said, in much too loud a voice, so that everyone in the shop turned their heads, that if he ever mentioned her again in my presence, I would kill him. Bodenheim stared at me as though stunned. An extraordinary phenomenon took place, which I have never seen again. Both of his ears turned white. Then, as though ducking a blow, he spun around and ran from the shop.

In the end, it was not I who killed him. Years later— years of small triumphs followed by years of degradation, in which he scrawled impromptu verses in Village bars for fifty cents or a drink—he was shot to death by a crazy friend, who also killed the woman Bodenheim was living with. I saw him the night he was killed. He emerged from a cafeteria on Sixth Avenue to wave to a man across the street, who waved back. I have always thought it was the man who shot him several hours later.

3

It was John Farrar who introduced me to Hervey Allen in the offices of the *Bookman,* a literary monthly of the time in which many of my poems appeared. Mr. Farrar, who was only eight years older than I, had the old-fashioned notion that new writers could be, or should be, helped on the road to fame by older and more established ones. He introduced me to several; he even sent me to call on Louis Untermeyer, with a folder full of poems, old and new, under my arm. I cannot say with precision how many editions of Mr. Untermeyer's anthologies there have been since that time and this, but I have never appeared in any of them.

Through Farrar I also met Henry Beston, from whom, a week or so later, I received a warm, amusing letter full of Latin embellishments. It was an invitation to visit him in

Massachusetts—not for a weekend, but two weeks. It was summer; my friendship with the young woman who loathed Bodenheim was over, or on the wane, and I accepted.

Beston was sixteen years older than I—a tall, restless, handsome man, and a bachelor. He afterwards married the poet Elizabeth Coatsworth. He had been born in Quincy, attended Harvard and the University of Lyons, and was as much at home abroad as in his native Massachusetts or New York; he was, in fact, a type, almost even of the generation, of those worldly provincials portrayed by Henry James. I have often pondered the secret of their charm; one is at ease with them, even when they are strangers. Is it a non-competitive aura? The type is not confined to the Eastern seaboard.

Beston's home was at Eastham, between Cape Cod Bay and the Atlantic. He had written to say that the best train was the one arriving at eight o'clock at night, and that dinner would be held up for me; it may be that he wrote "supper." Waiting for me at the Orleans station were Beston and the overseer of his farm. They had come in a truck. In went my suitcase, up I clambered, and we drove away.

We arrived at Beston's house and were greeted by the overseer's wife, who had prepared our meal. I saw a trestle table on which were three huge buckets, heaped to the brims with steamed clams. I followed Beston upstairs with depressed feelings. I was hungry, but not for steamed clams. I had never eaten them. I did not eat them that night. I have never eaten them. Beston, having deposited my suitcase, explained jovially that we would all feast on steamed clams, then top them off with hot apple pie and milk. When we returned to the dining room I had a plan.

I said I was too exhausted to eat very much, and that apple pie and milk would suit me fine, and would I please be forgiven if I did not attempt more? There were incredulous looks—what, not eat steamed clams? But nothing was said. I was given a generous helping of pie, a large glass of milk, and the four of us commenced eating. The three buckets were dispatched by the time I finished my pie. It was like a corn-shucking contest. If only their little necks didn't stick out so! The room was redolent of steamed clams and the sea.

The sea! At ten o'clock, Beston led me to the great beach fronting the North Atlantic.

We walked in utter darkness. There were no lights anywhere, not even stars. Huge shapes swarmed forth to meet us, somewhat on the moist side, then receded but still hemmed us in. I had begun to wonder where the sea was, when we came to a rise in the ground; I heard a low, continuous roar, and felt rolling over us the salt combers of the air. We stood at the top of the rise, and there below us was a vast beach; light dwelt there—on the dunes, on the water, and in the sky. We ran down to the water's edge.

Offshore, the sea heaved and undulated, massed and formed, rolling, toppling, receding, then trailing its lace of foam on the firm-packed sand. From time to time a wave huger than the rest rolled landward without pause, depositing a long line of glittering fish high on the beach.

I do not recollect anything I said that night. Perhaps I was awestruck. Beston, on the other hand, was transformed. He shouted, he sang, he quoted Horace and Virgil—in Latin —and he talked. Sitting on the dunes, or walking with great strides up and down the length of the beach, he kept up an unceasing commentary. He had been in the American Field Service with the French army in World War I and had an astonishing repertoire of *poilu* songs. He also knew a great many chanties. One of these he sang many times; he had a good voice, and the words of that song on the beach were beautiful and haunting:

> A long time, and a very long time, a long time ago,
> I made up my mind to go to sea,
> A long time ago. . . .

I was living abroad when Beston had the memorable experience recorded in *The Outermost House,* his journal of a year's residence on the outer dunes of Eastham. The house in which he wrote it is now a national literary monument. I married—he married; great distances separated us, particularly when he went to live in Maine. It is difficult to keep friendship in repair.

4

Farrar was the most generous of editors. You could bring a poem to him, and he would read it, then call up the treasurer to make out a check; you waited, almost overcome by joy and pride, all the while regaled by his talk of the literary world, the problems of running a magazine, his own desire to continue writing poetry. He was also a generous friend. He gave me the unbound pages of Amy Lowell's *John Keats,* which she had sent him in advance of publication, and I had them bound in blue calf. It was a two-volume work, but the index was so immense that I had it bound separately. How beautiful that three-decker looked on my shelf! I sold it when I was short of money.

Once he took me to dine with him at the Yale Club, which was then on West 44th Street, and although it was during Prohibition, we had some drinks at the bar; they may have been soft drinks, but somehow I doubt it.

At the bar he explained the theory of the left hand, how we are all born with certain things which the left hand delineates, but the right hand reveals what we have made of ourselves; and indeed, when he displayed his hands, there was a remarkable difference.

"I was born with a weak left hand," he said, "but my right is strong—I have made it that way."

From hands he went into genealogy; his forebears had come over on the *Mayflower,* or perhaps he said the *Lion,* the second ship, and he told me the story about Will Rogers who, when asked if his ancestors had come over in the *Mayflower,* replied "No, they went down to meet the boat." My own hands were square, with blunt fingers, and appeared to me to be quite similar; they still do, but perhaps to a practiced eye there is a difference. As for my ancestors, none of them "came over" when it counted; my mother brought me, together with five other children, and my father met us with his eldest sons at the Battery. Often, when walking there, I have tried to pick the spot where I first set foot—a very little foot—on American soil.

After dinner, but before the coffee was served, Farrar took me to the tobacco counter and chose a cigar, and though I wanted to smoke my pipe, never having smoked a cigar, he urged me to try one, recommending his own choice, a Corona Corona, long as a pencil and almost as thin. It was delicious. It cost seventy-five cents. I did not pursue the new pleasure.

It may have been that night that he took me to a play by a new British playwright named Noel Coward. It was called *The Vortex,* and we went to the second night performance, which fixes the date as September 17, 1925. Coward had not only written it; he had an important role.

During the first intermission Farrar pointed out some of the celebrities in the audience. Charles Chaplin was one of them, but I saw only the back of his head, for he remained seated. As we stood at the back of the theater, a beautiful young woman greeted John; they shook hands, and he introduced me. She was very modishly dressed. I thought her features too perfect, so much does strangeness play a part in attraction; but this was only a momentary glimpse, for soon she was gone. Her name was Mary Astor.

We returned to our seats. I had been greatly impressed by the vigor of the first act; the second I thought more Wilde than Coward, the third more Ibsen. I took away with me one seemingly unforgettable image: Coward at the piano, eavesdropping on his doom, and playing frenziedly as the lights grew dimmer. He went on to write other plays, and also wrote, produced, and acted in a wartime movie in which he quoted one of my metaphors. This gave me great pleasure, particularly as I was far from home when I saw it.

Chapter Two

1

Confirmed Villagers seldom ventured uptown. All had a favorite meeting place, and I had mine.

On the corner of Thompson Street and Washington Square, in a late eighteenth-century building with sloping roof and squat chimney, up a flight of wooden stairs on which I tried to kiss a pretty girl but didn't make it, there was a candle-lit room with a long and broad table, spoken of reverently as the "Poets' Table," and beyond that another, larger room with windows overlooking the park. This was Romany Marie's "tavern," where nothing stronger than tea or Turkish coffee was served.

Marie's clients did not come for her black bread, peasant fare, and in fact ate it only when they could not afford to dine elsewhere. Young, old, famous or struggling to achieve fame, the writers and artists who congregated there nightly found in her presence and her talk, her sympathy and advice, rest and relief from their daily cares. She was also a matchmaker, and some of them found new lovers or new mates.

She was a handsome woman, who seemed larger than life but was in reality of average height, though amply formed. She dressed in gypsy fashion; spangled and bangled, dripping with earrings and bracelets, she clanked when she gestured with her powerful, beringed hands, and her eyes flashed fire. Her rages—both real and feigned—were directed against her husband, whose name was Marchand, and who looked, and perhaps fancied himself, a perfect type of brigand, with huge mustaches and glowering eyes under shaggy eyebrows. He was, in fact, one of the kindest of men. While Romany Marie read tea leaves and coffee grounds, Marchand read palms. He once read mine.

I had gone there with my friend. Marchand joined us. Perhaps he was bored; it was late at night, and there were few customers. For a while he talked to us about the sea and love; in deep-throated Balkan English he implied a mysterious connection, but the connection eluded him and us, though we listened with respect, proud of his attentions. I am certain he had never read Sir Charles Sedley's

Love still has something of the sea
From whence his mother rose.

It was enough that he was talking to us. Suddenly he took my right hand and began to examine the palm with great concentration, turning my hand this way and that, and then checking it with the other. This was an honor that all who came to Romany Marie's longed for, for he bestowed it but seldom. Pulling the candle stuck in a bottle closer, he looked directly into my eyes and said: "You think you're great, don't you?" I thought—Lord, he is going to humiliate me before my sweetheart. His next words exploded in my face. "You are greater than even *you* think you are!"

I had supposed as much. Marchand had spoken. I nearly expired for joy. I would be famous; my sweetheart would be proud of me. With fame would come riches.

It has not panned out. The Hudson and Harlem Rivers are still wet, though a lot dirtier. I still have difficulty paying my bills.

As for my sweetheart, I gave her a ring. Hand in hand we went to a party on Staten Island. On the return voyage, in a crowded ferry, with the sea wind blowing, she began to berate me; I looked at her in astonishment. She handed me the ring. I looked at it, at her, and tossed it into the waters of the bay.

I returned to Romany Marie's without her. It was there that I met many people who throng my early years in the Village. Another honor had come to me: I was directed to sit at the "Poets' Table."

2

Not all who sat there were poets, even some who wrote verse. Vilhjalmur Stefannson was an explorer. Buckminster Fuller was an engineer and designer (I understand he took Marie for a ride in his dymaxion car). Edgard Varese was a composer. Paul Robeson was a singer turned actor. Harrison Dowd was an actor, singer, and composer who looked strikingly like his friend Eugene O'Neill. His settings for a number of Housman's poems were very melancholy, and he used to sing the words to his own accompaniment on Marie's upright piano as though they expressed a personal grief or despair. I still hear his low-keyed music in my mind whenever I read Housman.

Glenway Wescott came occasionally with his friend

Monroe Wheeler. My recollection of them is of elegant passers-by, of visitors "dropping in" from a more opulent world
—from uptown, in fact. And yet I remember a story told by
Wheeler on one of those brief visits. He had gone to a concert in Paris with a French composer. They sat in the balcony.
The theatre had two staircases in the lobby facing each other,
and as they were descending one of them after the concert,
both staircases flowing with people, Wheeler had remarked:
"Is it not like a mirror we are descending in front of?" His
friend stopped in his tracks, smote his forehead and exclaimed: "Mon Dieu! How badly we are looking tonight!"
But whether this particular visit took place before or after
Wescott's Harper Prize novel, I no longer remember.

Mark Tobey was another rare visitor. I mention him
here, and not in the painters' section which follows, because
he seemed to be, like Wescott and Wheeler, from another
world; also, like them, he was much fussed over by Romany
Marie. When I met Tobey again it was on a ship at sea.

Orrick Johns, the author of *Wild Plums,* a much admired
and much anthologized poem, was often there; and most
often, Harry Kemp.

Harry Kemp was probably responsible for my being
placed at the "Poets' Table." It was his girl I tried to kiss on
the wooden stair, ascending one day as she was descending.
I did not know her to be his girl. Her name was Frances
McClernan, and she had come to the Village from Bronx-
ville. Her red hair was bobbed, and her peasant dresses smash-
ing. She married Kemp, was swept up in his exploits, and
retired from the marriage as she had entered it, on a sea of
newspaper headlines. She paid him this compliment: "I
thought the marriage would last a year. It lasted three." She
afterwards married Maurice Hindus.

Kemp had been married once before, to a frail and beautiful young woman named Mary Pyne; there is a drawing of
her in Djuna Barnes's first book. She died of consumption.
His most spectacular exploit, a sensation in its day, was run-

ning off with Upton Sinclair's wife. They told reporters that their love was recognized in heaven and so they did not need to get married; unfortunately, it soon petered out on earth. Another of Kemp's ventures was even less successful. He stowed away on a liner going to England; he told me, years after it happened, that he felt he could not live another moment without seeing the land and birthplace of the poets he loved. He was discovered, put to work in the kitchen, and arrested as soon as the liner docked. Ezra Pound tried to get the Home Office to let him stay—without avail. He was confined and sent back on the first outgoing liner.

Kemp lived the role of poet; what he lacked in talent he made up in poses. He spouted his own lines and the lines of others. He spouted mine, and praised me when others were present. He was a great spouter, with his head thrown back, and his right arm upraised like a Roman's. I remember his arms; I used to box with him at Philadelphia Jack O'Brien's gym uptown after a workout on the roof around a track of slats which rattled and bounced. His arms were as long as tent-poles; he towered over me as well, and he kept me off by one glove on my head. He was built like Bob Fitzsimmons—broad shoulders, no hips, and slender legs. His back was covered with freckles. He ended his days in Provincetown, where he had been a colleague of Eugene O'Neill and a founder of the Wharf Players, afterwards the Provincetown Playhouse.

His literary fame rests on a single book, *Tramping on Life,* his autobiography. It was a bestseller. He was, in many respects, the American counterpart of England's William H. Davies, the "tramp poet." Davies's lines have not yet become embarrassing. It is a curious fact that most men who have played the role of poet have not been up to the mark. Good poets seem always to have been competent in the world of affairs, beginning with Chaucer; in our time two of the best have been a vice-president of an insurance company and a bank clerk.

3

The painters who congregated at Romany Marie's until fame, marriage or money swept them uptown and into the country were, on the whole, more light-hearted than the writers, and they seemed to have a great deal more to talk about. Some of them were to form the core of the once renowned Daniel Gallery, and then of the Downtown Gallery which, with prosperity, moved uptown: Peter Blume, Stuart Davis, Yasuo Kuniyoshi, Niles Spencer. I recall quiet conversations with Marsden Hartley, before the evening became loud with explications; or, rather, I was a quiet listener. He spoke gently and kindly; looking back, I can see that his fame had even then a durable aspect. Alexander Brook . . . Ben Benn, who is only now beginning to be recognized . . . William Zorach . . . there were others, of course, whose faces blur, whose names elude me. Had I been as interested in painting as I was to become I might now have a little collection of early works, for I was often pressed to take a drawing and sometimes even an oil. I had a stock reply: when I was rich enough I would buy one.

I went to a dance at Webster Hall with Peter Blume. There we picked up a girl who wore glasses. I do not remember whether she came alone or lost her escort in our concerted attack. We took turns dancing with her. We laughed and danced and drank the night and the midnight hours away in her company, Peter and I vying for her final favors, which he got. I was neither jealous nor unhappy. If I had Thomas Wolfe's gift of rhapsodical invocation, I would invoke that girl and rhapsodize. She dwells in my mind, laughing and alive, more desirable than all the beauties dancing past us in their pride.

Niles Spencer looked like a strayed aristocrat among the Bohemians, smiling good-naturedly over incessant chatter about "form" and "significance"—many theories, but few works of art. Spencer's sister, Marjorie, who was very pretty, and petulant or sulky by turns—though either would have sufficed since both became her—once told me how Hart Crane wrote his poems; she knew him, I did not. He would type two lines and leave the paper in his typewriter. A day or two later, sometimes a week, he would add another couplet or stanza. Rereading some of his verse recently I recalled her observation. It may explain the lack of transition everywhere evident in his work; I do not know what else can.

Much has been written about Crane's dissipations and tantrums—notably, and sympathetically, by Malcolm Cowley. I have sought in vain to find the following story in print. It was related to me by William Slater Brown.

Crane was living in Mrs. Addie Turner's frame house on the New York-Connecticut border. Everyone seems to have lived there at one time or another—Brown himself, Allen Tate and his wife, Caroline Gordon; Cowley; Peter Blume. Of one sojourn—there were several—Crane's biographer, Philip Horton, was to write: "Besides decorating his rooms, it was necessary to prepare for the winter. He ordered boxes of canned goods from the city, as well as a pair of snowshoes; he joined Tate in chopping wood," etc. Brown's story is about the snowshoes.

It seems everyone had them, except Crane. With money from Otto H. Kahn, he sent for a pair, the handsomest depicted in a Montgomery Ward catalogue. They arrived. This was in the early fall. By late fall he had taken them from his rooms and placed them in the hall; somewhat later, he carried them downstairs and left them in the vestibule, or possibly outside. He spent much time, when he was not writing, brooding or drinking, scanning the sky.

"That was the year," Brown said, "that not a single flake fell on the Atlantic seaboard."

One night, frustrated to the breaking point, Crane carried his beloved snowshoes to the middle of the dirt road, strapped them on his feet, and flopped about, up and down, uttering strange cries.

Suckling of sailors, who gulped the sea at last.

4

Marjorie Spencer came often to Romany Marie's, but sometimes sat alone, the candle on her table lighting up her loneliness. She never lost the look of a little girl, which was enhanced by the calico dresses she wore—straight out of the nineteenth century, such as one sees on dolls or in the portraits of itinerant painters of that time. I took her to a speakeasy one night. She was wearing one of those dresses, banded at the wrists, with a high-banded neckline. Staring at a tiny ribbon on her wrist, I noticed a scar, which was partly covered by the band. She drew the band back, and I saw that the scar was as big and round as a dime. It was also fiery red.

"Would you like to know how I got that?" she asked. Her childlike eyes stared innocently at me under her bangs.

I was more inclined to rush her to a doctor.

"I was here two nights ago," she went on calmly. "The man I was with bored me so much that I took my cigarette and held it there."

And she smiled.

Her life, which could have been a brilliant one, was unhappy. She found the company of homosexuals exciting, and at length committed the ultimate folly. She married one. She died young. In her last years she was fat and thin by turns, and her eyes held a fixed stare of defiance and agony.

Another painter: Joseph Stella. One night he lashed out at a certain school, and his rage seemed to fill the room.

"They paint women with the breasts down here," he exclaimed, pointing to his waist. "But I, when I paint the women, I put the breasts here!"

His fingers alighted on his shoulders like five-legged bantams.

Arthur Lee was a sculptor. There is a little torso of his in the Metropolitan Museum of Art; it is called *Volupté*. He was the very image of an artist—big, blond, and sturdy as most sculptors are when they are not starved. Far from starving, Lee destroyed food; at Romany Marie's he used to take bits of dough from inside a loaf and roll them around in his strong fingers. Then he proceeded to sculp them, strewing the table with tiny torsos made of dough, with only an occasional glance at what he was doing, for he was busy talking. He had taken all art, perhaps all knowledge, as his province, and he talked more about literature than about sculpture. We sometimes disagreed, and I have been told that he wrote things about me in his notebooks for posterity.

Antonio Salemme was another sculptor, an exception to the rule, since he was slim, but not because he was underfed. On the contrary: there was a chop house on Third Street, called Small's, I think, where he used to go to eat oyster cocktails and a grilled steak for lunch. The steak was accompanied by hashed brown potatoes. That kind of meal, he would say, gave one a new perspective, a new lease, on life. An admirable philosophy; I was often with him. He ate *con amore*.

Salemme was very attractive to women, and was an indefatigable and experienced pursuer of them. He had that perdurable Italian charm which age cannot wither; being slim seems to go with it. Somewhere in the background was a blonde Irish wife, but I never saw them together. One of the few times I saw her she was with Paul Robeson. In Salemme's studio off Washington Square there was a lifesize statue of Robeson, with supplicating arms upraised; but Robeson, magnificently built, was his own monument. I knew Salemme well into the thirties, when a visitor I brought around made mischief between him and his second wife, and between him and me.

Another sculptor: Isamu Noguchi, who was, like myself, one of the youngest of the habitués of Romany Marie's. Whenever he arrived, there were exclamations over his extraordinary good looks and panther walk. Some of those who exclaimed were then or later connected with museums. I once worked in a building adorned by a relief sculpture by him.

Another handsome man who came frequently to Romany Marie's was Holger Cahill, neither a painter nor a sculptor, but later the director of the WPA art program. I used to watch him and Salemme at their game of dazzling pretty young women whose innocent and astonished eyes went from one to the other in happy bewilderment. Cahill afterwards married Dorothy C. Miller, the most beautiful woman ever seen there.

Saturday night was the great night at Romany Marie's. How thronged it was—how lovely the women were, and emancipated. Their faces glowed in the candlelight. On Sundays, if you had lunch or brunch at Alice McCollister's tea room ("shoppe," I think she called it) on West 8th Street, you could see who had slept with whom the night before. It was enlightening. Many eggs were consumed.

One night, Romany Marie entertained a visitor from France. In that candle-lit rendezvous I was introduced to a man who seemed all beard and smile. He had gentle, gesturing hands. He took the homage of American writers and artists like a benign potentate. Although I was to live in

Paris for a long time, I did not renew our acquaintance there. Now, having read many of the memoirs of those years, with that charming man always preparing chicken broth in his studio while his guests talked on, then grilling the chicken for a second course over a charcoal fire, I sincerely regret it. His name was Brancusi.

Chapter Three

1

Jefferson Market was bounded by Christopher Street, Greenwich Avenue, and 10th Street. It stood behind Jefferson Market Court on Sixth Avenue where, earlier, Jane Heap and Margaret Anderson, editors of the *Little Review,* were tried —and found guilty—for publishing an instalment of Joyce's *Ulysses.* The courthouse building, with its clock tower, is now a public library, which took some doing; but the sprawling market, a place of immense windows framed by Roman arches on the street level, Victorian Gothic in its upper story, with gables and little spires, was torn down. In its place, under the magistracy of James J. Walker, a prison for women was erected—some said to punish the Village, which had voted against him; but I prefer to think that the idiocy which prevails in bureaucracies was normally at work. What could be more normal to the bureaucratic mind than a prison for prostitutes in a residential neighborhood?

To enter that market, with its scores of stalls, was an experience unlike any other. One stepped from quiet Village streets into a bustling area, in summer cool and shadowy, where wholesalers and retailers, dairymen, butchers, and grocers displayed their wares and also partook of them. I recall sandwiches and chilled buttermilk eaten and drunk in an atmosphere redolent of beeves, hams, venison, plumaged game birds, cheeses, and fresh loaves, surrounded by aproned men as honest as their wares.

Directly across Greenwich from the apex of the triangle formed by the market, on the south corner of Christopher Street, stood Luke O'Connor's Columbian House, a saloon where John Masefield had worked as a handyman, and where Eugene O'Neill spent some of his leisure hours. I once talked with O'Connor's nephew, who told me that when he was a child Masefield had held him on his knee. I never met O'Neill, although he was a close friend of Romany Marie, as well as of Harrison Dowd, but I met Masefield at the home of Thomas S. Lamont when the poet laureate was his guest in the thirties.

A few steps into Christopher Street, at no. 4, was Frank Shay's bookshop. Mr. Shay was another founder of the Provincetown Playhouse and a publisher of sorts. The first time I went into his shop he brought out a pamphlet he had published and urged me to buy it—it would be worth a great deal one day, he said. It was *The Ballad of the Harp-Weaver* by Edna Millay, and cost seventy-five cents. Later, his shop was bought by two sisters name Koenig, both pretty, but of a virginal cast. They had a door at the back which had never been painted and led nowhere; on it all the writers wrote their names, and by the time the Misses Koenig gave up the shop the door was full of signatures. They took it with them. It was tracked down a few years ago, and is now in some collection. When I was asked to write on it I had to hunt for a space. I thought it a great honor, and was certain it was when I saw the name above mine, or perhaps it was below: Edwin Arlington Robinson.

Next to the bookshop was the Pirates' Den, a restaurant

for tourists and slummers. The waiters were dressed as pirates and slammed their cutlasses on the table to startle clients into ordering. The fiercest-looking pirate was the one who stood guard by the basement entrance and growled you inside. He had a patch over one eye, a sash around his waist, a cutlass in the sash, and tattered breeches above hairy shanks. His name was Nathaniel Dirk, a painter who earned his living this way. A gentler soul was not to be found; at Romany Marie's, on his night off, he said not a word. I have been told that he and De Hirsh Margules were the first to hold an outdoor exhibition in Washington Square.

2

Across the street from the Pirates' Den and the Shay-Koenig bookery was the International Book & Art Shop, Joseph Kling, proprietor. I had known Mr. Kling only a short time when he took me into his confidence. He said that he knew of no one he could trust; that he believed me to be honest; he had to go to Europe for three weeks—would I run the shop for him? The prices were all marked, not only in the books, but on the prints, etchings, and lithographs, which he also sold, many of which he got from old volumes, worthless in themselves, but whose illustrations were made from the original plates or stones. I do not remember whether he offered me any compensation; I did not need it—I had an income of one hundred dollars a month. It sufficed. This may have been decisive with Kling. He told me that he had made inquiries about me.

All that I knew about him was that he had been the

publisher of one of those little magazines that died to make verse free, as the old phrase had it, and for a time had had as an associate editor Hart Crane, whose earliest poems appeared in it; it was called the *Pagan*. He was also a publisher of books; *Minna and Myself* bears the imprint of the Pagan Publishing Company. His shop was a meeting place for writers and painters; he himself was a skillful painter, and a self-portrait adorned the premises. He was always reading. In part this was due to his own predilection, in part to the fact that customers were not always clamoring for books, and there they were—the books, not the customers. He read with an eyeshade which he kept at a slant, so that he appeared to be reading with only one eye, keeping the other on the store.

Reading as much as he did, no day without its full quota, he came across many curious things, and was fond of reading them aloud, particularly to his girl, who had a lisp, and who flitted in and out of his shop like a sprite. She was very thin, very pretty, and always laughing. Her laughter was unlike any other person's; a perpetually pealing carillon accompanied her. Although he had told me he had to go to Europe on business, perhaps to find and dismantle more illustrated folios, I also knew that he had promised his girl a trip to Paris. Lisping engagingly, she had told everyone. They went. As soon as they arrived in Paris I received an urgent cable for money. It was summer, and I had barely sold anything; many browsed, but few bought, and some asked for umbrellas or handbags, which were neither on view nor in stock.

I told two of his friends; having them, he needed no enemies. They discussed it outside; inside, they said they would organize a sale, but it would handicap their efforts if I were around. Just leave it to them, was their advice to me. I peered into the shop while their sale was in progress; it was probably a Saturday night. Both were busy showing and wrapping books, prints, etchings, and lithographs. I was glad that Kling and his girl would not be left stranded. When locking-up time came, I returned to the shop, and was handed $32.50; even to me it did not seem like a large return for all that bustle and salesmanship. They merely exchanged glances, almost smiling; no doubt they saved their laughter for outside. One of them, a slouching slob of a man who painted, but badly, was the lover of a well-known poetess; the other later married an heiress. I cabled fifty dollars, and was glad when the three weeks were over and I could return to my private world. It turned out to be not much of an improvement.

3

De Hirsh Margules, who astonished the world more at his death than during his whole life, was a friend of Kling's and of the volunteer salesmen. Through him I met a man on whom, to some extent, he afterwards modeled himself; alas, *his* forte was not talk, although he could be loquacious. His prototype was different; I can only recall him with his mouth open. But sometimes it was a snarl as well as talk that occasioned it. He was destined to become famous in a role that suited him more than writing—the writer-as-TV-entertainer.

On TV he was paid for the kind of talk with which he stunned his friends and acquaintances for nothing, day in, day out, fiercely and tirelessly, in those far-off Village years. I tuned in on him one night; it was enough. The role of buffoon was natural to him. He was vulgar, outrageous, and entertaining. He had not changed one bit. He continued to publish, continued to appear on TV, and became rich. He was not much of a writer.

When I first met him he was thin, nervous, and almost crackling with pent-up energy. He had a kind of aggressiveness which—perhaps because of him—I tend to associate with short men. He was five feet seven, with a sharp nose and eyes like smoky blue marbles. His hair was unruly; a tuft of it, in front, moved about like a cockatoo's crest. His yellow mustache, which was eyebrow-thin, was stained with nicotine.

Some people's wits are merely sharpened by experience; his were well honed. It was rumored that he had stolen a Whistler etching from the Metropolitan Museum of Art and sold it to the dealer who had sold it to the museum; if idle tales are to be believed, he also spent some time in prison. He had a perpetual rage on; Bodenheim excoriated poets—he excoriated everybody, including Bodenheim. His voice was harsh, with a shrill edge. He had set himself up as a judge of art and *belles lettres,* or anything else, and was sought out on the chance that he might bestow commendation instead of criticism. It never came to pass. Every time a poor, struggling writer read him a story, he listened intently, if impatiently; when the reading was over, he invariably said, "Bah! Call that a story? The way to tell it is . . ." and he was off on a long, involved, often brilliant re-telling which held his listeners spellbound.

His wife was amply made. From the way she touched up her eyes and eyebrows, from the way she dressed, and from something she once said to me, I think she fancied herself a *femme fatale*. She was not. She was a type of suburban housewife who lived in the city. She had found herself in a literary and artistic world, and made the most of it, reigning as queen at the cafeteria tables where her husband held court. She came to see me once; I was startled when, after her knock, I opened the door and saw who it was. I was expecting the girl whom Bodenheim had termed his former mistress. I doubted that. He may have made a pass at her.

I asked my friend's wife to sit down and offered her a cigarette. When I tried to light it for her, she stood up, put the cigarette down, and placed her hand on my shoulder.

"Why do you run around with little girls," she asked, "when you can have a woman of the world like me?"

She was redolent of cheap perfume. She pulled me toward her, but I broke away.

A reader will not believe the phrases I used were I to set them down. I spoke like a hero in a three-decker novel. I told her, in effect, that as I did not love her, I did not wish to make love to her. She brushed it all aside. She led me by the hand into my bedroom. Still holding my hand, she pulled down the windowshades—it was mid-afternoon—and made me sit down on the edge of the bed. She then proceeded to un-dress me—shoes, socks, trousers, drawers, then tie and shirt. She swished off her clothes in a single lightning movement. She called attention to the beauty of her breasts; I saw no such beauty as she praised. I not only did not wish to make love—I was incapable of doing so. She was not to be deterred. She had a method and applied it. It was successful. She stretched herself out, and drew me over her.

I stayed away from the places where her husband held forth. I stayed away from Kling's. She may have telephoned once or twice; if she did, I made excuses. I never saw her alone again.

Some months later I met her husband in the street. He asked me if I was doing anything. The reader will not believe me, but I said "Nothing." It was the truth; I had not yet learned that it was not always necessary. He said: "Come with me."

We entered an apartment with shuttered windows. The shutters were inside. His wife emerged for a moment, greeted us, and disappeared. I wondered about the quizzical look she had given me. I ascribed it to modesty. We ate; we also drank. We drank longer than we ate. I found myself hours later in a huge upholstered chair with wings. He had talked inces-santly.

"It's two o'clock," I heard him telling me. "You don't want to go home now. We can put you up."

His wife listened—expectantly, I thought in retrospect. In my befuddled state they appeared very hospitable. It was clear I wanted to stay where I was. They left me. I heard furniture being moved. Then he reappeared.

"You can come in now," he told me, and helped me out of the chair.

I followed him into the next room, and realized dimly that twin beds had been pushed together. He was standing beside his wife on one side, and gesturing toward the other. I understood that that was the side for me. She tried to look demure; he turned out the lights on the wall. I began to undress. I undressed down to my undershirt and drawers. I found the edge of the bed and lay down, as close to the edge as I could get without falling off. I lay on my left side, with my back to them. I do not know if I had assumed he would get in first, and let his wife be on the outside; but I knew instantly that this was not the case. She was between us.

I tried to sleep, but became wider awake with every passing second. Though I was turned away from her, I knew that she was coming closer; I did not know she was being pushed until she pressed against me. In pushing her again, his hand slid past her and touched me. I seized it and sat up. I asked him what he was doing.

Instead of answering, he leaped out on the floor, turned on one of the lights, and sat down at the foot of the bed. In his hand was a revolver. He said: "If you don't do it, I will kill you both." I saw that she had buried her face in the mattress.

With my back to him, I put on my trousers, my socks and shoes, and followed it with my shirt and jacket. I thrust my tie into my pocket. I walked to the door, but he had leaped up again and was barring the way, the revolver pointed toward me. I spoke to him as I had to Bodenheim. I did not even bother to double up my fists. My words were: "If you try to stop me, I will kill you." He did not try. I brushed past him. I left the room and the apartment. I found myself on the street in the moment before dawn when the light is purplish and the air cool and sweet. I walked home breathing in that sweet, cool air as the air lightened.

4

De Hirsh Margules was poor, but he seemed used to it. Everybody was used to it. His friends fed him when they could and sometimes when they couldn't. But oddly enough, when they themselves needed feeding, or a small loan, or a small service, Margules provided food, money or his services. His reputation as someone on whom one could rely, who was always there in a pinch, who would not let you down, grew with the years. He maintained that reputation until his death.

When I met him he had a room on MacDougal Street, directly across from the Provincetown Playhouse. It could have cost but little, and with the landlord he had, perhaps not even that. His landlord was Albert Strunsky, who was never known to evict an artist or writer. The room was not only De Hirsh's home and studio; it was his private hostelry for waifs and strays of the Village, of whom there were not a few. They slept on the floor.

Margules knew everyone in the Village, and when he came to Paris, which happened while I was there, he got to know everyone there, too; his friends included Norman Douglas, which is more than I can say about myself, although I admired the author of *South Wind* and *Old Calabria* immensely and glimpsed him often. When Bodenheim was found murdered, the police looked for someone to identify him; it turned out to be Margules. The newspaper stories which followed that crime featured his recollections of the poet, of the Village, his view of art, of life, and the delights of cookery—his own.

De Hirsh was a peripatetic chef. He walked and he talked. He walked to friends' houses to cook for them, and he talked about his cooking. If you asked him to your house to dine, he would offer to prepare the meal for you; told that the meal was already planned, he volunteered to prepare the next one if you purchased the ingredients, listing them at once, and the places where they were to be had. He always began the same way; Cézanne had his apples, but Margules saw in onions and garlic the beauty and well-being of the world. In listing ingredients his Eddie Cantor eyes took on a faraway look in a trance of steams and savors. No woman who ever lived loved a kitchen as much as he did, or was so eager to stand over a stove, and afterwards at the sink.

His loyalty was fierce, like a woman's; it teetered on possessiveness, and often toppled over. Had the world been what he wished it to be, everyone would have been commanded to be happy, and given the wherewithal to achieve his heart's desire. With him, cheerfulness did not merely break through —it was like a cataclysm. Although he did not grapple his friends to his soul with hoops of steel, he did the next best thing—he crushed them to his chest with muscles of iron. He hugged them on the street, always at the ineluctable moment when his echoing hello had turned all heads in his direction. He hugged them in their homes where, on arrival, he lifted husbands from the floor and then their astonished wives; but sometimes he scooped both up together in a one-armed hoist that would have made a wrestler pregnant with envy.

Indoors or out, he might suddenly burst into an operatic air; his voice was good—good and loud—and he could have become a singer had he not become a painter. But perhaps he should have been an actor. His father had been a director of a Yiddish theater, his mother an actress in it; his sister, Annette, created the role of Tondelayo in the 1924 Broadway hit, *White Cargo*. A great deal of this pervasive theatricality had rubbed off on De Hirsh; but perhaps he was born with it.

He had a droll face, like a showman's, in which was stuck a nose that might have come from one of those shops where they sell party novelties. His chin was square, with a cleft in it. I have mentioned his eyes; large and doll-like, they were apt to roll like marbles doing close-order drill.

He dressed with a flair for sloppiness. Everything he had on was either too loose or too tight, but uniformly ancient; occasionally, bow ties and open leather sandals proclaimed to his friends that he was going to a party. Winter or summer, a blue beret, studiously rakish, capped the ensemble. His flamboyance extended to his autobiography. From a booklet about him which bears an introduction by Alexander King, I quote part of a sentence: "Burdened (or bolstered?) with six names, Isaac Edward Cecil De Hirsh De Tannerier Gilmont Margules was born in Jassy, Rumania, in 1899," etc.

De Hirsh! *Was ist das Isaac Edward Cecil mit De Tannerier und Gilmont?*

He cannot answer.

5

His watercolors were greatly influenced by John Marin, whose friend and pupil he was. Marin seized the essential man in a blurb he wrote for a show:

Margules—
> Youth in its prime,
> rampant, exultant,
> an art-lover with abounding faith and
>   sincerity,

with much intelligence and quick seeing,
striving always to understand this seeking.
Go and see his work.

Examples of his work are in many museums and private collections.

Associated as he was with certain cerebral poets—the kind who perennially impress their admirers with the idea that a revolution is imminent in the world of letters, but have thus far left literary innovations to men of lesser talent, like the Pounds and Eliots—Margules began to pursue, in secret meditations, an intellectual root for his painting, not liking the sidelines. After much cogitation, his mind burdened by literary concepts and endless talk in which he was perforce a mere listener, he evolved a concept of his own, and gave it to the world—or, more specifically, to his cerebral friends. He called it "perspective of time." A new phase followed: "time painting."

Working in oil, he divided his canvases with horizontal and vertical lines which gave him four quarters, then further divided the quarters into eight triangles. To show the progress of time, he painted, in clockwise order, and with the colors of the spectrum as a basis, blue-green and green for morning, yellow and orange for noon, red and red-violet for evening, and blue-violet and ultramarine for night. Occasionally he set both a sun and a moon as seals upon the movement of the hours, and spoke of "color-lights" and "color-time." The triangular wedges, each representing three hours in the "time painting" cycle, became "circular time perspective."

"I see all my scenes both by day and by night, and I want that to show in my paintings," he said.

Now, exegesis may be useful, though not very, in poetry; but in painting? A painting is unlike any other work of art in that it does not depend on interpretation, for it is not the image of anything, being only itself. Art critics termed his work "semi-abstract." "Semi," from the Greek "hemi," means half, and "abstract," among other meanings, is the essence of a thing. A half-essence. . . . Margules enjoyed reading about himself, and left meanings to others. He was a celebrity, and made the most of it. Bow ties and sandals were worn more often.

It appeared he would be a bachelor forever. One day his friends learned that he had acquired a wife. She was a Bostonian, quiet-spoken, not at all pretty, but solid, sober, in love with De Hirsh and a perfect foil for him. She seldom spoke. In addition to living quarters on Christopher Street, he now had a studio on Sixth Avenue. He turned out a great many pictures, and sold them. He was written up in the art magazines. It was his most flourishing period. His fixed price for a watercolor was $600 or $800—I forget which, since I never bought one. I was told you could offer him $599 or $799, as the case may have been, and he would refuse to sell. I thought this admirable.

His wife died, I never learned of what: perhaps his cookery. Margules ceased to paint in a frenzy. He was seen more and more often in the streets, in cafeterias, and in Washington Square; there, one day, he sat down beside Dawn Powell. She told me: "He talked so much, that I never got to know him."

Another surprise was in store for his friends. In his last years he became a contributing editor to *Art Voices*. His editorial duties were limited to one page; the idea for it was a brilliant one—and his own. Painters wrote; he himself was scribbling poetry like a man possessed. Why not a piece of writing by a painter, with a picture by that painter reproduced on the same page? Writers painted; why not, etc. He approached his writing-painting, painting-writing friends. Alexander King complied; so did I. When the issue containing my poem and painting appeared, De Hirsh sent me a case of wine, more impressive in appearance than taste, but an astonishing present all the same. He helped to drink some of it.

After that I saw him less and less. I was busy, too. I also

disliked being hugged by him in my own house, not only because it offended my masculinity, but because I knew he had cracked someone's ribs in one of his displays of affection. Nevertheless, old associations die hard; I had him to dinner, I went to see him on Christopher Street, where he displayed his pictures and read me his poems, which were full of wonderful lines in a crazy context distinguished by a total absence of syntax. He seemed as poor as ever. The top of his hutch table had curled up on all sides, so that it resembled a giant wooden bowl. Chairs with missing legs leaned forlornly against cracked walls; some lacked a seat as well. His washing hung from wire coat-hangers.

On one of the last occasions that he came to see me he spoke with sincere affection about me to my wife and about my wife to me. He said that he planned to get a house in Italy, and that we must come and live with him. I was incredulous; was he losing his mind? I even wondered if he had enough for that month's rent on his Christopher Street flat. A kinsman of his wife's was paying for his art supplies, and occasionally purchased a picture from him "to keep him going."

I had almost lost contact with him when I learned he was in St. Vincent's Hospital. My wife and I went to see him. He was very cheerful; always surrounded by people, whether at home or in a cafeteria, he was surrounded by them in his hospital bed. One night, not liking the solitude that followed the close of visiting hours, he rose, dressed himself, and left. He barely made it back to Christopher Street. He was very ill; and it was to prove his last illness. He died in another hospital uptown, where a friend with whom he had gone to stay had taken him. He was sixty-six years old.

A few months after his death I received a letter from a lawyer. Enclosed was a list of De Hirsh's friends. There were forty-five names; mine was among them. He had left me a thousand dollars. Kling, still in the book business on Greenwich Avenue, was left five hundred. The estate was valued at more than a hundred thousand dollars.

It was while De Hirsh was in St. Vincent's Hospital that I met one of the men who was to become co-executor of his estate. He is Harrison D. Horblit, a collector of note. One day recently, while I was visiting him and his wife in Ridgefield, Connecticut, Mr. Horblit recounted some of the difficulties he had experienced. One of the residual legatees wanted a "cut" of the pictures as well as the money, and took ten, although Mr. Horblit had paid for all to swell the estate.

Stranger still was the behavior of another friend. This man, of whom De Hirsh always spoke highly to me, but whom I never met, sent Mr. Horblit a letter. In it he said that he had fed De Hirsh over a period of twelve years, during which time De Hirsh had also consumed a considerable amount of his liquor. He enclosed a bill for six thousand dollars.

Mr. Horblit, I am happy to report, threw letter and bill into the wastebasket. He was still indignant when he told me about it.

6

The man who married an heiress was for many years my friend. I am convinced now that he was not laughing at me— not even at Kling—but at the extraordinary opportunity which had been presented him, and of which he was bound to take advantage, when he took over Kling's shop. He was a born opportunist. It did not always pan out. The heiress he married came of a socialite family. She died; I heard she had committed suicide. The money he spent like a prince on voyages, hotel suites, and champagne parties ceased flowing; it was income from a trust fund. The goal of unearned riches eluded him.

All this was in the future. He was another Rumanian, very handsome, with expressive eyes; suave, cynical, and always neatly dressed. He spoke fluent English—with a charming accent, of course; French, Italian, and Russian. He could have entered the foreign service; corporations would have welcomed him. He despised work. He wound up with an unsavory crowd: peddlers of faked masterpieces. His suave and worldly air were of inestimable value. It did not seem to bother him. Money was money; it did not matter how you got it. He told me about the mob's stable of painters, always on call. One furnished a street scene by Utrillo, another Utrillo's signature; one a nude by Renoir, another his signature. Sometimes in a landscape, one merely brushed in the background, while another provided houses or figures, and a third the signature. All were specialists. I listened and felt sick. My friend merely sneered at the suckers of this world.

Years later, I was a shy participant in one of his exploits. He had met, he told me, Rodin's last secretary. The sculptor, as is well known, spent much of his time while his models were resting in sketching them in bold and graceful lines, sometimes adding a wash. There had been hundreds, perhaps thousands, of such sketches, many of them on large sheets of paper. They were all signed. The secretary had brought over about a hundred. By some arrangement, my friend got hold of perhaps fifty. I am no expert; to me, they looked—they had the "aura" of being—genuine, and I believe they were. (Margules thought so, too, although skeptical at first.)

I introduced my friend to several eager collectors, who bought some of the drawings. He offered me one free, and even suggested I look through his portfolio—which was immense in size and contents—and make my own selection. I chose a pencil drawing of two nudes, had it framed in a narrow raw wood frame, and hung it on my wall. It was much admired.

One day a charming woman came to tea. She was not only charming—she was rich. She kept looking at the nudes. She brought them into the conversation. Finally, she said that if I ever wanted to sell the drawing, she would like to be the purchaser. Just call her up, she said, and tell her the price.

I held out a long time. Then I called her up. I said I would take five hundred dollars for it. She was delighted. She invited me to dinner at the Lafayette, where she was staying. This was all to the good, as I did not have the price of a meal. "Bring the picture along," she added.

I removed it from my wall, washed the glass, saw I had nothing to wrap it in, and took it to my Chinese laundryman, who wrapped it in brown paper—very neatly, I thought. He was no ordinary laundryman. I had once told him that my name, like his, was Charles, and he always told customers in his shop, pointing to me: "Him Charley too." He also had a sign which read: "Shrits 25¢." From Charley's laundry I walked the five or six blocks to the Lafayette and was invited upstairs for a drink.

I ascended, placed the picture on the bed, and sat down facing my hostess. A waiter appeared with Scotches-and-soda, and we talked and drank, and the waiter appeared again, and we drank and talked some more, then went downstairs to dinner, and when the dining room was shut down for the night, she suggested we have a brandy in her room.

Nothing had been said about the picture. But when we were again in her room, she wrote out a check and handed it to me. Her writing was large, broad, and flowing, and the check almost sagged from the amount of ink on it. I placed it on a radiator. An hour or so later, as I was leaving, I snatched it up—it was almost floating—and put it in my pocket.

It was not until I was outside, on University Place, alone with the lamps of midnight and the warm check in my pocket, that exultation filled me. Five hundred dollars! It was an enormous sum to me, and like all such sums which have come my way, it seemed unspendable.

A block from the Lafayette lived my Rumanian friend. I walked to his house, rang the bell, and was admitted. He had been asleep. He came to the door in a flowing foulard dressing gown, and on his face was the most astonished expression I have ever seen. He was not used to callers.

I quickly poured out my news.

"Now," I added, "I am going to write *you* a check for $250."

I proceeded to do so.

"But," I pleaded, "do not be at my bank at nine in the morning to cash it. I have to deposit this first and let it clear."

And I waved the five-hundred-dollar check about.

As for the other Kling salesman—the slouching slob—he simply disappeared; I heard he had gone to live in New Jersey, perhaps off his parents. I saw only one picture by him; it sufficed. He also told me how he had come to paint it. He said that the poetess he was sleeping with was a Catholic; the first time he made love to her she had carried a rosary into the bed. The painting showed a nude, with a cross pendant between the legs. Worse than the subject was his execution.

Chapter Four

1

Montgomery Evans 2nd sported an enormous Kaiser Wilhelm mustache and never appeared in public without a stick, usually one with a silver or ivory knob. When he made his nightly appearance at Romany Marie's he used to rap it on the floor, then stand for a moment in the doorway to survey the room, and be surveyed. He had a collection of sticks, some merely weird, others obscene. His apartment was full of art nouveau objects and African masks. He was curious about many things, and he also had shelves of esoteric books. He was an admirer of Aleister Crowley, the diabolist. He liked people, but termed himself a snob, and afterwards wrote a book on the evolution of caste.

I found him a pleasant companion, but at times a disconcerting one. When he coughed or laughed—his laugh usually turned into a cough—a slide of gravel went down his gullet and came to rest God knows where. He did not laugh at the agonies of the young. I was unhappy; I spoke of enlisting or suicide. He thought both excellent solutions for almost anything, but advised me not to try either until I had got myself laid (elegant though he was, that was his expression). I followed his advice, and kept on following it. I ran into him on Waverly Place. His eyes lit up, his Kaiser Wilhelm mustache bristled, and his stick did a drum major's rat-tat-tat on the pavement.

Several weeks passed. I was the happy recipient of a check from the *New Yorker*. I called him up and asked him to lunch with me at the Brevoort. It was April; he recommended shad roe, and I was once more delighted with his judgment. When, years later, I enlisted, it was not to run away, but to serve.

I probably saw a great deal more of Evans than I have recalled. Recently, I learned that a shop on Cornelia Street had a book called the *Independent Poetry Anthology, 1925*. I had a poem in it. I asked the bookseller how much he wanted for it, and he said ten dollars. That put a damper on it; nevertheless I asked to see it. Tucked inside was another poem by me, addressed to "Mon Ami M. Montgomery Evans 2nd,"

a monarchist:
Observe his ankle and his wrist,

etc. The book was, in fact, his copy, inscribed by me in 1927 between my two sojourns in Paris.

I saw his bookplate again for the first time in almost forty years. I am unable to do it justice. In the worst late art nouveau style, which was bad enough when it was early, he is depicted as a devil, with claws for hands, a wig with two bumps suggestive of horns, and a hint of Tiresias where his chest should be. He is standing in a black pool, probably the depths of iniquity, up to his hips; behind him, a Tiffany sunset sends its black-and-white beaded rays heavenward.

I bought the book. I have been looking through it. Joseph Kling is in it; Gwendolen Haste and Clement Wood; Countée Cullen; Dawn Powell. Louis M. Eilshemius, the painter, is in it with two poems. One is called *The Soul's Own Dell*, the other *Sweetness*, beginning:

> 'Tis sweet to gaze at rosy maiden-cheeks
> Athrough a vision-veil of tender smoke....

2

The lines awoke memories. I recalled a visit to a private house, 118 East 57th Street, still lit by gaslight in 1937. There I saw a man with deep-sunken eyes and a bristling white beard who was seated by a window. There was a shawl over his shoulders and a blanket around his legs. On the floor by his feet lay a scatter of canvases—big, little, and of various shapes. There were also canvases in spilling piles, canvases stacked against the walls a score deep, canvases perched on chairs, hiding a sofa, engulfing a piano and overflowing to the open door and seemingly to the hall beyond. As the man with the beard and the shawl peered out over the swirl of stacked and scattered canvases he appeared for a moment like King Canute ankle-deep in the tide. He was Louis Michel Eilshemius, the "supreme Parnassian" and "transcendent eagle of art," as he liked to term himself. Above him, from a towering cabinet, two stuffed pelicans, with the dust of decades on their plumage, looked down placidly.

The canvases in the room were but a fraction of his output. He had painted nine thousand pictures, he said. But that was nothing. He had also written two hundred books—most of them, unfortunately, as yet unpublished. He had consoled himself by composing at least a hundred pieces of music, among them "Six Musical Moods" and "Oenone and Eight Other Tone Pictures by Louis Michel Eilshemius, M. A., Marvel Musician-Composer, Improvisatore, Soulful Master." On a card which he handed to strangers in the street he was more explicit. It read: "Louis Michel Eilshemius—Painter, Poet, Composer, Marksman, Inventor and Ex-Fancy Amateur Dancer." But when he had occasion to send letters to the newspapers, which was often—they were chiefly about modern art—he signed himself "Mahatma Louis M. Eilshemius" or "Dr. Louis M. Eilshemius, M. A., Wonder of the Worlds," and—for variety—"Mightiest All-Round Man."

The "mightiest all-round man" had fallen on evil days. Four years before, a taxi had backed into him; he had been chair-bound ever since. He ascribed the accident to the evil spirits of his enemies, of which he seemed to think he had a great many.

At seventy-three, he no longer painted or wrote or composed. In the old-fashioned, unwired brownstone house where he lived in lonely bachelorhood with a bachelor brother, he sat all day with his back to the window, in the room cluttered with his canvases and with some of his writing and music on a table beside him. It was there that fame, long in coming, had found him at last. Retrospective shows were his lot, and his nudes and landscapes hung in the Metropolitan, the Boston Museum of Fine Arts, the Cleveland Museum, Detroit Institute, Phillips Memorial Gallery in Washington, and the Luxembourg in Paris.

He spoke with pardonable glee; after all, he had known his own worth all along.

"I used to go to the galleries and shake my stick at the canvases," he told me. " 'Phftt,' I would say, 'these canvases are terrible. Come up and see my stuff.' Well, they came. When they saw my paintings, they said I was a Futurist. What's *that*? I was one hundred years ahead of my time. But don't put me down as an eccentric," he warned. "I'm a great man." His shaggy white beard thrust forward dramatically. "Great art is vision, imagination—nothing else. Nobody can beat me for nudes—I'm bigger than Michelangelo."

A moment later he reminded himself that a critic had called some of his nudes wooden.

"Why," he exclaimed, "all my nudes are wonderful! Why, the biggest men say they sing. Wood doesn't sing. What makes me so wild are these critics. They don't know anything about me. Wooden nudes! Why, they sing!"

Limpid blue eyes flashed fire, gnarled hands gesticulated. I observed that he had the look of one deliciously surprising himself by the things he is saying. When he had recovered he said: "Here is one of my books. Poe wrote his in ten years. I wrote mine in ten hours. Poe? Bah! I'm better than Poe."

I looked at the title page: *Creation's End, A Four Page Epic and Two Other Poems, by Louis M. Eilshemius, Poet-Painter-Composer, Born 1864 at Laurel Hill Manor, now part of Kearny, N.J.* One of the poems was *Rhapsody of Regret*. It began:

> Mary, golden tressed Mary!
> I was innocent athen.
> Mary, tender eyed Mary!
> Would those love-days glow again?

As the poem unrolled the lines grew longer, the language more intense:

> As we spake thy Dido-body languishment bespoke.
> Thy neat limbs were dapper, as the dainty elves
> Crossed anow; now tightly pressed against each other.
> Mary! The window-panes they glared like storied delves!

And so forth. Poor Poe, I thought, with his paltry

> Helen, thy beauty is to me, etc.

"Some of these fellows make fun of me," said Eilshemius. "That doesn't pay. You don't make fun of Milton, do you? Or Shakespeare? Well, I have the brain of Milton and the versatility of Shakespeare. Sometimes my language is better than Shakespeare's. He was slipshod, you know."

Poor Shakespeare, who never "blotted a line."

He paused for breath. Suddenly he said: "How do I look?" and reached for a mirror on the table beside him; peering into it, he picked up a pair of scissors. He then proceeded to trim his beard.

"I'm a genius," he said. "Genius is very sensitive, you know. Everybody that comes here says 'You're a master.' Well, that settles it."

For a moment or two he turned his gaze on the open door, staring at it with an impatience that bordered on agitation.

"Look at him!" he suddenly jeered. "He can't walk!"

He pointed derisively.

I looked up and saw a thin, bent figure dressed in the fashion of another age painfully moving down the hall while supporting himself on a handrail. It was his brother. Slowly, painfully, the bent figure shuffled past and disappeared around the bend of the stair.

"He can't walk," Eilshemius repeated, and there was a note of joy in his voice.

"What do you like to do now that you don't paint?" I asked him.

"I like to swear like a trooper," he replied. "Gol ding it, damn, I'm a devil. I'm the biggest devil the world has ever seen." Somewhat lamely he added. "I like devil-people."

Did he like any other painter?

"No, only my own self. I don't favor any living human being. There are no great artists today."

It was somehow understood between us that there was an exception.

"Here," he exclaimed, "look at this art magazine!" He waved it aloft. "I wrote to them to print some good stuff—not Picasso and that sort of thing. By golly, they obeyed me. Look! There's my picture and two of my paintings."

He paused to let that sink in.

"Art," he suddenly exclaimed, "is like a bird flying through the air—you know that, don't you?"

Again I looked up, and saw the stuffed pelicans gazing down with lacklustre eyes.

3

Dawn Powell's poem is entitled *Dead Things*. Dawn was one
of the first friends I made in Greenwich Village. We picked
each other up, though not in the street. It happened in Kling's
bookshop, where our browsing came together over a new
periodical; a sonnet of mine was set large on the front page.
She was pretty, slender, and shy; the tragedy that was to op-
press her life and her husband's was still in the future—
the near future—and the wit for which she was to become
famous was not yet in evidence. Her husband was the wit.
She invited me to their West 9th Street apartment to meet
him.

Joseph Gousha (pronounced "Goo-shay") was a Penn-
sylvanian of French extraction, with very blond hair, very
blue eyes, and charming old world manners. When he greeted
you at the door the greeting was princely; even when he did
not actually bow, a bow seemed to hover between his guest and
himself. He had been a newspaperman and wanted to become
a writer. "But I married a girl with more talent than I have,"
he told me, "and I think she should have the chance to develop it."

During the thirty-five years that I knew him he worked
in an advertising agency. Time and his sedentary occupation, together with drinking, bloated his figure; but his
princely manner never left him. They had one child, a boy
slender as a wand, and beautiful as a boy can be; by the time
he was five it was apparent that all was not right with him.
It may explain the drinking, in which Dawn joined, and
sometimes led. She drank gin, and it is extraordinary that she

COLLEGE OF THE SEQUOIAS
LIBRARY

should have produced so much, and of such high quality, considering the number of tuns of gin she must have consumed in the years that I knew her. Like Joe's, her figure, in time, rounded out, while her tongue got sharper. But, unlike most literary lushes, she never attacked her friends. I see her two images in my mind—the warm, eager, pretty, and ambitious young woman from Ohio, and what she became.

It was in the Gousha apartment that I met Edmund Wilson, who later was to write a long, thoughtful, and appreciative account of her work. I also met Eugene Jolas, whom I was to see again in Paris. Another writer I remember meeting at the Goushas was Jacques LeClercq, whose daughter, Tanaquil, born in 1929, was to enchant ballet lovers.

There were many literary discussions. Present at most of them was a man with luxuriant sideburns that seemed to merge with the coarse tweed Norfolk jacket that he always wore, which gave him the appearance of a shaggy turtle. His name was E. Ralph Cheyney, and he was the sole begetter of the *Independent Poetry Anthology, 1925* which, as the title page states, was "an unedited collection of contemporary American verse never before published." Once was enough for most of the work in it, including my own; I except only Genevieve Taggard's *Mirror*. Cheyney's *Dialogue By Way of Introduction* is a crashing bore. So, come to think of it, was he. How could those interminable discussions about poetry have been so exciting and so upsetting?

Dwight Fiske, another friend of the Goushas, was a nightclub entertainer. His specialty was a risqué monologue which was half sung, half narrated from the piano. His hands were usually on the keys, but his body was twisted toward the audience, so that the salacious import of his composition could be beamed from his eyes and flashing teeth, punctuated by occasional bursts or tinkles on the keyboard. He was a witty conversationalist, but in retrospect I cannot separate his wit from his mannerisms. One night I was with him and Joe Gousha in a restaurant on Lexington Avenue. I do not recall other diners being present, and it is possible we were alone, dining and drinking late because Joe was working late. A cat belonging to the establishment went by our table with tail straight up in the air. Fiske instantly dubbed it "Snowflake" from the view it exposed. Again, flashing teeth, flashing eyes, and gesturing hands played their part in our common hysteria.

I think Dawn picked up some of Dwight Fiske's mannerisms; I know she admired him greatly. Another friend whose wit she admired was John Mosher, a charming man and one of the early editors of the *New Yorker*. He told her once: "You must come see my new apartment—I have a bed like a bruise!" From Fiske or Mosher, or both, she picked up the use of "My dear" to mock the speaker:

"My dear, I have discovered the most wonderful beauty parlor!"

"What do they do there, my dear?"

"My dear, you wouldn't believe it!"

"Do, do tell me."

"They use soap and water."

She afterwards developed and used this in a play.

At a party I gave on Perry Street there was a woman who sat on the floor. Dawn was in a chair yards away from her, but little by little the woman came closer, crawling with a glass in her hand, and looking up admiringly at Dawn. Soon she was beside Dawn, who jumped up.

"I didn't want a lapful of ears," she told me.

4

I no longer remember when I first learned that Dawn had a lover. As they were so much together, for so many years, there must be many people who never knew that she had a husband. Her lover looked all his life like a combination country squire and man-about-town. He was the editor of a travel magazine, and it may be that it was under his tutelage that Dawn became such a steady drinker, since the only traveling he ever indulged in was a pub crawl. His name was Coburn Gilman. They grew stout together.

Gilman possessed one of the most boisterously cheerful personalities I have ever known, and merely to be near him was to banish gloom. Even his accidents had their cheerful, hilarious side. He was accident-prone.

The accidents that befell him were recounted by him with charm and wit; but occasionally they were serious enough to lay him up. I recall going to see him in a hospital on East 19th Street, after he had been run over in proximity to it. He was quite unabashed and cheerful. Sometimes, after a party, when he was foolhardy enough to leave by himself, a search had to be instituted for him. He was usually found on the parlor floor, back of the stairs, having slithered over the banister on contact.

His most spectacular feat in this line did not result in any injury. At a large party uptown—I think it was on Park Avenue—he was, as usual, the last remaining guest, and in fact did not leave at all. His host put him to bed. The next morning, host and hostess went to their respective jobs, leaving him to sleep it off. Cobey awoke. Stark naked, he walked down the hall, saw a door, opened it, closed it, and found himself in the hall. Turning back, he now saw that there were several doors, any one of which might be the right one. He tried them all; all were locked. This, to be sure, was bad enough; but what was worse was that he did not know the name of his hosts. He had been brought there by a friend.

He rang for the elevator.

The elevator man took one look, yanked him inside, and descended nonstop to the basement. Gilman's charm worked. He was given an old pair of trousers, perhaps a shirt as well, and thus garbed, with bare feet, made his way to the open air, determined to walk to his apartment on Lafayette Street. There was a police prowl car on the corner, and he was halted. Again his charm worked. He was driven downtown.

I asked Dawn once, after Joe's death, when she was coming to dinner, if she would like me to ask Cobey to make a fourth.

"No," she replied in a flat tone of voice. "I don't want to carry him back."

A final glimpse of them, and of her husband.

Early one evening, a few years ago, I went into the Cedar Tavern—the original one, on University Place near 9th Street —and saw Joe Gousha in a booth. He was drinking a martini and reading the *World-Telegram* with a scowl. In another booth sat Dawn and Cobey Gilman, glowing with gin and laughter. Perhaps he had just recounted one of his mishaps.

5

In the Gousha apartment, in that still happy year of 1925, I met a young couple who were poor and ardent. He was a dark Irishman, very good-looking, with piercing eyes and curly black hair. His suits were always elegant; perhaps they were also frayed. Her dresses were on the simple side—tight bodice and flaring skirt. She was very intense. Her intensity charged the room; sometimes, when he was talking, her breathing became rapid and rapturous, her bodice seemed on the point of bursting, and one half expected her to cross the room and fall into his arms. He was an entertaining talker. They lived together. Both wrote poetry; hers was very passionate—reading aloud, she almost swooned before she got to the end.

Poverty at length compelled them to get jobs; books were their life, and both went to work in Brentano's, which was then on Fifth Avenue near 26th Street. I dropped in one day.

He was in the fine bindings department, she behind a counter. He saw me come in and led me to her; a few words were exchanged, and he led me back to his domain. We chatted awhile; then, before I knew what he was about, he had thrust two leather-bound books—they were very small—under my arm. Taking me by the other, he escorted me to the door and out into the street, where he said goodbye and left me.

I stood rooted to the ground, or sidewalk. I expected, and half hoped, that someone would emerge—the store detective —and arrest me on the spot. The enormity of the deed, to which I had been made an accomplice, almost overcame me; it would have been a relief to be seized and conveyed to prison.

Thus I stood, I do not know how long; then, on leaden feet, I started to walk southward. I walked very slowly, reluctant to go too far. In this manner I came to Madison Square. I told myself I would go no farther; I would sit down on a bench and wait for the blow to fall.

I sat down. The books were still under my arm, clamped as in a vise. I put them in my lap; they were getting uncomfortable. Now, surely, I would be seen; the stolen property was in plain view. A minute passed. Another. I felt too weak to stand up. Almost without thinking I found myself holding one of the volumes in my hands. It was a Keats, bound in smooth blue leather. It was not a rare book; in recollection I am certain it was one of the little Oxford World Classics editions, which sold for fifty cents; but, of course, it was bound. The other little book was Housman's *Last Poems*, another reprint: this one was bound in brown calfskin.

I read in one first, then the other. I woke from my enchantment to the reality of Madison Square and a wicked world. I was no longer weak in the legs—I was hungry. Clutching both volumes in one hand, I left the little park and walked back to the Village.

I was not followed, and was not arrested. When I saw my friends again they hoped I was getting pleasure out of the books. I had to admit I was. I never called on them again during working hours.

I saw the ardent couple in Paris during my first year there. We drank a bottle of cognac in their hotel room, and recited poems to each other, full of tenderness for our words, expressed in quavers.

I wish I could write a happy ending to their story. They returned to New York. I do not know what became of their love of poetry, or their love. They married, but not each other. He went to Hollywood, where his good looks and abilities were useful. She has two poems in the *Independent Poetry Anthology;* both are of the bodice-bursting variety. Reading them over, I saw her flushed face again and almost heard her breathing.

Chapter Five

1

I try not to think of the buildings that have been torn down and of the widened streets which, capable of holding more traffic, brought that traffic in. The widening of 8th Street, in particular, seems like a crazy bureaucrat's dream. To widen it, the sidewalks were narrowed; there was hardly space to walk two abreast, and parking meters were added.

8th, between Fifth and Sixth Avenues, was once a distinctive street. There were always three or four bookshops on it, and no neon signs, no pizza palaces. I have mentioned the Washington Square Book Shop; another was that of Francesco Bianco. Though in a basement, it was wainscoted and elegant, and was a favorite "hangout" of George and Ira Gershwin.

Bianco dealt in first editions. He also did some publishing on the side. His books were beautifully designed and printed; one of them, *Natives of Rock,* a collection of poems by Glenway Wescott, was illustrated by Pamela Bianco—"that wonderful painting child," as Richard Hughes termed her. She had become internationally known at the age of twelve with an exhibition at the Leicester Galleries in London. Walter de la Mare wrote a series of poems to "illustrate" her pictures, and the result was a book, *Flora,* now extremely rare.

The past weaves its own spell, making everyone look backward. Hughes, author of that durable masterpiece, *A High Wind in Jamaica,* had started out to pay tribute to Robert Graves on his seventy-fifth birthday, then found himself invoking other early friends—T. E. Lawrence, Masefield, "all the Nicholsons," De la Mare, Davies, Blunden, Sassoon, and "the Biancos."

At the time I met them they were living on the top floor of a brownstone on Grove Street; now, as I write, that apartment glows again with tranquil hospitality—high teas and talk, Mrs. Bianco, with a Dutch boy coiffure, pouring with a cat in her lap (later, she had a Pomeranian). Margery Williams Bianco was the author of many children's books, among them *The Velveteen Rabbit* and *Poor Cecco.* A niece of hers married Eugene O'Neill, and their daughter, Oona, married Charles Chaplin. I happened to meet Bianco on 8th Street the day of the wedding. Grinning happily, he asked: "Did you know that I am the uncle of Charlie's aunt?"

One saw famous writers and painters at the Biancos; but the focus of attention was always Francesco. Perhaps he was such a good host because he was himself such good company. He had a ready wit, and was quick to see the ridiculous lurking everywhere, for he seemed able to invoke it at will. In the deflation of pompous persons he showed real artistry, for he always began tentatively and even deferentially to differ before going on to quibble or spoof. But when he was once fairly launched there was no stopping him, and it was sometimes a question whether his eyes were flashing indignation over an opponent's stupidity or triumph at his own feats of demolition.

On a more sombre note he sometimes repeated his own aphorism: "There is a cure for everything, except stupidity."

He admired Cummings greatly, and Housman and De la Mare. He often quoted Moréas, and had made a translation, for Eugene O'Neill, of Rimbaud's *Bateau Ivre*. Boswell's *Life of Johnson* was a book he read over and over, and he was fond of reading aloud the famous passage in praise of Iona in Johnson's *Journey to the Western Islands of Scotland*. I owe to Bianco my first introduction to the *Life;* I have had, and have given away, many editions, but can never, I suppose, forget the feel and look of the two-volume, blue-bound Oxford edition he gave me when I was a young man.

Bianco was an accomplished linguist. I have been with him in strange restaurants, discovered on our rambles, when he pinpointed a French, German or Italian waiter's *birthplace* by his accent. He belonged at one time to a club where all business was transacted in Latin. He spoke English fluently, and was extremely well read in it.

Like all true classicists he despised shoddy writing, and could be devastating over a single inept sentence. I must confess that his strictures were sometimes humorless as well as merciless. He was also contemptuous of writers who used foreign phrases in their work without a real knowledge of the language they were borrowed from. Generally, however, he wore his learning lightly, though he could never resist a malicious pleasure in correcting intellectuals. In simpler company he never tried to overawe those whose education and tastes were different from his own.

This was one side of him. On the other, he had that almost extinct social grace which confers on the person just met not only warmth of welcome but interest in his or her concerns. It was sincere; he had a real feeling for people— to which, of course, they responded. All who knew him recall him with affectionate phrases, and recall almost as a special gift of his how often he had made cheerfulness break through. He had another gift which seemed hardly of our time—letter-writing; his letters were lengthy and prompt, and they were written in a beautiful script, like copperplate engraving.

I have saved, for later telling, the greatest gift of all.

2

In one of the houses on the north side of 8th Street, near Sixth Avenue, was the press of Samuel Aivaz Yakob Sheraaobode Azerbajode Muradkhan, a stocky, swarthy, dark-suited man with black hair and large melting but nevertheless inscrutable eyes. The East dwelled in them—the Middle East. He was a Persian. Slow, suave, with a low-pitched, rasping voice, he was impatient with strangers, sycophants, and Bohemians in general. He was a printer—with a difference. Upon his types he lavished the affection of a lover; he set copy, whether on a linotype machine or by hand, as a diamond-setter might set a row of diamonds, caressing each. His types were his jewels. He had large, caressing hands.

At the time I met him he was "typographer to E. E. Cummings," a title bestowed on him by Harry Hansen in the New York *World*. Francesco Bianco introduced him to me as "Mr. Jacobs," and Samuel A. Jacobs was the name that appeared on his business card and books. Mr. Jacobs had just printed a book by Cummings entitled *&* in two editions totaling 333 copies, one numbered and signed and consisting of 111 copies on Vidalon handmade paper, the other on De Coverly rag laid, and merely numbered. The poems in *&* were thought to be daring; but that was in 1925. The book was shown, on request, by Josephine or Chase Horton of the Washington Square Book Shop, but only if you were known to them; it ceased to exist for snoopers and other suspicious-looking characters, in particular the radar-nosed John S. Sumner, secretary of the Society for the Suppression of Vice, who had a habit of dropping in, on mischief or his favorite reading bent.

Mr. Jacobs told Cummings about me; Cummings asked him to bring me to 4 Patchin Place, where he lived in a single room on the top floor. I was introduced with the remark, "Poets should know each other," and a bow from Jacobs for both poets, and perhaps all poets. Cummings smiled; his hair was blond, and his golden smile and hair seemed to light up the unlighted hall. Then he stepped to one side so we could enter. I took in the whole room at a glance. I have never seen another like it.

From the door a path led to an easel at the far end, which was not very far. The path was a bare expanse of floor about a yard wide, bordered on either side by burnt-out kitchen matches, heaped inches high, and criss-crossed like the twigs of a charred hedge. The twin hedges were similar in texture and depth; he must have dropped a match on the left side, and alternated it with one on the right, as he stepped back and forth from easel to door, from door to easel, day after day. At that time, and for years afterward, Cummings smoked everything—a pipe, cigars, cigarettes. Then, on his doctor's orders, for a decade and a half until his death he stopped; but as long as twelve years after he had stopped he told me he still missed smoking.

As for his painting, he always painted more than he wrote, both in New York and at his New Hampshire farm. When he won the $2,000 *Dial* Award for his poetry in 1925 the announcement stated "he has become more and more absorbed in painting," and it surprised no one on that publication, least of all the managing editor, when Cummings submitted a picture to mark the event. Marianne Moore told me:

"Winners of the award were supposed to contribute to the issue announcing the award. But instead of a poem, Cummings preferred to publish a painting. He invited me to his Patchin Place studio, on the top floor of no. 4, to help him choose one. It was not a very big piece of work. We let him choose it; *he* was to like that issue. He was very careful about his reproduction, its proportion and size."

"Not very big." It was very little—approximately 6⅛ by 8¾ inches (measurements from the inner edge of the gold frame). The subject is a somewhat formal yellow rose with stylized, pointed green leaves rising gallantly from an opaque pitcher in tones of red, green, and gray on a table splashed with red. The medium is watercolor applied thickly. Cummings gave it to Miss Moore in 1938; it hung in her Brooklyn apartment and is now in her West 9th Street apartment above a shelf full of his books. She wrote him about her present: "After studying this very noble rose—the turquoise under-leaf and touch of red reflected back even to the petals, I can surmise why botanical gardens and over-flowered shops do not abound in yellow roses. Yet they might, and still lack this one."

I have always been an admirer of Cummings's paintings, and in the late thirties, when I came into some money, I purchased four. Later still, when I wrote his biography, I devoted an entire chapter to his painting. Nevertheless, people generally have not grasped the fact of the amount of painting he has done, or of the beauty and competence of his work. He, too, must have pondered the disadvantages of being a poet *who also paints*. The foreword to one of his catalogues, in dialogue form, ends:

> Where will you live after this war is over?
> In China; as usual.
> China?
> Of course.
> Whereabout in China?
> Where a painter is a poet.

3

He was thirty-one years old when I met him. Although he was only five feet nine or so, he gave the impression of being taller by the way he carried himself, shoulders squared and head thrown back, as in the bust of him by Gaston Lachaise. His eyes were hazel, his mouth full and sensual. He had an extraordinary attraction for women, then and later. I once had tea with him and his third wife; present also was a Bennington alumna with whom I fancied myself in love. The fancy passed. When we left she said:

"I'd like to live with him for three years."

I was considerably startled, for I had had the same idea about her, without setting a time limit.

"Why?" I asked. "And why three years?"

"Because I would like to know him well, really well, and it would take that long."

Many years later I took my daughter to tea with the Cummingses. On the way to Patchin Place I asked her not to smoke when we got there, because he had given it up, and it might disturb him.

"Oh, Charles," she exclaimed, "you'll make me dislike him."

She did not smoke while we were there. I think she forgot all about it. Cummings had welcomed her, and continued to talk to her, as his guest, as someone in her own right. When we were safely in the street she turned and embraced me.

"Charles!" she exclaimed. "I love him!"

She returned to school—Chapel Hill, not Bennington.

On an earlier visit, just after the war, when I was living on the top floor of 66 Bedford Street, a large studio apartment with a raised living room reached by a short flight of steps, I gave her a party. I invited all the young people I could muster, and asked Cummings, too. After much dancing and a great deal of eating, the youngsters decided to see the Village and trooped out. Cummings and I sat amid the wreckage. He was very pensive. Suddenly he said, "You know I have a daughter named Nancy, too."

I did not know; I was astonished. He told me the following story.

A year or two before, while at his New Hampshire farm, he passed on the road near his house a young woman he did not know and who did not know him. In the country manner both said "Good morning." This occurred several mornings on his walks; he saw that she was a visitor at the farm next to his, which belonged to the family of William James. The young woman was his daughter by his first wife. She had been brought up under another name. She had since learned who her father was, and there had been a reunion at Patchin Place.

The image of a father and his daughter passing each other like strangers on a country road brought tears to my eyes. We sat in silence in the silent room.

In 1946, Cummings published a one-act play in blank verse entitled *Santa Claus: A Morality*. Although I deprecate in others the reading into literary productions of ideas and symbols which are seldom present, I believe that this play contains, in poetic and symbolic form, the autobiographical fragment given above. In it, a little girl recognizes Santa Claus even though he has exchanged masks with Death, but without knowing he is also her father.

The farm in New Hampshire, which Cummings inherited from his mother, consisted of three hundred acres of woodland. There were only two crops—birds, and the landscapes he painted on immense canvases. Over the years, regional lumbermen tried to buy some of his stands of trees, but he would not sell. He did not even cut the grass around his house because thrushes' nests were so thick on the ground.

The porch was hung with vials of sugared water for hummingbirds. He told me once, in New York, that the hummingbirds bade him goodbye when they set out on their incredible flight from New Hampshire to the Caribbean. One day, at the farm, I observed them doing it. He had remarked quietly: "They're bowing goodbye." I looked, and there they were, ascending to the top of the screen and descending, five or six times, like tiniest helicopters. Then they turned and flew away.

4

Cummings was unlike most of the poets I have known. He was interested in people. His poetry reflects that interest, and *The Enormous Room,* of course, is not so much autobiography as a celebration of people under that peculiarly twentieth-century form of duress, the concentration camp.

One day at Patchin Place, during God knows what kind of discussion we were having, he suddenly said: "You are not very fond of people, are you?"

I asked uneasily: "Why do you say that?"

"Because you haven't written any prose," was his reply.

I have often pondered this seemingly simple statement. A man who writes prose is more likely to be writing about people than a man who writes poetry. To write about people, one must be interested in them. I have since written a great deal of prose; but perhaps it was of the wrong variety.

Cummings went where people congregated. He liked prize fights and burlesque, about which he was an expert. Wrestling appealed to him because of its pictorial quality; he used to make little line drawings at the old Madison Square Garden on the backs of checks and envelopes. He went to an occasional movie, although he despised the medium. To him, Hollywood "distantly resembled a rather undersized hen's egg into which has been introduced a rather oversized ostrich chick." I remember a remark he made during a newsreel. It was just after the annual Irish Sweepstakes winners had been announced, and now some of them were being shown on the screen. Suddenly I felt a nudge; Cummings had inclined his head toward me.

"Want to know why you and I can never win one of those things?" he whispered.

"Why?" I asked, startled; also, someone was hissing. He replied:

"Because we don't look like that."

There is a more or less widespread myth that he was antisocial, but I believe the opposite was true, and that only work or illness ever kept him away from people or a party (provided, of course, that he wanted to see the people or attend the party). But like every intelligent person he was jealous of his privacy; although even this has been exaggerated. He was once stopped on Sixth Avenue by a man who afterwards complained to me that Cummings had simply said "I don't know you" and walked on; but it is always risky to interrupt a poet in meditation, and perhaps sheer vanity or optimism to assume that one will be remembered after a single meeting.

Cummings wished to be free, on his walks as elsewhere, and he had only himself to keep himself so. Freedom was, in fact, a kind of obsession with him; hence his remark, at dinner once in my apartment, that he had just passed Ossining on the train, that he always felt a chill going past a prison, and—with a shudder—"I still feel a chill." He had not forgotten his own confinement in France during World War I.

He was a great observer of occasions. If someone did something unexpected and pleasant he sent flowers, to male and female alike. When he learned that I was going abroad he deemed that an occasion which ought to be marked in some way. He decided to give me a *bon voyage* dinner at Marta's on Washington Place. He also asked Jacobs. Although it was during Prohibition, there was a bottle of wine on the table.

Cummings was a charming host, an entertaining companion. Even at his most serious his mind was never far from humor or burlesque. He had a light voice which seemed to go with the whimsical side of his nature; it was a very cultivated voice, but though light, was capable of extraordinary modulations—from Harvard to hoodlum—and it made an excellent accompaniment to his habitual mimicry. The waiter lingered by our table, the owner came to beam at us. When Cummings took out his checkbook, I said:

"If I were the owner, I'd keep that check with your signature."

Cummings laughed.

"I hope it will happen," he said, "but I believe otherwise."

He exchanged glances with the owner, who laughed, too. The eyes of Samuel Aivas Yakob Sheraaobode Azerbajode Muradkhan rolled ecstatically.

5

Joseph Ferdinand Gould was the subject of several poems by Cummings, who also painted his portrait. One of the poems gave him the lasting sobriquet of "little Joe Gould."

Five feet four—bald, bearded, and spectacled—Joe flapped like a scarecrow when he walked, for everything he had on, from his hat to his shoes, were handouts from friends. He had many, and regularly paid his respects to all in one grand circuit of Greenwich Village.

Weather never deterred him. I saw him once from a doorway during a summer downpour that had cleared the streets. He trudged past me like a diver, jets of water spouting from his shoes, and twin waterfalls cascading fore and aft from his turned-down hat. It happened on 10th Street; I guessed he had just been to call on Cummings. I got home in time to hand him a dollar in the hall.

After one of these circuits he returned to the dives which were his usual haunts in lower Greenwich Village, where he was pointed out to newcomers and sightseers. For them he had a gambit suited to the place.

"I believe in democracy," he would say to a stranger. "I believe everyone has the right to buy Joe Gould a drink."

The right was frequently exercised.

Joe was no ordinary panhandler. He was, to begin with, Harvard *magna cum laude,* of that famous class of 1911 which included Conrad Aiken, T. S. Eliot, and Walter Lippmann. I used to feed him, too; but a time came when he was so bedraggled that I began to intercept him outside my door. The first time I did this I gave as my excuse that I had a girl inside; his eyes lit up behind his spectacles and he looked as though he thought me a very gay dog indeed. Thereafter, the pattern was set; he rang the bell, I went into the hall.

I took him to dinner once at the San Remo on Mac-Dougal Street. He told me then that his last square meal was in June, 1936, when he attended a class reunion. I would give anything to see a film of that event, with Joe gorging himself in the midst of awestruck educators, financiers, corporation heads, and other illustrious alumni, including poets. But I can report on the dinner I gave him.

Clams again! New England to the core, Joe preferred clams to Italian cutlets. He devoured a plate of them, and then another, and was so bespattered that a paper napkin applied to his mouth and beard disintegrated, leaving his beard like a hedge in winter when the first snow falls. He drank beer with the clams.

"British beer," he commented, "has only hops. American beer has hops, skips, and jumps."

When coffee was served, he asked me for a cigarette.

"I feel naked without a cigarette," he said.

Those eyes behind the spectacles—how merry they were!

He smoked with a holder.

Joe's wit was greatly enhanced by the way in which he delivered his lines. He spoke slowly, with a nasal Yankee twang. He was born in Norwood, Massachusetts, the son of a doctor and the grandson and namesake of a professor in the Harvard Medical School. His father, he said, "held the pessimistic belief that the Americans were the best people God ever made." His own views were more generous. In one of the notebooks which he carried around with him, under the heading, "Why I Never Expect to Marry," he had written: "I never expect to marry because my horoscope says I will marry outside my own race, and I have never met a human group that I did not think of myself as belonging to."

He never married.

His interest in racial groups led him to another startling conclusion.

"The greatest invention in the world," he also had written, "may have been the wheelbarrow, because it taught the Irish to stand on their hind legs."

Although Joe was little, he told me that he thought of himself "as at least six feet tall." It may explain why he declared, in another of his notebooks: "I have delusions of grandeur; I believe myself to be Joe Gould."

I asked him if he had really said: "The Goulds were the Goulds when the Lowells and Cabots were clam-diggers," which was going the rounds. At first he regarded me with suspicion; but suddenly the eyes behind the spectacles began to gleam, and he replied in his slow, nasal Yankee twang:

"What I really said was, 'When Sir Ferdinand Gould was returning from the Crusades, he stopped off at Hanover to buy a loaf of pumpernickel from the ancestors of the present kings of England.'"

He now complained to me that he was "the most quoted and least published author" he knew. He also quoted himself.

"I have slept with the Lady Poverty," he told me, "but I am a conservative person and do not consider that an introduction."

I had just read that sentence in one of his notebooks, which he carried around with him in a battered portfolio, under his arm in summer like a businessman, and against his chest in winter. I never saw Joe without his portfolio; Cummings told me he remembered the start he got the first time he did.

6

The notebooks contained portions of an enormous work whose existence has been questioned, and whose full title was *An Oral History of Our Time*.

"My general idea," Joe said, "is that every human being is as much history as a ruler or celebrity because he illustrates all the social forces."

The concept led him to take down conversations overheard on park benches, in bars, and in subways and flophouses. The manuscript at one point towered seven feet, which led Joe to boast that he was the only author in history who had written a book taller than himself. Some pages from it appeared in the *Dial,* the *Little Review,* and in Pound's *Exile.*

A few years ago the *New Yorker* published a series of articles by Joseph Mitchell which cast doubt on the existence of Joe's major opus. Recently, Dr. Theodore Grieder, head of the Special Collections at New York University, showed me half a dozen of the notebooks, which he had just purchased. The handwriting was Joe's; the stains were vintage Gould. I predict that more of them will turn up.

Joe also wrote poetry.

> "Who killed *The Dial?*
> "I," said Joe Gould,
> "With my inimitable style,
> I killed *The Dial.*"

An oft-quoted couplet is:

> In winter I'm a Buddhist,
> And in summer I'm a nudist.

With Maxwell Bodenheim as his sponsor, Joe became a member of the Raven Poetry Society of Greenwich Village and took part in its exhibitions of poems tacked to West 4th Street billboards. Criticized for not being serious enough, he retorted that "neither were most of the members, since they wrote only on such trite themes as life, love, and death."

He was thrown out.

It was M. R. Werner, author of *Barnum* and *Tammany Hall,* who gave Joe his most spectacular handout. Werner had just closed a deal with Hollywood and was understandably cheerful. The bell rang. He guessed who it was.

"Tell you what, Joe," Werner told him. "I'm going to give you a check for twenty-five dollars."

The two men studied each other in silence. Then Werner went to his desk, wrote the check, and handed it over. Joe looked at it and at him, and remarked nasally: "Reckon this lets you out for quite a while, doesn't it?"

He stayed away six months.

Almost everyone he knew achieved, in time, some fame, some money, or at the least, a fixed abode; Joe alone remained a vagabond—in his own phrase, "the last of the Bohemians." The Village was his home; a doorway to sleep in sufficed. One trip away from it made an indelible impression.

"I once spent seven years in Philadelphia one Sunday afternoon," he told me.

When I asked him why he had never been to Europe, he replied: "Why should I go slumming? In the United States I meet a better type of European. If I went abroad, I would only run into second-rate Americans."

7

I went abroad in November, 1925, bearing a letter of introduction from Cummings to T. S. Eliot. I did not deliver it (but mailed it later).

All I remember of London is the funeral of Queen Alexandra, the cold, and a book. All the men wore black ties; some also wore black armbands. It was a city of bowlers, furled umbrellas and black ties, black armbands. It was impressive; it was England.

There were icy sheets in my bed in a Bloomsbury hotel, and I paid an extra shilling a day for a coal fire in my grate. One morning in the dining room, where I ate enormous breakfasts of hot cereal, grilled sole, and chops, a new waitress addressed me.

"You are American, aren't you?" she asked.

"Yes," I said. "How did you know?"

After all, I had only ordered breakfast, and I may even have pointed to the menu with a numb finger.

"Because you are wearing a muffler," she replied, a little smugly, I thought.

One day in my wanderings around London I found myself in a book shop holding a long, thin, buckram-bound book. Opening it at random, I began to read: "Inquisition indented taken at Detford Strand in the aforesaid County of Kent within the verge on the first day of June in the year of the reign of Elizabeth by the Grace of God of England France & Ireland Queen defender of the faith etc. thirty-fifth, in the presence of William Danby, Gentleman, Coroner of the household of our said lady the Queen, upon view of the body of Christopher Morley, there lying dead & slain."

I went back to the opening paragraph. I read from the beginning. I read the whole book through in the shop while people came and went, perhaps stared at by them and the proprietor. I bought it. It was the Nonesuch Press edition of *The Death of Christopher Marlowe* by Leslie Hotson, who had discovered the coroner's inquest, and other documents. The thirty-fifth year of the reign of Queen Elizabeth was 1593. Marlowe had been killed "within the verge," that is, within twelve miles of the sovereign's person, and the inquest was held under royal supervision. The mystery which had surrounded Marlowe's death for more than three centuries was over.

All that I knew of Marlowe's work at this time was what I had been taught in high school—that is, the passage from *Doctor Faustus* beginning:

Was this the face that launched a thousand ships?

Now a great desire to know all of it seized me. I bought the *Works*. It was the great Oxford University Press edition by Professor C. F. Tucker Brooke of Yale. When I opened it at the hotel I was dismayed. It was based on the first editions, and the text was in the old spelling. I persisted; afterwards I could not bear to read Marlowe modernized.

I carried this book with me everywhere. I carried it into the army. It was a secondhand copy, and cost four shillings. The original owner's name is on the flyleaf; the handwriting is upper class and I am unable to read it. Under his name he wrote

60th Rifles
1910,

the year the book was published, so he must have been, like myself, a Marlowe enthusiast. When I went into the army I wrote my name underneath, and under my name

338th Infantry Reg.
1942.

But first I took it with me to Paris. One night, a night of loneliness and rain, under the rain-drenched awning of the Dôme, I sat on the deserted terrasse with Marlowe and a drink. Inside, all was gay, all was loud, and waiters with trays drifted to and fro through smoke as through fog. I became aware, at length, that the terrasse had another occupant. I looked up and saw, at a nearby table, an American with an amused expression on his handsome face, which told me he had been watching me for some time. I said "Hello," and he suggested I bring my glass over.

"What is the book?" he asked.

I handed him Marlowe's *Works*.

"Oh!" he exclaimed; "that!"

He began to look for something, and finally found it and read it aloud. It was the description of Leander. When he got through, I took the book and read, from the facing page, the description of Hero.

He looked pained.

Chapter Six

1

I had gone to England to write, perhaps to study—to spend, in fact, a long time there. Such had been the earnest advice of my friend and patron. How lucky I was; how irresponsible I turned out to be. I had fallen in love on shipboard, and was pining and fretting in London, waiting for a letter from Italy. Mark Tobey was a witness to my agony. He was traveling with a family (related to Muriel Draper) which was chaperoning a beautiful young American woman from Reading, Pennsylvania. He was very sympathetic, and I fear I must have bored him with my daily and nightly confidences.

In London, I saw Tallulah Bankhead in *The Green Hat,* after pacing back and forth between two theaters trying to make up my mind. Thomas Hardy's *The Dynasts* was playing at the other, and I finally persuaded myself I was too unhappy to see such a serious work. Another missed opportunity! And one Sunday I went to the Albert Hall to hear Vladimir De Pachmann. He began a Chopin prelude, then stood up abruptly and came to the footlights. "Wasn't that wonderful?" he asked breathlessly. The audience stomped, whistled, and applauded, and he returned to the piano very pleased with himself.

The letter came. I rushed to get a visa and crossed the Channel. We met in Paris. She returned to Italy. I stayed where I was, still in love, and somewhat the worse for wear.

My American friend from the Dôme terrasse was a painter who painted reclining young men with Easter lilies sprouting from their loins. He was not a bad painter. He came to my pension to invite me to a party. It was not his party, but one given by Janet Flanner. There were a lot of strange people there, and I became defiantly drunk. Miss Flanner's friend was Solita Salerno, a dark-eyed novelist; they were standing near a table full of bottles when a phonograph started up, and I simply walked over and put my arm around Miss Salerno and began to dance with her. A look of astonishment or outrage passed between them, but it was nice to be dancing, and it added to my intoxication. Mark Tobey told me when I saw him that Miss Flanner disliked me, but admired my work. He thought this a stunning compliment. I have read Miss Flanner steadily through the years, and admire her immensely.

The next thing that happened was that my Dôme friend invited me to go with him to Villefranche to stay with Jean Cocteau, he said. I declined. And then, one day, he called to tell me that he was going to another party, but would not ask me to go with him because I had not enjoyed the first one, but that he would leave the key under his mat, and that if I were not there when he returned he would kill himself. He left a present with me, a gold lamé turtleneck sweater. I never wore it. I was not present when he returned. He did not kill himself.

Countée Cullen arrived with his clergyman father. They wanted to see the Folies Bergères and bought three tickets so we could go together. When the time came I could not go; I was in bed with a fever. They were not to be put off. They came to my pension and tried persuasion. Then the Reverend tried healing. He pushed up the top of my pajamas and rubbed my back. It worked. I leaped from the bed and dressed. We made the show.

The great attraction, of course, was Josephine Baker. She came onstage clad only in a tail-feather. A gasp of admiration, followed by prolonged applause, filled the theater. I thought that not even the Greeks had ever fashioned such a figure. The Rev. Mr. Cullen seemed pleased that God had. When Countée nudged me, I saw that his father was on the edge of his seat. His eyes held fiery gleams.

The Cullens left, and I continued to mope. Harold Stearns sent me to a doctor he knew. The doctor was charming; it was almost worth while being ill to meet him. He said to me: *"Pourquoi êtes-vous triste? Vous êtes jeune, vous êtes poète, vous êtes à Paris; c'est le printemps."*

I pondered it.

I met Harold Stearns at the Select. He was another member of the class of 1911 at Harvard, and famous once as the editor of *Civilization in the United States.* His pronouncements were admired in intellectual circles. One of them was: "There is something the matter with a culture whose youth is eager to desert it." Then he left, too, to join the expatriates. He is Harvey Stone in *The Sun Also Rises.* He was also "Peter Pickem" in the Paris edition of the Chicago *Tribune.* He told me that he had evolved a foolproof system for playing the horses. His appearance belied this. I treated him to drinks. He drank champagne cocktails.

One afternoon Brett slid onto the stool next to mine at the bar. She said: "Will you buy me a drink, chappie?" I said: "What would you like?" She liked a champagne cocktail, too. She had on a floppy, drab-looking hat. I did not think her very pretty. But Harold Loeb has a drawing of her he made which shows her as she must have appeared to him and Hemingway. Loeb is Robert Cohn in *The Sun Also Rises.*

I never met Hemingway; later, when I went to live in Saint-Germain-des-Prés, I used to see him bicycle up to the curb at the Deux Magots, have a bock, and leave. He was a handsome man, red-cheeked and smiling. His smile was for everyone. It was nice to have seen him with his big apple-cheeked smile.

It was easy for a young man living in Montparnasse to fall into a pattern of strenuous unproductivity. One rushed to the Select in the afternoon, and drank. Then one went to dinner somewhere, and returned to drink some more. Then one went to the Dingo, to have scrambled eggs and listen to Hilaire Hiler play the piano. One went home to sleep into the middle of the next afternoon.

There was a beautiful blonde American girl who came to the Select every day. She was always the center of attention, surrounded by men, each of them full of hope. She had a husband, usually there, too, but on the outskirts of the circle, crowded out by the men who wanted to sleep with his wife. I do not remember his name; her first name was Grace. I had occasion to remember it.

Her husband was despised by everyone. He may have been all right sober, but nobody ever saw him except when he was drunk. He got drunk in the most miserable way. After several drinks he was abusive and combative—not too combative, or he would have been mauled about a bit. His abuse was directed against everyone, and lacked style. It was built around four-, seven- and eleven-letter words. One night, as he was tirading, everyone sick over it because of the look of anguish in his wife's eyes, I saw her raise her *fine à l'eau* to her lips and bite off the top of the glass.

2

I was living in a pension in a cul-de-sac near the Boulevard Montparnasse. After several weeks on the ground floor I decided I needed a quieter location. Old ladies with black shawls gossiped in the parlor, and a little girl, whose mother went to work, roller-skated in the hall.

The *femme de chambre* told me I could have the room above. I asked her if the occupants had moved out. She looked surprised, and assured me it had been empty a long time. It was my turn to look surprised. My things were moved up. My first night there was also my last. When I got into bed and put out the light—the switch hung from the ceiling like an old-fashioned toilet pull—I heard something leap from the windowsill and start toward me. I quickly pressed the button. I saw nothing. I pressed the button again, and the leap from the windowsill followed.

After several such pavans and excursions I resolved to see it through. I switched off the light. The footfall followed; whatever it was, it came toward me. It reached the bed. It sliced through my body like a cold knife and disappeared into the wall, which was papered over with monstrous maroon flowers. I switched on the light, and spent the night reading and dozing by turns. I left the pension as early in the morning as was decently possible. I fled the quarter. I went to live in Saint-Germain-des-Prés.

One Sunday evening, as I was sitting on the terrasse of the Deux Magots as idle as could be, a man whom I did not recognize stopped by my table and said hello. With him was a beautiful blonde girl who also said hello. I recognized her. I asked them to sit down, but he made a counter-proposal. They were on the way to a nightclub; would I care to join them? He did not appear to be drunk. I said I had no money on me. He had an answer to that, too—I would be his guest. I went.

The nightclub was on the rue du Lappe. There was an orchestra in one corner, and linen-covered tables around the walls. My host ordered champagne. It did not take us long to consume the bottle of champagne, and he ordered another. We drank that, too. He ordered again. His wife was between us, and it was pleasant sitting there with her next to me. She was radiant. I looked forward to dancing with her.

He would not mind, I thought to myself, if I had one dance with her, and perhaps another before we left.

The orchestra began to play. I waited for him to get up and dance with the radiant girl who was his wife; instead, he ordered another bottle of champagne. He now suggested that I dance with her. A fleeting, troubled look passed over her face. I thought him a boor, but was eager to comply.

She was a good dancer. We danced a great deal. The only time we were not dancing was when the orchestra was not playing. While we danced, he drank.

A little after three in the morning, as we were all sitting at the linen-covered table on which several empty bottles stood forlornly, he announced that he was going out to get some air. The troubled look passed over her face again. We watched him walk the length of the dance floor. As soon as he had reached the door, she turned to me. I saw the old look of anguish in her eyes.

"You had better go," she said. "There's going to be trouble."

"What kind of trouble?" I asked; but perhaps I had guessed.

"I know him, he's not coming back," she said. "And I have no money with me, either."

"Do you really expect me to leave you here alone?"

"No," she whispered.

I saw that the waiter was looking at us. I called him over and asked to speak to the proprietor. The proprietor came; he was well-fed and had a flourishing mustache, much loved and much stroked. I explained. My host had left; he was a little inebriated, and might not come back. I had no money on me. I would, however, identify myself. I would return the next day and pay him. I had money in my room; meanwhile, I would leave my watch. I displayed it.

"Monsieur," he said, "if you have money in your room, I will accompany you home and you can pay me there."

His reply incensed me, and I refused. What—take a man to my room at three o'clock in the morning?

"In that case," he said, still calm, "I will have to call the gendarmes."

His mustache swung around; following its course I saw two gendarmes in the doorway.

"Call them," I said.

He called them.

The gendarmes escorted us to the door and into the middle of the rue du Lappe. Walking with them in the middle of the street we arrived at a police station. One of the escorting gendarmes explained to a gendarme behind a shabby desk. He pointed to a wooden bench against a wall. It was narrow, and turned out to be hard as well. We sat on it until morning. Squads of gendarmes reported for duty, or went off duty. They looked at us and shrugged. I sat stiffly on the bench, her head on my shoulder.

At nine o'clock we were ordered to get up. Once again we were escorted to the middle of the street, this time by two gendarmes in front, and two bringing up the rear. Everyone looked at us, but we did not mind. The air was cool, and we enjoyed stretching our legs.

I do not recall how many blocks we traversed in this manner. Perhaps the police station was near the courthouse. We found ourselves in another room, this one representing justice instead of crime, and there was a gleaming desk instead of a shabby one; it was also high, and a magistrate peered down at us. In addition to the gendarmes, there were several civilians. One of them was the proprietor of the nightclub, another our waiter.

The magistrate demanded to see our *cartes d'identité*. He seemed surprised when both of us admitted we did not have them on our persons.

"But you must have them on you at all times!" he blustered.

We were meek and silent.

He now asked my companion her name. She gave it. He had no trouble with her surname, but could not get the hang of Grace. He asked her to repeat it several times. She and I put our heads together. What could Grace be in French? Perhaps a hard "a"? She growled it out in what she hoped was Gaulic fashion:

"Grr-ah-ss."

"Ah," exclaimed the magistrate; *"Grâce, alors!"* He wrote her name down. He smiled, and we smiled, to him and to each other. I think he liked the idea that a young American woman bore such a name. He now asked for mine.

"What is your occupation?"

"Je suis poète," I said.

The words, which rang out in that tiny courtroom, appeared to take him by surprise. He stared at me. A clerk ran up, whispered and pointed to the proprietor and waiter. The magistrate shrugged. He was not interested.

He dismissed the case.

Vive la France, where a man can term himself a poet and be taken seriously. I believe it is the only time in my life that I have so termed myself. It is not a word to bandy about. Neither is *grâce*.

We reached the street without an escort. I hailed a taxi and took Grace to her hotel, where I dropped her off. It was the Hotel Lutetia, where the North Vietnamese negotiators first stayed when they arrived in Paris. I went on to my pension and plunged into bed like a diver. I never saw her or her husband again.

3

One day, as I was going past the Café des Deux Magots, I saw Cummings. He was sitting at a corner table on the terrasse with Michael Larionov, painter and designer for the Ballet Russe. We saw each other at the same time; in a moment he was up and we were shaking hands. I said: "I am glad to see you." Instead of replying, he smiled and pointed. There was an automobile at the curb, and on the automobile a pennant with the word "Forever" on it. And forever it was.

Cummings was living in a courtyard studio at 248 Boulevard Raspail with his second wife, Anne Barton. She told me later how they had met Larionov, and through him, Picasso, at the Russian Ballet. She had gone with Cummings and Lewis Galantière, and as they were standing in the lobby she became conscious of two men staring at her. Galantière knew Larionov, and introduced him.

"Picasso then asked Larionov for an introduction," Anne told me, "which led to tea in his studio and a private showing of some seventy-five paintings. I was awed and petrified, to say the least; finally, Picasso said to Cummings: 'She reminds me of a rabbit eating cherries.'

"He had the simplest sort of apartment—it was over the Galerie Paul Rosenberg. There was an old upright piano and on it one of those glass paperweights with a figure design by him inside, and in one corner a large rubber ball which he had covered with paint; this was for his son Paul. Not a single picture was visible.

" 'I paint here,' Picasso told us, 'then I just put the pictures on the elevator, they go down to Rosenberg, and that's the last I see of them. Very handy!' "

Picasso's first wife, Olga Khoklova, was present at the tea, as were several other dancers from the Russian Ballet, and Larionov's wife, Nathalie Gontcharova. Later, Picasso, Anne, and Cummings went down to the gallery, where they sat on a sofa while an attendant showed them the master's works. Picasso stood behind the sofa, and from time to time leaped in front to peer into their faces.

I saw the Picasso show after it was hung. It may have been a retrospective, because the first picture in it was an early, representational one, small, dark, done in Spain and, I think, signed "Ruiz."

Despite the fact that Larionov was married, as was Anne, he began to call on her, bringing long-stemmed roses, sometimes leaving them by the door when she and Cummings were out.

"He was a wonderful man," she told me, "but not my cup of tea."

Another couple: more trouble.

Walter Lowenfels was a poet. He once shared a poetry prize with Richard Aldington. Aldington's wife, Hilda Doolittle, signed her poems "H. D." When Lowenfels published his first book, he signed it with his initials. He looked over my earliest blank verse poems in a condescending sort of way, and remarked that if they had been his he would have eliminated every third or fifth word. It was not a basis for friendship; what happened next increased the distance between us.

One day, far from my usual haunts in Paris, I met a young American woman. She was slender and dark, and when she smiled it was as though every feature smiled; even her teeth. It is what I chiefly remember—that wonderful smile, and not her features. I was instantly enamored. Idiotically, when I saw Lowenfels that night, or the next day, I raved about the dark, strange, and smiling beauty I had met. The more I talked, the more thoughtful he became; at last he asked me her name. He not only knew her; he was going to marry her.

Our friendship was over.

Another drinking spree.

Eugene Jolas invited me to have a drink with him at a café near the Eiffel Tower. It was very pleasant sitting in the open, with the Eiffel Tower magnificently straddling air in plain view. I was greatly impressed. This was before I went up it.

From time to time I have encountered people curious to learn how much liquor I can hold. I think Jolas was one of them. He recommended a Pernod, which I had not previously sampled, but did not have one himself. It loosened my tongue. Looking at me brightly and admiringly he said: "Well, I thought you were an aesthete, but I see now you are a regular guy." With the Pernod inside me it sounded good. He suggested another. At the end of that one nothing sounded good, possibly because I could neither see nor hear, and had to be lugged to a cab. He sat beside me to prop me up.

Chapter Seven

1

My new home was a pension on the rue St. Benoît, next to the Impasse des Deux Anges. It was behind an iron gate; a path bordered by shrubbery led to the house, which was shuttered and serene like a house in an Impressionist painting. My room was under the eaves. When the bells of Saint-Germain-des-Prés struck the hours their fading ripples of sound filled the room.

A short walk up the rue St. Benoît, left on the rue de l'Abbaye, brought me to the Place St. Germain and the Café des Deux Magots. It was there that I spent most of my first year in Paris. Winter or summer, it was pleasant to sit there and sip drinks and look and jot down lines.

I never ate in the pension. I had petit pain and coffee at the Deux Magots, and lunch and dinner at the Pré aux Clercs on the corner of the rue Bonaparte and the rue Jacob. The food was very good, inexpensive, and the waiter cheerful and friendly. His name was Emil; later he became the proprietor. But sometimes I went to the Deux Tours, on the Boulevard St. Germain, where there was a wonderful scallopine of veal Florentine, with ham rolled up inside the veal, and creamed spinach inside the ham.

Julian Green used to come into the Deux Magots around nine-thirty in the morning, order a coffee, and start a page in his schoolboy-size notebook. When he got to the bottom of the page he stopped writing, possibly in the middle of a sentence, and shut the notebook. The waiter brought his coffee, and he sipped it like a man who had done his day's work, which he had. He wrote in French; his novels had to be translated. Many years later, as I continued to ponder the phenomenon of such a morning's work, I made some calculations. If he wrote three hundred words in that notebook every day, in thirty days he would have nine thousand words, and in six months more than fifty thousand. Mr. Green was handsome and distinguished, and no doubt had many calls on his time. He never looked bored, and was treated with great respect by the garçon. I never saw anyone interrupt him. He is now Julien Green, and a member of the French Academy.

I saw other celebrities, without meeting any of them. I did not go to the rue Fleurus to pay my respects to Gertrude Stein; it might have been useful, but I never thought of it, and no one suggested I should do so. I met her brother, Leo, however, at the café, but no longer remember how that happened. All I remember of our talk was the impression he left with me, no doubt by design: that it was his taste, not his more famous sister's, that started her on her famous collection.

With Leo Stein was a man with whom I became friends in New York, many years later. He was John Cournos, a member of Pound's Kensington circle, who inherited Pound's Church Walk flat when the poet went to live in Paris; now he, too, was there, a slender, self-effacing man with several novels to his credit and a poem in Pound's *Des Imagistes* anthology of 1914. A gentle soul: H. D., Richard Aldington, William Butler Yeats, Pound himself, thought the world of him, as I learned thirty-three years later when I was gathering material for my biography of Pound.

2

There lived in the pension a young woman, a student at the Sorbonne, who had many friends, young as herself, some of them English. She was American—from Georgia, I believe. She was a slight, pale girl with luminous blue eyes and straw-colored hair who looked exactly like a Marie Laurencin. There was a poignant as well as delicate quality about her. The group as a whole, waiters at the café and restaurant, and trades-people in the shops of the quarter, accorded her a kind of unique homage—solicitous and protective at once. The young women in her circle did not look on her as a rival; as for the young men, there seemed to be an understanding about her —they could share her company in public, but no private, individual pursuit would have been tolerated. She always left the café early, and always alone.

Her best friend was an English girl named Elizabeth Montgomery. Another member of the group was Edward Lockspeiser, the future biographer of Debussy. Through them I began to be aware of a man, whom I shall call Mr. Flaherty.

Mr. Flaherty was six foot one, broad of shoulder, massive as a walrus from shoulders to waist, but with tapering legs. He moved with the weight and authority of an irresistible force. At the café, where he ordered a vermouth before din-ner and sat gazing out with ambassadorial detachment, everyone—waiters, customers, passers-by—beheld him with admiration and seemed to brighten at his presence. He was so big, so *magnifique!* After his vermouth he set out for the restaurant. Emil bowed, rubbed his hands together, and escorted Mr. Flaherty to a table which was reserved for him; then, taking up an empty bread basket, Emil filled it with *croutons*—heels of loaves—and was rewarded by Mr. Flaherty's smile. It was a daily ritual; Mr. Flaherty liked the heels of fresh loaves, and Emil liked to provide them. Next, they put their heads together. Emil disappeared, and Mr. Flaherty tucked an immense napkin into his collar.

He began his dinner with a bowl of Potage St. Germain, a specialty of the house, and followed it with a thick Chateaubriand garnished with watercress, a dish of boiled potatoes and string beans, a demi of wine. A green salad, for which he mixed the dressing himself, while Emil handed over in their proper order mustard, salt, pepper, vinegar, and oil, topped but did not quite conclude the repast. Emil now opened a trap door and descended to the cellar, whence intimations of his errand were wafted to the restaurant, which had begun to fill up.

He emerged with a round, open wooden box which he bore before him as once a duke might have borne, on a velvet cushion, the crown of his liege lord. He waved the box under Mr. Flaherty's nose, and smiled with pleasure and relief at the approval in Mr. Flaherty's countenance. No one else in the restaurant approved. Emil set before Mr. Flaherty a wedge of cheese the size of a pie cut, and the last *crouton* accompanied the cheese. Coffee and a liqueur followed, and there began to be perceptible on Mr. Flaherty's face a kind of incandescence which was as much an exudation as a glow.

Replete with food, wine, coffee, and liqueur, he now brought forth from his tightly stretched waistcoat a silver cigarette case, tapped a cigarette on it, and permitted Emil, who had been hovering by the table for this moment, to strike a match and light it. It was only then that Mr. Flaherty, throwing back his head to exhale the first puff, deigned to look around at the other diners. His eyes sought and found what he was looking for. It was the pale American girl, sitting with her friends at two tables which had been pushed together. I was at one of the tables. The talk was about Mr. Flaherty.

Once a month, without fail, Mr. Flaherty disappeared from his usual haunts, and was absent three days on a magnificent drinking spree. During this time he walked sideways like a crab, progressing by zigzags. At this particular juncture, I learned, he should have been absent; but there he was, a puzzle to all. Some members of the group were actually impatient with him for falling behind on his schedule. What they did not know, and what I afterwards learned from Lockspeiser, was that Mr. Flaherty had fallen in love with the Laurencin girl, and feeling love's redeeming powers, had vowed not to go off on another bistro crawl while she was in Paris.

3

Mr. Flaherty rose, and weaving his impressive way past our tables as though unaware we existed, left the restaurant and returned to the café. Ostensibly, it was to sip a cognac; actually, it was to await our coming, to feast his eyes once more on the blonde girl. When we arrived, Mr. Flaherty glanced at his watch. His pleasure was tinged with dread of the moment when she would leave, which would be exactly half an hour later.

On this particular night another couple, known to some

members of the group, arrived at the café at the same time and sat down with us. Some minutes later, the newcomers were greeted by a man who was a stranger to the rest of the group; he was introduced, and drew up a chair. After scanning the faces of all present, his eyes returned to the face of the blonde girl. I did not like his stare; neither did Mr. Flaherty, as it turned out. I saw him signal the garçon for another cognac.

As the garçon turned away from Mr. Flaherty's table, quite suddenly the blonde girl got up to go. The stranger rose with her and said that he would see her home. A stunned silence followed his announcement. She looked perplexed and, with the stranger at her side, left the bright terrasse and was lost in the darkness beyond.

Mr. Flaherty had shared our astonishment and indignation. He set his glass down on the marble-topped table and strode with piston-like precision to the rue St. Benoît. Peering into the black depths of the garden between the gate and the pension he saw them almost at once. To a casual observer they might have been in an embrace, but he knew otherwise. Her hands hung limply, her head had fallen forward. The man who was with her exclaimed: "I only tried to kiss her." He pushed her toward Mr. Flaherty, who quickly scooped her up, at the same time giving the man a sharp cuff that sent him reeling from the garden into the street.

I learned the next day that the girl had been taken to the American hospital at Neuilly. I did not see Mr. Flaherty for three days. On the night of the third, I went to the Deux Tours. He was there.

His head and massive shoulders were hunched over a tablecloth on which a monstrous rose had blossomed from an overturned wine glass. A cigarette was burning itself out in his right hand, which hung over the edge of the table. The cigarette burned down to his fingers, and he dropped it; at the same moment he raised his head slowly and opened his eyes, which were not focused on the immediate scene.

Stubble shadowed the usually florid steeps of his face.

The corners of his mouth were smeared, and there were wine and other stains on his shirt, tie, and waistcoat, all of which were crumpled as well as soiled. His eyes found my table. At Mr. Flaherty's signal the waiter brought another bottle of wine. He set it down reluctantly, I thought; there was pity in the glance which he gave me. Seeing the bottle, Mr. Flaherty roused himself.

"Care to join me?" he asked.

It was several minutes before he spoke again.

"I am glad it is you," he said, "and not one of the others."

A look of pain passed like a cloud over his face, and he moistened his lips several times. The gathering spittle began to glisten unpleasantly. I looked down at my glass. He poured some more wine into his with an unsteady hand, managed to get it to his mouth, not without some loss, which he wiped away with an angry gesture. When he set the glass down, it turned over, and the new stain merged with the old in the middle of the tablecloth. He bowed his head.

"Do you wonder why I go off like this?" he asked, his eyes fixed on the dark pattern before him.

"It doesn't matter," I said. "It's all right with me."

"When I was a boy," he persisted, "my father asked me to saddle the mare. He had business to attend to before nightfall. I saddled the mare," he went on relentlessly, "but I forgot to tighten the cinch-strap. Night fell and my father did not return. We went looking for him with lanterns. We found the mare first, with the saddle under her belly, then my father. He was lying in the road with his head bashed in."

Staring straight ahead Mr. Flaherty began to cry. I took up his silver cigarette case and extracted a cigarette. He thrust it into a corner of his mouth, where it fell apart.

"Let me take you home," I said.

Mr. Flaherty rose slowly, painfully raising the burden of himself, and let me take his arm. The waiter ran to the door to hold it open. As we reached the street, Mr. Flaherty began to walk sideways, and at every four or five steps had to be pulled back from the curb.

4

Edward Lockspeiser was a year younger than I was, but compared with me he was a man of the world. He had run away from home and school in England, and had been in Paris several years when I met him. He spoke French fluently; in the summer of 1926 he went to the Lago di Como, and came back to Paris speaking Italian.

He had, what may be rare, a cynicism which was charming. His comments on men and things were accompanied by a smile of such warmth that for a moment one thought he was praising someone or something instead of criticizing. To give his smile full play, he removed the pipe which he smoked constantly.

Lockspeiser's head bore a remarkable resemblance to the bust of Beethoven one sees everywhere, and often in his company I thought that this is how the young Beethoven must have looked. Another thing pleased me; I knew him to be a man of talent, and I observed that his fingers, like mine, were short and blunt. He was writing music when I met him, and he played the piano well. I recall a concert where a composition of his was played; the conductor was Vladimir Golschmann, to whom Edward introduced me. Mr. Golschmann was very young, too. Edward's piece was dedicated to the Comtesse de Noailles.

Edward was a good story-teller. Perhaps his effects were heightened by the way he had of modulating his voice, as though orchestrating it. He had that very enviable British characteristic of never beginning with the air of one with a priceless story to tell, nor at its end did his expression indicate he had just told it. On a visit to London he wrote a card or a letter which he did not mail because he had no stamp. That night he dined with a friend who admired his work and wished to show him a good time. Several pounds were spent on it. Edward asked him for a halfpenny stamp. He got it. At a late hour, after walking his friend home and saying goodbye at his door, he was called back. His friend said: "Oh, I say, Edward—can you let me have the ha'penny for the stamp?"

The modulation and mimicry of this remark were sublime.

I went with Edward to the Eiffel Tower. I do not like heights, and I was a fool to ascend. We found ourselves on a little platform. Edward threw one leg over the railing, and half turning to me, said: "What a wonderful place to conduct an orchestra!" And he flung his arms about. I wanted to sink to the floor, and had to be helped down the steps to the elevator.

On another occasion we went to a cinema. There was a three-piece orchestra there. First he annoyed me by making strange sounds, as of trumpets, horns, and flutes, under his breath. I was relieved when they ceased. Then I saw he was not there. I became apprehensive. I got up to look for him. He was standing in the aisle a few rows back; his arms were moving up and down rhythmically, and I could hear as I approached, the *sotto voce* orchestration of his mouth. His face was flushed and ecstatic. He stopped abruptly and followed me to our seats.

Before he went to the Lago di Como there was a stupendous musical event in Paris. I wish I could say that it was his idea to attend it; I suspect, however, that I thought it up myself, for it was connected with literature, in the person of Ezra Pound. The event was the first performance of George Antheil's *Ballet Mécanique* at the Théâtre des Champs-Elysées, Mr. Golschmann conducting. Antheil was Pound's protégé.

It took place on Saturday, June 19, 1926. I saw Pound for the first time, and looked with awe at the undisputed ruler and law-giver of English and American poetry. James Joyce sat in a box, distant and detached, with a black patch over one eye. I did not see Eliot, present, I have read, as the escort of Princess Bassiano. Sylvia Beach, of the famous Shakespeare & Company book shop at 12 rue de l'Odéon, wrote later that Pound was in the gallery, surrounded by Left Bank friends, but I distinctly remember seeing him below, where the action was; but perhaps he flitted about and we are both right.

I sat in the orchestra. The theater was packed with, as Lincoln Steffens noted, "all the queer people in Paris, French and foreign, men and women. Wild hair, flannel shirts, sticks, no hats, and big hats for both men and women, and, note well, many intelligent faces." He overlooked umbrellas.

On the stage there were eight pianos and one player-piano; at the player-piano was Antheil himself. He wore bangs. There were also xylophones, electric bells, whistles, loudspeakers, and in the center of the stage an airplane propeller. Nobody believed it would go on, but it did.

Everyone was stunned when the performance began. The din from eight pianos and the player-piano made that tightly packed audience heave in anger. Cries of "Enough!" "Enough!" filled the air the first minute, and the aisles over-flowed with protesters; but whether they wished to get at the musicians or get out, I cannot say.

Suddenly, without warning, the airplane propeller began to whir. Its blast blew right down into the audience, and a gasp of surprise or rage was heard above its roar. Umbrellas were opened for protection; those without them climbed over seats to get out of range. Adherents of Pound and Antheil swarmed into the aisles, shouting encouragement, and there were duels with sticks and umbrellas, both open and shut, and many fist fights. Above the din of the *Ballet Mécanique* and the orchestration of hisses, insults, and applause, was heard Pound's voice. He was hanging, according to Miss Beach, head downward from the top gallery.

5

Guy Endore was another young man with whom I became friends. When I met him he had not yet published anything, but when we were back in New York I took two of his stories to the *Bookman,* and "Two Stories by S. Guy Endore" duly appeared, in the issue of January, 1929.

Endore was very slender, with the kind of features which are termed "chiseled." His hair was golden and curly, and he also looked like a Greek god. There was nothing effeminate about him. But he had one peculiarity, which was to make trouble between us. He was a vegetarian. He also liked snails. I cannot now reconcile this with his vegetarianism. I was also to have trouble with him over snails.

One day, when he and I were at the Deux Magots, he told me about a Columbia University professor he knew. The professor was an ardent Francophile. He could not bear to see France in trouble. France was in great trouble; her governments fell almost daily, and the franc fell with them. The franc was about forty to forty-five to the dollar. He could not bear to take all those francs for the dollars he exchanged. When he went to a bank to exchange his dollars he counted out the prewar total and shoved the rest back.

I was moved by this story. It was the kind of thing one dreamed of doing one's self. The government had called on all patriotic and loyal Frenchmen to turn in their paper francs to bolster the gold reserve. Here was an American who had heeded the call. I felt proud of him. I wanted to meet him. But Endore told me the professor had gone to Portugal.

"Why Portugal?" I asked.

"There are no Americans there," was the reply.

"You mean to say there is no American Express Company in Portugal?" I asked.

"No," Endore said.

I said, "Let's go."

He said, "I'll go pack."

We called the garçon, paid the bill, and separated. He went to his place on rue Monsieur le Prince, I to my pension on the rue St. Benoît. We met at the Gare de Lyon and took the express to Marseilles.

Why Marseilles? Because we were out of our minds. Our plan was to get to Lisbon or Oporto by sea; was not Marseilles the great seaport of the Mediterranean? Were there not many ships there? Perhaps we could even get a sail boat to Oporto.

The truth of the matter was otherwise. All the seaborne traffic between France and Portugal left from Boulogne, a short distance from Paris.

We did not know this. We were in a compartment of the Marseilles express, blissfully speeding through the French countryside. Sharing the compartment were two other passengers, one a countryman, Morris White, on his way to visit Frank Harris in Nice. The other was a Frenchwoman, perhaps thirty years old. She had a seat by the window, facing Endore and White. We tried not to look at her.

I had met White in New York, and had seen him briefly in Paris. He was a dark, spectacled young man with jet-black hair. His hands were long, with tapering fingers. He wanted to be a writer, and a great deal of our talk on the train was about writing. We also talked about food; at Lyon there would be a five-minute stop, and it was our plan to be ready to hop off the moment the train slowed down, dash into the station, purchase sandwiches, and dash back.

The train slowed down. We sprang up. The Frenchwoman grasped my hand.

"*Allez! Allez!*" she commanded Endore and White. "I will look after *bébé*."

She pulled me back beside her. They gave us astonished glances and ran pell-mell from the compartment.

A basket, which I had not seen before, appeared. From it she took a cold chicken, bread, pears, grapes, and a bottle of wine. There were plates, glasses, and napkins. We were feasting when White and Endore returned. They munched their sandwiches in silence.

Night fell. The lights went out. White and Endore slept sitting up. When I took her hand, she snatched it away. But she was not angry. When she was certain the others were asleep she rose and left the compartment. I followed her. She led the way past other dark compartments to the platform. In that swaying enclosure we embraced, clinging to each other in sweetness and love while the train poured its black length through the exploding night.

6

The next day Endore and I trudged up and down Marseilles, seeking out shipping lines for the voyage to Portugal. There were no such shipping lines. We were tired and depressed. We discussed our situation.

We could still get to Portugal by train. It would take about three days. It was August. It would be an uncomfortable journey. Endore was willing; I was not.

We then decided we would find a place on the Riviera that was not too expensive, and spend several weeks there. Our plan was to stand on the platform of the local train and get off at the first attractive place. This is what we did, after spending the night in Marseilles.

We went to dinner. Enter snails. When Guy ordered them he saw my expression. He became angry.

"I wouldn't mind," he said, "if you had ever tried them."

"Will it be all right if I try one and don't like it?"

"Yes," he said, vehemently.

I called the waiter back and ordered six snails. Our orders came at the same time. There was a pungent garlic and herb sauce. I pried a snail out of its shell; it took some doing. I dipped it and took a bite. It was like rubbery chicken.

"Nothing doing," I said.

"At least you tried one," he said, smiling.

He proceeded to dispose of both orders. He also had a *bouillabaisse*.

The next morning, lugging our suitcases, we took the Côte d'Azur local. We came to a pleasant-looking place. We paid the conductor and alighted. It was Juan-les-Pins. The hotel was magnificent as a palace. Endore went in to inquire about rates. He came out and we resumed walking. We walked to Golfe Juan and rented a rundown villa. There was also a fig tree. When I told Endore I was hungry, and suggested eating, he said he had eaten.

"You've eaten?" I asked incredulously. "When? What?"

"Tomatoes and figs," he replied, pleased with himself.

I walked out and found a restaurant.

It was from this villa that I sent Eliot the letter of introduction from Cummings. Mr. Eliot was then editing the *Criterion,* and I enclosed a poem. It was called *Dead Men Under Buildings*. He did not take it. It afterwards appeared in the *Bookman*. He had very kindly suggested that I might have misused a word in the phrase "silver bird." If I let the adjective stand, he said, someone might see a mystical connotation which I had not intended.

I did not accept his suggestion. I was not yet a bird-watcher, and I liked the sound of "silver bird." Years later I changed the line.

Only one thing marred our stay. The villa was run down; it was also in rags, so to speak—there were cracks in the wall, leaks in the roof; after each rain, and sometimes without it, the ceiling in our huge bedroom became a mat of mosquitoes. All they asked was to be let alone until the light went out; then, that's all we asked. The problem was solved in an ingenious way.

Endore was athletic; perhaps he had been a basketball player at Columbia. There was a beach-ball in the garden. Our strategy was simple, and exposed great masses of the enemy to slaughter at one time. We put out the light and pretended to be asleep. At a signal, we leaped from our beds. I pressed the switch. He stood in his basketball stance with the immense beach-ball raised. With a piston movement of both arms the ball landed on the ceiling. The result was carnage. The maneuver caught planes just alighting on their home base, and made a thicker squash.

Our sojourn in Golfe Juan lasted seven weeks. I found Endore a good companion despite his idiosyncrasies about food. He had an analytical mind. I was greatly impressed by a chart he drew for me one day; by means of it he showed me that it was well-nigh impossible for anyone to go back more than four or five generations when tracing descent. Five generations back there were 62 ancestors; six, 126. He doubted that anyone could thread such mazes. He expressed regret that knowledge could not be transmitted; every generation had to learn certain things all over again, things that could not be passed on by word of mouth or even books. His conversation was brilliant. He was to become a fabulous story-teller, a true practitioner of the art of non-fiction novels.

7

In Golfe Juan I wrote a poem entitled *Côte d'Azur*. Because of it, several years later, agreeable tidings reached me about the Poetry Society of America. My informant was Henry

Goddard Leach, editor of the *Forum,* in which some of the best critical writing of the day appeared—by Mary Colum and Edith H. Walton—and some of my poems as well. Mr. Leach told me that he had attended a meeting at which editors in the audience were asked to define poetry. He said that when he was called on to speak he told the gathering that he did not have a definition but had brought something he thought was poetry, and would read that. It was my poem.

> Westward the galleys moved, the long oars shone,
> the slaves' chains clanked upon the oars;
> and captains cloaked in gold stood at the prows
> looking on Africa.
>
> Between them and Phoenicia the sun
> smote the fragile air like a burning gong,
> and past the golden beaches of the shore
> clouds like bright mountains piled beyond the hills
> glittered like imaginary lands, and birds
> streaked the blue sky with swift white cries.
>
> And tall black men with wooden gods
> came down to see them pass
> chanting for wonder by the warm
> magnificent Mediterranean.
>
> The wind by day blew gold, by night
> the wind blew silver.

Whether anyone remembered my name, or even the fact of a youth who had once attended as a member of a night, I cannot say. Endore wrote me recently:

"Several times I have been to Juan-les-Pins, to Vallauris and all that area, but I could never find the place we lived in. Everything has changed there so tremendously. A number of times I've been to Paris, and that hasn't changed much around the Saint-Germain-des-Prés area. Rue Monsieur le Prince is the same except that instead of whorehouses and little hotels it is all medical supplies and bookstores and one Vietnamese restaurant."

Chapter Eight

1

Morris White returned from his visit to Frank Harris. He had made notes of their conversations and was thinking of writing Harris's life. One night, on the terrasse of the Deux Magots, I said to him: "If you turn your head slightly, you will see the most beautiful woman in the world." He stared longer than I thought necessary, smiled with elaborate condescension, and said: "One of the most beautiful." His comment angered me.

I had seen her a number of times. She always came to the café with a German shepherd who sat by her table patiently, with well-bred boredom. His name was Wolf.

Her name was Anne Rose Morton. She had been studying music in Paris. She shared an apartment on the rue Jacob with another young woman from Asheville. Her friend's mother and her own were coming to fetch them back.

I met her mother. She was tall, with more than a trace of

the beauty she had bequeathed her daughter. She was a widow. When she died, and her daughter and I went through her papers, we found letters from Julian Hawthorne, son of the novelist; he had proposed to her, and had been rejected. I admired her firmness. He was a writer, too, and writers are notoriously poor providers. I leave the reader to imagine how she looked on me.

I returned to the United States with Anne and her mother and her friend and her mother; and Wolf. They went on to Asheville, I to a tiny furnished room in a rundown house which stood at 82 University Place, where the new Cedar Tavern is now located. There were three mail deliveries in those days, and my time was spent chiefly in running up and down the stairs.

I must have gone back to one of my old hangouts, for recently, when I had occasion to write Peter Blume in Sherman, Connecticut, he reminded me of it; he also reminded me about a transaction I had completely forgotten, just as I had forgotten about Montgomery Evans and the *Independent Poetry Anthology*.

December 31, 1969

Dear Charlie:

It was nice to get your note. You know it must be about forty-five years ago that we sat at a table in Romany Marie's and you offered me a blue serge suit which you had made for yourself in Paris by a very elegant tailor, but which you somehow never wore. Your natural style at that time was the loose-shaggy Harris Tweed. You wanted a modest ten dollars for it, if it fit me. Of course, I never, in those days, had as much as ten dollars in my pocket but I promised to get it from my dealer, the Daniel Gallery.

The suit was everything you said it was, the rich weave and the exquisite tailoring in every detail (Ebie still remembers how the pants fit the small of the back). It had wide lapels of a kind which were uncommon, an international cut and a buttoned flap for the inside pockets as a guard against pickpockets. Oh, yes, I paid you the ten dollars, and you threw in a Dunhill pipe to close the deal.

I wore it for years and years until it got mixed up at the cleaner's and I ended up with a miserable pair of serge pants—someone else's—a misalliance which was utterly disastrous.

If you have any recollections of that suit you might be amused by this.

As ever,
Peter.

I did not recollect the suit until I received Peter's letter. I still do not remember where I had it made, or how I could have afforded to do so. Most puzzling of all is that I should have bothered to bring it back, since I disliked it. I chose the durable cloth it must have been with pleasure; but when I put the finished product on I felt like a knight in armor. I must have put it away carefully as well as promptly.

I am glad Peter had such good use out of it. I only wish now that I had taken it back with me to Paris. Those buttoned flaps on the inside pockets!

Anne and her mother went to Provincetown for the summer; I followed. It was there that I wrote many of the poems that are in my first book. And it was there that I met Norman Perry, a young man from Newburyport, who was studying painting with a woman who did not paint any better than he did, and who had a voice that would frighten a crow from a fair meadow. I know, for I had to listen to it every day from the next room.

For I no sooner set foot in Provincetown than I was caught up in a crowd of young people from Greenwich Village thronged on the pier. Perry, who was with them, thought them the most wonderful people he had ever met; on the strength of our meeting in their midst he promptly invited me to stay with him. He was rich, he had a cottage, and would not hear of my looking for lodgings elsewhere.

Anne and her mother stayed at the other end of Provincetown, the genteel end, far from the madding, Bohemian crowd. I used to walk there; but sometimes I took the bus. That is how I became acquainted with a Portuguese girl who one day alighted with me in front of Perry's cottage. I asked her in. Perry's eyes lit up. She was spectacularly fleshed.

Now, Norman Perry was one of the handsomest, masculine men I have ever known. I add "masculine"; every woman in New York will know my meaning, for the city is full of handsome men, alas of no use to them. He had jet-black hair, flashing blue eyes, and a nose the equal of John Barrymore's for purity of line. But for some reason—I think it was my red hair—she preferred me. She had made this quite clear, and when I did not respond, she taunted me about my masculinity. But I was adamant. I was, and remain, scornful of promiscuity.

Our drinking and talking continued, and I began to think that Perry's charm was beginning to register. I seized the opportunity by announcing I would flip a coin for her. I lost. I hope I did not show too much joy. I slipped out.

Anne and her mother left. Perry dismissed his teacher. One evening, he and I loaded his convertible with canvases and drove to the ocean. The tide was going out. Standing there in the windy darkness, Perry took one of his canvases and tossed it into the water, then another, and another; soon a bobbing caravel of his paintings was bound for the open Atlantic. When the last one was launched he turned to me and said: "I know I am a bad painter. But I mean to learn all about good painting." And this is what he did; I met him in Paris the following year while he was making the rounds of museums.

From Provincetown we drove through the night to Newburyport, to a mansion with a circular driveway where there was no one at home except servants, Norman's parents being in Florida. A nightly ritual: every night before dinner he or a butler—I do not remember which; perhaps they took turns —poured martinis from an enormous German silver shaker. On one such evening, after dinner, Perry felt a great urge to go to Boston. We got into his car and drove there, going so fast that occasionally, when he passed a car on the right, I could look down into it.

Perhaps we stayed at the Ritz, for it was at the Ritz the next day that we joined a group of revelers who departed, with us in tow, for Lincoln, an opulent suburb. Our hostess was a pretty young woman whose escort was a young Italian count. Although I remember his name, I will not give it here. They had been quarreling, and the quarrel continued when we reached her house. In a large room lined with palms I heard her say: "Oh, if you mean Michael, I love him like a brother."

I leaned over and said: "You understand, Count—like a lay brother."

Heads popped up from drinks, the room froze. For an instant I thought I would be asked to leave. Then someone laughed or shrieked, and everyone joined, including the Count and myself. The quarreling ceased.

2

Anne and I were married in New York, and returned to Paris without Wolf—her friend got him. We found an apartment on the rue de Vaugirard.

The Museum of Modern Art recently displayed a rusty bed-spring splashed with plaster. I do not know why it was displayed; some people have always to be *à la mode,* no matter what the *mode* is, and the Museum people, perceptive and charming though some of them are, lend themselves to perennial frenzies for fear of skipping a footnote to the history of art in our time. I have skipped many such footnotes. When I saw that bed-spring I recalled another. It was in the apartment which my wife and I had rented from a little old woman dressed in black to the band around her throat. She lived in a wall near the entrance, in a cubicle just big enough to contain her cot. When we came in answer to her advertisement she showed us around. How cordial, how charming she was to us—young, American, and just married! She inventoried everything. She opened a cabinet full of lovely glasses; the moment she did so the top shelf crashed to the floor and several little glasses perished in splinters. She saw in this a good omen.

"Ah," she exclaimed with upraised hands. *"Quelle bonne chance!"*

We approached the bedroom. She hesitated. She drew back a step and looked up at us. She was embarrassed.

"Mais, Monsieur et Madame," she declared. *"Le lit—il chante!"*

She reached into the room and pressed her gnarled little hand down on the bed. It was true.

I did not tell anyone I was getting married; my wife told her mother on the phone before we sailed. Mrs. Morton made some inquiries about me; one of them was to Professor Munn. I bring him in at this juncture because in one of the rooms in the apartment there was a table eight feet long at which I did my writing; I had told him about it in one of my letters, without mentioning my bride. Paris seemed to me more expensive on my return, and I also asked him for more money. He wrote back, knowing I was married, but not telling me he knew:

Dear Charles,
If I were a young man in Paris, and had such a table as you describe, I should not only be happy to write on it, I should be happy to sleep on it.

Yours very truly, etc.

It was a great blow.

We continued to live as well as we could on a hundred dollars a month, supplemented from time to time by small checks for poems. On Thanksgiving Day we went to Foyot's. Waiters glanced at us admiringly; one of them led us to a table with a linen cloth which was stiff and sparkling and at least a quarter inch thick. In his eyes I was a rich young American; French logic told him that, else why had I come there with a young American woman of a beauty he had not seen for many a day, if ever?

Alas for Franco-American relations, always precarious; when I looked at the menu he had handed me with a smile and a bow I felt like an impostor. We did not have turkey, or goose, duck or even chicken; I ordered what I could on the money I had, which was not much, it being near the end of the month. It turned out to be a pâté de foie gras, of an excellence beyond compare on Paris's incomparable bread; but it was not what I had envisaged for my bride and me.

At a table not far from us a covey of politicians—who had been eating when we came in, and who were still eating when we left, napkins tucked into collars or unbuttoned waistcoats—glowed like the lamps in the Place Furstenberg from a profusion of pâtés, hors d'oeuvres, soups, fillets, vegetables, cheeses, wines, brandies, and liqueurs.

We should have gone to the Pré aux Clercs, where Emil made every day a holiday. Norman Douglas was a frequent diner there with Walter Lowenfels. Lowenfels always nodded, but did not introduce me; Douglas, on the other hand, always bowed to me and my wife, or perhaps just to her. There was a kind of poetic justice in this—she gave me the first copy of *South Wind* I ever saw, and I read it on the *De Grasse,* in which we crossed.

If only De Hirsh Margules had been there! He knew both men, and would have hugged my wife and me between the hors d'oeuvres and the Potage St. Germain, introduced us to Douglas, and to the people at the next table, and perhaps the one beyond, extolling my talent and her beauty, and waving his arms about like Prince Mishkin. Alas; it was one of his poor periods, and he did not dine out.

Small checks.

I sold three poems to *transition,* then called Eugene Jolas to ask him to pay me for them—it was an incredibly small sum, but I thought he sounded annoyed. He sent the check.

I sold a poem to the *Dial* and received twenty dollars for the eight-line stanza Marianne Moore used—there were, originally, three such stanzas and sixty dollars would have been better. She preferred to use only the first; it may have been the best stanza, but looked a little skimpy when it appeared under the title I had given all three, which was *Ode.* She was a stern editor, and in addition to dropping my second and third stanzas had made pencil marks around two words in the first; their omission, she suggested, would further improve my poem. I asked her, by return mail, to leave them in, and she did.

She was not stern when I met her. Her pink and white complexion was a marvel, and her braided red hair was heaped high, worth mentioning perhaps because the young tend to forget that the old were not always old and topped by tricorn hats.

3

Frances McClernan arrived. She had introduced me to Willard R. Trask before I left New York for London, and now I met him again in her company.

In an apartment on the Île de la Cité there lived a friend of theirs and mine named Marvin Lowenthal. Mr. Lowenthal was writing a life of Montaigne; it turned out to be excellent and unusual: *The Autobiography of Michel de Montaigne.*

His books made an imposing sight in the moted air of that charming apartment.

I am not one to inspect other people's shelves. Trask, I discovered, had no such scruples. All books are his business. He is a formidable finder of them. He took down one or two of Lowenthal's, then several. They were all English, eighteenth and nineteenth century, in the original bindings, the earlier ones in calf; inside there was a label which read "Boyveau & Chevillet, 22, Rue de la Banque."

The next day Miss McClernan, Trask, Anne, and I descended on the establishment near the Bourse. It was dark with books: shelves from floor to ceiling, and tall ladders against the shelves. We brushed aside polite inquiries. Were we perhaps looking, Messieurs, Mesdames, for Beeron or Veelda? No—*merci*. But now I regret not asking to see the Wildes. They were probably all "firsts."

Everything had been priced before World War I, when the franc was worth twenty cents.

Like Dauber & Pine on Fifth Avenue, there was an upstairs and downstairs. Downstairs, there was a little old woman in black perched on top of a ladder busily dusting books. Our entrance startled her. She spoke apprehensively.

"Ne dérangez pas les livres!"

Miss McClernan put it to us: were we there to derange the books? We got up on ladders ourselves. It was all a little intoxicating.

Trask was the first to spot a prize, and gallantly let Miss McClernan have it: *The Works of Mr. Alexander Pope,* 1717, full calf gilt, and a first edition. She still has it.

Another day, at a book stall on the quais, he spotted a copy of *Ulysses,* which was then selling for around sixty dollars. He looked at the price: 3.50 francs. Had the bookseller made a mistake? The bookseller glanced at the price and then at Trask.

"Monsieur," he said with acerbity, *"c'est le même prix pour tout le monde."*

Trask bought it.

Frances McClernan returned to New York. Trask stayed on in Paris. Shortly after Anne and I left, Trask became Ford Madox Ford's "literary secretary" and went to live with him at 32 rue de Vaugirard. I did not meet Ford until I was once more settled in the Village, this time for good.

4

One night, after a Stravinsky concert, in which the composer conducted his own works in his angular and strenuous fashion, my wife and I rode back to Saint-Germain-des-Prés in a taxi. We got out at the Café des Deux Magots to have a *chocolat* before going home. I paid the driver, and put my wallet back in my breast pocket. It contained all my money and our joint passport. When the time came to pay for the *chocolat* there was no wallet. I went back to the curb where the taxi had stopped; a kiosk was there, and the woman who sold newspapers, who had always been friendly, avoided my eyes. No, she had not seen a wallet, Monsieur.

Perhaps the loss of the wallet was a portent. I wanted desperately to stay on in Paris. But time was running out. I applied for a Guggenheim Fellowship. I did not get it. I applied for a job on the Paris *Times,* and got it.

The *Times* was up a flight of dark stairs at 33, rue Jean Jacques Rousseau, on the right bank near the Bourse. It boasted of being the only afternoon paper in English on the Continent. It was owned by an American. Its editor was G. H. Archambault, in later years a correspondent for the New York *Times.* The "G" stood for Gaston. He was a stout man

CHARLES NORMAN

Pamela Bianco

The author, age 20. Drawing by Pamela Bianco, 1924.

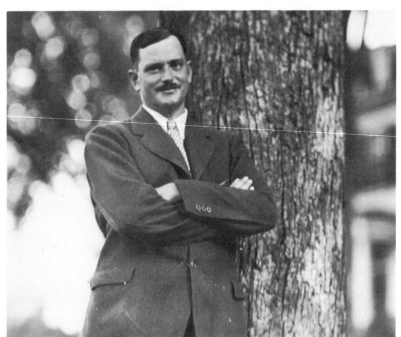

Hervey Allen and DuBose Heyward at Folly Island, S.C.; John Farrar; Henry Beston (bottom).

E. E. Cummings, self-portrait, pen-and-ink, 1927; Joe Gould, oil by Cummings.
Bottom: *Anne Barton in Paris, oil by Cummings.*

Stockton, N.J., 1928; Francesco Bianco; Margery Williams Bianco, with Suzy, a Pomeranian.

"*Brett,*" *line drawing by Harold Loeb; Dawn Powell, gouache by Diana Norman.*
Bottom: *Guy Endore, Harold Loeb.*

Romany Marie by John Sloan, oil on canvas 24x20 (1920). Collection of Whitney Museum of American Art, N.Y. Bottom: *Provincetown, 1927.*

Nancy.

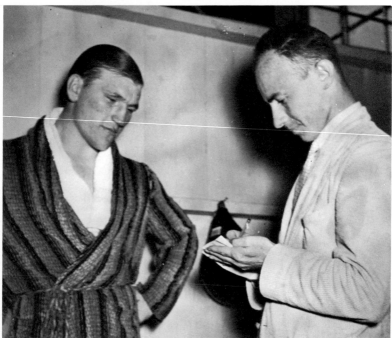

André Malraux in U. S., 1937, to raise money for Spanish Loyalists. Bottom: *Tommy Farr before going 15 rounds with Joe Louis. (Photos by Mary Morris).*

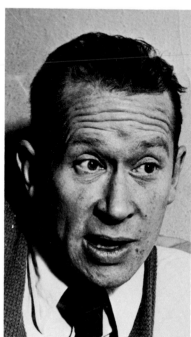

Edna St. Vincent Millay at her farm, 1937. Bottom: *E. E. Cummings talking to author, 1938.* (*Wide World photos by Mary Morris*).

Early water colors (photo by Mary Morris). Patchin Place, 43 years later (photo by the author).

Thomas Wolfe in Asheville, 1937 (courtesy of Charles Scribner's Sons). Bottom: *Willard R. Trask (photo by Bill Yoscary).*

*Mary Moore Cross at man and wife show, Gotham Book Mart Gallery, 1969
(photo by Bill Yoscary).*

Hirsh Margules and friends in Washington Square (photo by Arthur Swoger).

MacDowell Colony, l. to r.: *Carl Carmer, Helena Kuo, William McCleery, B. Diamond, C. N.* Right: *Alaska Highway, 1944.* Bottom: *George Gamow, in his garden.*

Mansfield Studio, MacDowell Colony, 1946 (photo by Margery Lewis). With Padraic Colum at Gotham Book Mart (photo by Congrat-Butlar).

The author, age 59. Charcoal drawing by Diana Norman, 1963.

who looked larded with pâtés; but whatever he ate at night, for lunch he had only a bottle of ale, which the office boy brought to his desk. With the ale to sustain him, he continued working—poring over French newspapers, and snipping items from them with enormous scissors. I rewrote copy alongside two future authors, Vincent Sheean and Hillel Bernstein. The job lasted only three weeks, but was to prove decisive in my career.

In May, 1928, my wife and I returned to New York and took an apartment on Patchin Place for forty-five dollars a month. It was the two-room apartment on the ground floor of no. 4, which E. E. Cummings and his third wife were to occupy for so many years. Cummings was still living by himself on the top floor; my wife used to see Anne Barton, beautiful and mysterious in a black wool suit, a felt hat, and a silver fox-fur piece around her neck, passing our window in the late afternoon to keep her rendezvous with him. She had her own apartment; he had the best of all possible worlds—his work, his solitude, and a beautiful wife-mistress. The arrangement had less to offer her, and she gave it up.

One night there was a knock on our door. I went to open it and saw, in the murky hall, a man with a cape and a gnarled stick, and a woman I recognized as Alyse Gregory, Marianne Moore's predecessor as editor of the *Dial*. She said, speaking rapidly: "I beg your pardon—we used to live here, and we thought we would like to see the old place again before leaving for England; it is so unlikely that we will ever return." She turned to the man in the cape. "This is my husband, Llewelyn Powys."

I asked them to come in and introduced my wife, who accompanied Mrs. Powys on her tour of the back room while I stayed in the living room talking with Mr. Powys. I heard his wife exclaim: "Fancy! There's a bathtub!" At that, Mr. Powys rushed to the back to have a look. They told us that when they were living there none of the houses in Patchin Place had running water; water was supplied by a pump in the middle of the street. There were no indoor toilets either, but a row of outhouses at the end of the cul-de-sac where the lamp post now stands. They recalled other occupants of the apartment for us; all were famous. Louise Bryant, the correspondent, was one; she had lived there with her first husband, John Reed, author of *Ten Days That Shook the World,* and then with her second, William Christian Bullitt, afterwards our first ambassador to the Soviet Union. John Cowper Powys, Llewelyn's brother, had been a neighbor of Cummings on the top floor.

Despite the improvements, the apartment was far from comfortable; my wife was pregnant, and she preceded me to Asheville, where her mother had a house. My patron, when I saw him, said to me: "Now that you have a wife, I am sure you will wish to support her yourself." He was quite right, except for one difficulty. I had no money.

Chapter Nine

1

When John Farrar went into book publishing at least one of the *Bookman* customs was continued by his successors, Seward Collins and Burton Rascoe. The new editors also read my poems fresh from the pocket, and paid on the spot. The treasurer, who brought the checks in, seemed very old to me, but probably was not more than fifty. I can still see him entering the editorial office with a slight stoop, smiling and holding aloft, like a tiniest pennant, a wet check which he waved to get dry. But whether he belonged to the old regime, or the new one, I no longer remember. Part of my honey-moon trip was paid for by the *Bookman* when, in my anxiety to add to the little money I had, I took a batch of poems in; they were read at once, totted up, and paid for. The check came to $260, a truly munificent sum. I had barely time to cash it; my bride and I sailed on the *De Grasse* the next day.

One of the poems was *Saint in Modern Dress*. A month after it appeared, in the July, 1928, issue, it had a memorable reading, probably the best it will ever have. It took place in Stockton, N. J., at the country home of John Gerard, a writer whose wife, Margaret Linley, was casting director of the Theatre Guild.

John Gerard was an American, born in Florence, educated at Winchester and later at Princeton, where his Continental air had earned him the sobriquet of "the Duke." He was, indeed, elegant in dress, speech, and manners. But what I admired was his erudition. His reading was enormous. He not only read Latin and Greek—he spoke them. I also admired the way he had of greeting me when I met him in the street; I seem to remember him walking a dog. I was always glad to see him, and perhaps was even effusive; he, on the other hand, with a priceless air of timelessness—ah, those Greek and Latin classics!—would resume a conversation we had had a month before, five months, and—once—at least two years before, as though we had been standing by the curb all that time. He invariably asked me to dinner, and once he asked me to Stockton.

The house in Stockton had espaliered trees against one whitewashed wall, and there was an Elizabethan garden with flagstone walks sown with herbs which gave forth their scents when you trod on them. Another guest was present on this particular weekend, the actor Claude Rains. Mr. Rains was asked by John or Margaret, perhaps by both, to read *Saint in Modern Dress* aloud. He glanced at the poem, and a pleased look passed over his face; it was a very long poem, and he settled himself in his chair, letting the lamplight fall on the page and his profile.

His distinguished bearing, his air of command, or of taking charge—his resonant but clear English speech, with which all are familiar—were greatly enhanced by such proximity. He read, patiently, to the end, and it was, to me, a stupendous performance. But while I was flattered, and have

not forgotten the flattery, I have another reason for mentioning this incident.

Some thirty-five years after the knocking on the door
at 4 Patchin Place, there was another such knock, this time
on East 11th, where I still reside. I opened the door. Before
me stood a man with a distinguished bearing who asked me,
in a familiar and resonant voice, if he could use my phone
to call his wife; they were subletting the apartment below
mine. It was Claude Rains, now aged and stooped; later, I
met his wife, who also came upstairs to use my phone. And
then? And then, alas, she went to the hospital, where she died.
Mr. Rains went to live elsewhere.

2

Oddly enough, it was not Mr. Farrar who published my first
book, but Alfred A. Knopf, who was the first to see the manuscript. It had been submitted by another editor of the *Bookman,* Dorothea Brande, who later married Seward Collins. I
recall her with affection and gratitude. She had not only
approached Mr. Knopf; she had recommended me to that redoubtable patron, Otto H. Kahn, who sent me a check for
$450. Why $450? I have often observed that if you ask a poor
man, or a man in moderate circumstances, for a certain
amount, he will give you that amount; but rich men always
give less than requested, out of some mysterious principle
born of caution. Dorothea undoubtedly asked Mr. Kahn for
a little sum to tide me over, and visualized a round one—say

$500; he sent $450, which looks lopsided. It was, nevertheless, a windfall. I inquired Mr. Kahn's whereabouts; he was on a ship at sea. I rushed to a cable office and sent him a message of thanks for which I paid with his money.

Dorothea was in her middle thirties when I met her. She looked like a heroine in a middle western novel—hair in a knot, but wisps of it blowing about, and more feminine than elegant in her choice of clothes. A few years later some disorder transformed her into a mountain of flesh; then, unable to move about, she stayed in her apartment overlooking the Queensborough Bridge, where she read manuscripts and worked on a book which turned out to be an enormous bestseller. It was called *Wake Up and Live.*

Seward Collins was rich and attractive, but had some strange ideas for an American. He told me once, when I asked him what his views really were—he was being attacked as an authoritarian—that our society was too permissive, there were too many gadgets, and a return to a simpler social order, perhaps guilds instead of unions, was what was needed. At the time of our talk he had dropped the *Bookman* and come up with a new publication called the *American Review.*

It was not literary.

Although I had an agent, Mrs. Brande continued the pressure from the *Bookman.* I received word from her that if I telephoned Knopf's editor on a certain day I would have a decision. When that day came, I realized with dismay that it was a Jewish holiday, one of those high holy days when everything shuts down in New York. I was faced with the prospect of a long, disconsolate weekend.

I was sitting in Washington Square with my suave Rumanian friend. Our talk was inevitably about my book. He said, "Phone them." It was, at least, something to do. We went to a store on MacDougal Street. The Knopf phone rang and rang. I was about to hang up when I heard a woman's voice.

"Are you calling about a poetry manuscript?" she asked.

"Yes," I said.

"In that case," the mysterious voice continued, "I have a message for you."

"Yes?"

"It has been accepted."

I rushed past my friend and did a jig in MacDougal Street.

The advance from Knopf was $250. Eric Pinker gave me a check for the whole amount, without deducting his ten percent commission.

"It's all right," he said. "I'll take it from the next sale."

Mr. Pinker was the son of the founder of the most famous literary agency in the world—J. B. Pinker and Sons. The home offices were in London, where Eric's brother Ralph was in charge; from time to time they took turns at running things, Eric going to London, and his brother coming to New York. Eric was very, very British, and was disliked by some for being, or seeming to be, a snob. I found him a good friend.

His wife was Adrienne Morrison, formerly the wife of Richard Bennett, the actor, by whom she had three daughters —Constance, Joan, and Barbara. Miss Morrison, a former actress, was distinguished and capable and was in charge of the play department. One afternoon in the Pinker office I was introduced to two of her daughters. They were merely pretty compared with her.

With the money from Pinker, I went to Asheville. My daughter was born there. She was baptized, with her hand on his shoulder, by the Episcopal Bishop of Western North Carolina in the living room of my mother-in-law's house. My wife, born in South Carolina, was related to DuBose Heyward. I once astonished his daughter, Jenifer, by telling her she was related to my daughter, Nancy. It was in her mother's apartment on Gramercy Park; also present were Betty and Carl Carmer. Dorothy Heyward looked astonished; then we all laughed.

A few months later, in that memorable spring of 1929, my book appeared.

3

The title was *Poems*. It was bound in green cloth stamped in gold, and had a distinctive green jacket, the typography of which was first-class Knopf; the poems, however, were set in italic Granjon, which I thought bad. Nevertheless, it was a handsome book. It exists in two states, which may be something of a record considering its sales. At the last moment I had made a correction in the proofs; the printer reset the two corrected lines but failed to yank the original ones out. The first state has both versions in sequence; in the second, there is a cancel or substitute page. (Elmer Adler, who knew how to please authors, once showed me a slip-case containing both volumes.)

The most exciting review was by Granville Hicks in the *World*. "He may well take an important place in the American literature of the future," he wrote of the author of *Poems*. "In the quality of his metaphors there is a strength that is often Elizabethan, and his imagination sometimes illuminates macabre subjects with a flash of lightning that reminds one only of John Webster."

This was probably a reference to *Dead Men Under Buildings*.

His review, together with others, was read at the breakfast table. I will never forget the surprised, pleased—nay, almost proud—look Mrs. Morton gave me; I had cut a sorry figure in her eyes until then, I am sure. Equally dazzling was a review by William Rose Benét in the *Saturday Review of Literature,* as it was then called: "*Dedicatory Poem* has the touch of finality that is usually associated with greatness. Its accent is unerring." It is brief, not overly familiar, and I give it here:

> Since whosoever builds with speech
> Fashions fragility from nought,
> These songs must be beyond men's reach
> To rend what I have wrought.
>
> The few, the scattered seeds of fame
> In the barbed woods of calumny,
> Will throw their light upon my name,
> Their shadow on my memory.

This poem was followed by *Saint in Modern Dress,* which numbered 180 lines. I do not intend to give it here. It opened with the phrase,

> Teeth of the rain nibble the night.

Poems was also favorably reviewed in the Asheville *Citizen* by Edwin Bjorkman, a Norwegian novelist who was a local celebrity. He was the book editor of that paper, and he gave me books to review. The wife of the man who owned the paper had a son by a former husband. She was rich, and the son was rich; he was fourteen or fifteen, and it was thought that association with me would help him. I was offered the job of tutoring him at fifty dollars a week for five two-hour sessions in the mornings.

I cannot say he was much of a scholar, or that I was much of a tutor. He soon developed a way of leading me into discussions which had nothing to do with our studies, but which consumed a good part of the two hours. The best of it, for him as well as myself, was our daily walk around the spacious grounds of the Asheville country club and golf links. It took us into the fresh air, from which both of us benefited.

Mr. Knopf had told Dorothea Brande that he did not expect to make money out of my book, but was "glad to publish it anyway." He did not make any money out of it, and neither did I. My recollection of the one and only statement I ever received is that it showed seven copies sold; perhaps it was nine.

I myself gave away about forty; I have a vision of myself stopping people on the street to do so, but I think this happened only once when I encountered Dwight Fiske on Fifth Avenue and drew him aside; I had just been to Knopf's, and had a bundle of books under my arm. I undid the bundle and passed a copy to him, after inscribing it with his fountain pen. (Years later, when the *New Yorker* included two of my poems in its first anthology and periodically sent one check to Knopf, because one of the poems had appeared in the book, and another to me, the smaller one, I became indignant because I was broke. I wrote Mr. Knopf. The reply —from Mrs. Knopf—had a sobering effect. I still owed the firm for the copies I had given away. Perhaps I still do for some of them.)

I wrote a great deal in Asheville, perhaps the bulk of my second collection, which Knopf declined and William Morrow accepted. It was the first book of verse to be published by that firm. The Knopf editor wrote Pinker that the new collection was not as good as the old; the Morrow editor told me that she and Mr. Morrow had not only liked it for itself, but were impressed by the growth it marked over the earlier volume, which she had sent for. Her name is Frances Phillips and one of her authors was to play an important role in my life, not because he and I became close friends, but because he got me a job in a profession I was to follow for about ten years, during which time, and longer, I published no more books.

The name of the second book was *The Bright World and Other Poems*. It opens with a sequence entitled *Sonnets to a Lady in North Carolina,* and concludes with a group of five dramatic monologues and dialogues in blank verse. Edwin Arlington Robinson wrote me: "I think you are writing altogether better blank verse than most that is being written nowadays." I showed his letter to Willard Trask, who commented: "He means all but his." After the book appeared, I applied again for a Guggenheim grant. I did not get it. Mr. Robinson was one of my sponsors.

One day, some five years later, while walking through Washington Square, I saw him for the first time. He looked exactly like the portrait in front of his *Collected Poems,* even to the way his legs were crossed. He was sitting on a bench facing the row of Georgian houses on Waverly Place. He was alone. I wanted to stop, to introduce myself, to thank him, to tell him how much I admired his work. I walked slowly past, unable to bring myself to a decision. A few months later he was dead.

4

I was in New York when *The Bright World* was taken. I not only met Miss Phillips, but William Morrow, the founder of the firm, one of those gentlemen publishers who seem to be a fast disappearing breed. With the Morrow advance, and other sums I was able to raise, I returned to Asheville; but not before some dismal months had passed. It was winter; I lived in a furnished room on 3rd Street in a building known as "Strunsky's Stables." The Elevated ran past its windows, and it was also known as "Desire Under the El."

Something was very much on my mind during this sojourn. It was this: one of the poems I had written in Asheville, too late for inclusion in the Morrow volume, had come back from the *Bookman* with a rejection slip. It was long and had a lengthy title—*A Poem To Commemorate the Three Hundred and Sixty-fifth Birthday of Christopher Marlowe.* At the end of it I had put the year, 1929.

One day, it occurred to me that Mr. Collins might not have seen the poem. It was like a vision, and as with all visions, it called for a pilgrimage. I walked uptown to the *Bookman* offices at 28th Street and Fourth Avenue and left it for him with a note. Five days later, in an awesome mixture of self-pity and self-righteousness, I went once more. This time, I asked for Mr. Collins, and was made to wait.

I looked at my watch. Five minutes had passed. I got up to go—wishing, however, to stay. Mr. Collins appeared. He escorted me to his office, talking all the way. First, he apologized for keeping me waiting. He had received a long-distance call just as my name was brought in. Then he asked: "Isn't it a beautiful day?" Although it was, I thought his remark incongruous. I also wondered when the blow would fall. I was now seated; he was standing, gesturing toward the sun-bright window. He began to apologize a second time.

"The reason we have kept your poem so long," he said, "is that we could not decide what to pay for it."

I stiffened in my chair.

"The poem," he went on, "will take up five pages, and our price per page is fifteen dollars. We did not think that enough. We went up to twenty, and still it didn't seem enough. We are therefore paying you twenty-five dollars a page, and if you will wait a moment I will have the check for you."

I could only sit there dazed and unbelieving, but multiplying rapidly. I even got it right: $125, an enormous sum, considering I did not have carfare back to the Village. Mr. Collins returned with the check, without waving it about, and I put it in my pocket.

"By the way," he said, "I noticed the date at the bottom of the last page. Why didn't you send it in before?"

Because I have often been curious to learn what followed the delivery of a climactic line in other people's books I will describe what happened. My mind was very clear. I was hungry and I was overjoyed. I did not want to hurt his feelings. I did not want to get anyone in trouble. He had not seen the poem before; when he saw it, he had bought it. I mumbled. I made it appear that I had been absent-minded. I left him on the best of terms, and went to the *Bookman's* bank, which was a walk of another ten blocks. I cashed the check, and looked around for a restaurant.

Just before I left New York, my wife asked me to send her a book by an Asheville man. I went to the Washington Square Book Shop and asked Mrs. Horton if she had it. Her eyes lit up and she pointed to a stack.

I returned to Asheville, where I continued to write. I also had leisure for reading. One day I took up the book my wife had asked me to send her. I did so without enthusiasm. A local man had published a book; I would see if he could write. I did not expect to finish it. It was immense—626 pages —and almost too heavy to hold lying down. I stretched out on the couch in my study upstairs and began to read. The book was *Look Homeward, Angel* by Thomas Wolfe.

I was not aware then of the storm that had broken over Asheville when it appeared. The only storm I knew was in my head. Later, my wife began to point out some of the book's characters on our trips to town. She told me Wolfe's mother had sat on the porch of her house in Pack Square, rocking, reading, laughing and crying, and ejaculating from time to time: "It's the God's truth! It's the God's truth!"

5

Charles Yale Harrison was the author to whom I was introduced by Frances Phillips in the William Morrow office. His book, which was to make him famous, had just appeared; it was called *Generals Die in Bed*. Miss Phillips told him I needed a job. Harrison asked me what kind of work I had done; he did not mean my poetry. I told him I had worked on the Paris *Times*.

"Good," he said. "I can get you a job."

"For three weeks," I added faintly.

He looked startled.

Harrison was on the copy desk of the now defunct *Bronx Home News*. Everybody passed through its city room en route to the big papers downtown; I could, too, he said. He told me how to go about it—in particular, not to mention how long I had worked on the Paris *Times*. He said I would be asked one question, to which the answer had to be yes: did I know how to write heads? I did not know, but Harrison was sure I could learn quickly. So was I.

I was interviewed by one of the biggest men from the waist up I have ever encountered—like Mr. Flaherty, in fact. In recollection he seems taller seated than I was standing up. He had a long cigar stuck in his mouth, and cold Catholic eyes that drilled through me. I believe his name was Fitzpatrick; he was the managing editor. He asked the question, at the same time taking stock of me with those cold eyes, of a pale, pure blueness. I answered as instructed, and was sent to the slot-man who showed me where to sit. I was on the copy desk. Shortly after, Harrison went to work for the *Evening Journal,* which was serializing his book. Before he left, he gave me another piece of advice, which I failed to follow.

"If you want to get ahead," he told me, "join the party."

To a writer of verse, writing heads was not difficult once type sizes and word-counts were mastered. In a few days I read copy and wrote heads so fast that I was asked by the slot-man to slow down so that some of the work could be done by others. One of the others was Harry Markson, afterwards president and match-maker of Madison Square Garden.

I never saw Markson fight, but he saw me. He was a thin,

whimsical young man with thick glasses and the look and savvy of the born newspaperman. In the years to come I was able to spot the breed without trouble; journalism was their life as well as vocation. Markson lived on the west side in mid-Manhattan, and from time to time we left the office together. The *Bronx Home News* was one block from the 149th Street station of the IRT.

One Saturday night, after putting the Sunday edition to bed, we got on the subway. The car we were in was almost full; at one end some passengers were standing. We found two seats at the other end, near the platform, and sat down, papers in our laps. Directly across from me was a Negro, perhaps about fifty years old.

At the 125th Street station two men came into the car at our end, looked around for seats, but seeing none, remained on the platform. One let his eyes rove over the passengers, examining each in turn. Suddenly he strode into the car and grasped the Negro by both shoulders.

"Get up, you black bastard," he snarled, "and give a white man your seat."

I stood up and put my paper down. The man was still stooped over the Negro. I tapped him on the shoulder and said, "We don't do that kind of thing here."

He let the Negro go and straightened up, turning toward me with an incredulous look in his eyes. It was also a look which said: "A fight? My pleasure." His right hand came up as I was turning away from him. I had already been punched in the ribs by his companion. Turning, I caught a glimpse of Markson's face. He looked startled; but his look also said I was a bigger fool than he had taken me for. He continued to sit there, a solitary seated passenger; all the rest had massed at both ends of the car to watch. They were mostly men.

In the glare of the lights in that oblong ring hurtling through darkness at one o'clock in the morning I was swept from one end of the car to the other, taking and blocking blows, almost always off-balance and unable to throw a punch of my own. I fell once; rolling, I saw a hobnailed shoe aimed at my head. It was probably the swaying car that saved me; as the two men wove and staggered to keep their balance, I was up. The onslaught began again.

The train stopped at 116th Street. The doors opened. Some passengers about to enter stepped back. The doors closed. The train pulled out without them.

Between 116th and 96th, I saw a new figure: the guard. His face was white. I heard him say: "My God, what can I do?" before I was swept, backing all the way, to the other end. At 96th when the doors opened police swarmed into the car.

There was a little procession to the 100th Street police station. The man who had assaulted the Negro turned several times to call me "nigger lover." Markson walked beside me, carrying both copies of the Sunday edition of the *Bronx Home News*. An ambulance was waiting outside the station; inside, a young doctor swabbed my face and head and placed a patch over my left eye. The two men were booked. Both, I now learned, had just been discharged from the navy. Markson and I resumed our interrupted ride. He suggested that I spend the night at his place, and I gratefully accepted.

It was now between two and three o'clock. I stripped and went into the bathroom. There was a full-length mirror on the back of the door and I found myself gazing in astonishment at a tattooed man: I was black and blue from my chest to my knees. My left eye was swollen, and there was a lump on my head.

I went to work on Monday, creating a mild stir by my appearance. Markson was able to fill everyone in, and no doubt did it wittily and whimsically.

About two weeks later I received a telephone call at the *Bronx Home News*.

"My name is Harry Sacher," the caller said. "I am a lawyer. I heard about your fight in the subway, and there is something in the story that interests me very much. I'd like to hear it from you. My office is at 11 West 42nd Street. There's no rush—come when you have a free hour."

I went to see Mr. Sacher. He listened to my account. When I was through he said: "I am still young enough to be interested in points of law. There is an interesting point of law involved in your experience. You were in a public carrier. The guard, when he appeared, not only should have helped you—I believe he had to help you even at the risk of his life. It can only be decided in a court room. My proposal is this: if you will let me bring suit against the IRT, I will pay all the expenses of the suit, and if we win, we'll split 60-40, sixty percent for you, forty for me."

I was agreeable.

"But," he went on, "if we sue for $10,000, it may not get on the calendar for five years. If we sue for $5,000, it may get on in three. However, if we sue for $3,000, it may be resolved in a year or a year and a half."

I told him the sooner it was resolved the better. We shook hands, and he said: "You'll hear from me."

I heard from him three and a half years later. I had long since left the *Bronx Home News*.

6

It was in "Strunsky's Stables" that I first met Owen Francis, a former steelworker from Pittsburgh who had turned short-story writer. He was tall, broad-shouldered, and very rough.

Item: we were standing by the Church of the Ascension at Fifth Avenue and 10th Street. A couple passed us, the woman clinging to the man's arm and talking baby-talk as she peered up at him admiringly.

"Fifteen minutes with her, and I'd kick her teeth in," Owen remarked almost before they were out of earshot.

I did not doubt it.

Owen's nose was slightly askew from a punch that had landed there; it made him look even more masculine. At a party we went to he was greatly admired by a very delicately formed young man who ran after us when we were leaving. The man followed us into the bedroom, where our coats were. At this time, which was before he went to Hollywood, Owen was still wearing his World War I horse-blanket overcoat; he was big, and it was big. It was also heavy. The little man who had followed us was determined to pay a final homage to my magnificent friend—he offered to help him with his coat. He took it from Owen, who was grinning, and sagged under its weight.

"Oh, my," he exclaimed, looking up helplessly. "You're not even *bi*-sexual!"

Several years later, Owen arrived from Hollywood and invited me to dinner. He was very restless. He asked me if I knew someone we could see after dinner—he was sick, he said, of actors and producers. I called Antonio Salemme, and we were invited to MacDougal Alley, where he and his second wife had a studio.

Salemme's wife was a buxom beauty with red hair which she looped into an enormous, crackling knot—at least, it appeared to be crackling. She painted under her maiden name; it was Corinna de Berri. Her friends called her Ginger. She was a good painter.

Owen and I spent a pleasant evening. We parted company on Fifth Avenue and 8th Street; it was then around midnight. The next day I learned a number of things, chiefly from Owen, who was in St. Vincent's Hospital.

After leaving me, he had gone back to his hotel, which was uptown, taken a revolver from his suitcase, and taxied downtown. I never asked him how he happened to have a revolver.

The Salemmes were surprised to see him. They were even more surprised when he threw his revolver on the table and told Salemme he was in love with his wife.

"You can have the first shot," he added.

Salemme did not take advantage of this sporting offer; I think I would have.

Owen was talked out of it and drank himself into a stupor, fell, and snapped his ankle. An ambulance came for him. Salemme was glad to see the last of him. Thereafter, he avoided me.

Owen went back to Hollywood. I must have seen him at least once after that, because it was he who told me that he had become enraged on location, one day, torn up his contract and tossed the pieces at Major Warner's feet. After that, I completely lost track of him. I heard, however, that he was much in Thomas Wolfe's company, then that he had married someone in Louisiana, and finally that he was dead. His father-in-law, I was told, was an undertaker, who may sometimes have measured him in his mind's eye. My recollection of his stories is that they were very good. Perhaps they will be collected.

Salemme and his wife separated. He married again, and moved uptown. She stayed in the studio in MacDougal Alley. I went to a party there once, when oysters were served right out of a barrel shipped to her for the occasion. It was a supper party: oysters on the half-shell, washed down by wine. There was a lot of washing.

I also recall a snatch of dialogue.

Pamela Bianco and I were talking with a woman who became vexed by my quips (such, in any case, is my recollection). She had on a horsy-set hat, like a derby; perhaps it was a derby. She said to Pamela: "I'd like to take him home with

me, take his pants down, and give him a good spanking."
Pamela said: "Or just take his pants down."

7

I met Wolfe at a party in Grove Court when my wife and
I were together again, this time at 262 West 11th Street. Like
him, I was appearing in *Scribner's Magazine,* but we did not
talk about each other's work—we talked about books. Wolfe
was steeped in English literature, and talking with him was
like talking with Willard Trask or Francesco Bianco. I do
not recall looking up at him; perhaps he stooped for me.
He was six feet four or five, with soft, expressive eyes and a
sweet smile; sometimes, when he smiled, he licked the corners of his mouth with his tongue, like an adolescent girl. He
appeared very gentle, and he was very friendly.

He was also homesick for Asheville. He told us he was
afraid to go back and showed us some of the scurrilous letters and postcards he had received. It was a recurrent theme;
we always urged him to go. He afterwards did, and was
lionized.

He came often to dinner. His capacity was enormous.
I used to carve and serve my wife and him, tell them not to
wait, and begin to carve for myself. His plate was bare before
I was through and he got a second serving before I had my
first. When, late at night, we ran out of liquor, as frequently
happened when he was there, he reached into a back pocket
and brought out his reserve, an enormous flask. The whisky
seemed to lubricate his mind, and he talked without stopping

until the early hours. He talked as he wrote, quickly characterizing people by his trick of repeating some person's peculiarity as he went along, and so vivid were these characteristics that I sometimes found myself looking around to see who it was who had joined us in that quiet and shadowy room at two or three in the morning.

I went to see him once in Brooklyn. When the door opened I heard him say: "That's not my wife—that's the janitor's wife." I was looking up, expecting to see him up there; now I looked down and saw a little woman with a broom in her hand enfolded by his bulk pressing from behind. He really towered over her. She had been sweeping the apartment when I rang the bell. The room was almost bare. I sat down on a beat-up chair, he on an up-ended case of beer. In a corner was the refrigerator on which he wrote standing up.

The janitor's wife resumed sweeping. While I talked, she swept away with might and main; once I even had to raise my feet quickly, so she could sweep under them. But when Wolfe began to speak she stopped sweeping and leaned on her broom to listen, a look of idiotic worship on her grimy face. She finally left. He asked me if I would like to see the manuscript of *Look Homeward, Angel*.

He led me into a room which was absolutely bare except for one object. It was a packing case, about six feet high, in which an upright piano had once been shipped. It was open on top. He stood beside it and looked down into its depths with a pleased, almost benign look. I tried standing on tiptoe, then shinnied up, as I had often done on fences when young, and peered in. It was three-fourths full of manuscripts tied by string. He reached down and brought up a portion of *Look Homeward, Angel*. The manuscripts of *Of Time and the River* and *The Web and the Rock* were also there, and God knows what else.

They are all at Harvard now, and I should like to see *Look Homeward, Angel* appear as it was written, without the hacking to which it was subjected merely—as I believe—

because it happened to be the first of the big novels. His other books would be improved, pared of the material quarried from their illustrious prototype.

About ten years later, when I was on leave from the army, I stopped off in Asheville. My daughter and I went to the Wolfe house on Pack Square, which had been turned into a museum, and then to the cemetery to see Tom's grave. The rectangular stone slab over it did not seem big enough for his giant form. Not far away was the grave of Elizabeth Montgomery, the English girl I had known in Paris in the pension on the rue St. Benoît.

Chapter Ten

1

One by one, the expatriates returned. I saw both Harolds again. Harold Stearns had found a haven with Evan Shipman, a tall, thin, pale withdrawn man, stooped by life, and later lost in the many young deaths of the Spanish civil war. He was like a shy wraith, startled when encountered, then standing pale and stooped, speaking hardly at all, his few words muffled in the pale, pursed mouth. It was not until I read Hemingway's portrait of him in *A Moveable Feast* that I learned why he spoke that way—to hide his bad teeth. There was an air of gentility about him, of faded elegance, too; his suit was shabby and too large for him, but not because it had belonged to someone else—he had simply become thinner. I wonder now what his writing was like; Hemingway speaks of him as a poet whose indifference to publication impressed him.

I never saw the apartment where he sheltered Harold;

it could not have been much, but it had books in it. I was working, and Harold used to bring me books to sell to me, the kind of books I was always looking for in the shops on Fourth Avenue. I paid him five dollars apiece for them, and only later realized they were not his to sell, and I returned them all so that it wouldn't make mischief between him and Shipman, who may have wondered at the growing gaps in his shelves.

My wife liked Harold, who was shy, quiet-spoken and courteous, and had a wry kind of humor. He also looked underfed, and we fed him more often than we fed anyone else. It was from him—not the other Harold, whose specialty it was—that I learned something about economics which writers in that field appear to have overlooked. Stearns assured me one day that it costs a poor man more for a shirt than it does a rich man.

"How is that?" I asked.

"It's very simple," he replied. "A rich man buys half a dozen good shirts and rotates them. They last almost forever. A poor man buys one shirt at a time, and being poor, buys an inexpensive one. When it has been to the laundry half a dozen times, he finds it necessary to buy another."

I think he was still playing the horses, when he had a few dollars, but his system worked no better here than in Paris. He afterwards wrote an autobiography called *The Street I Know*. The title was taken from Ralph Cheever Dunning's

> The wind blows cold in every street,
> But coldest in the street I know.

Dunning, another unfortunate, was much admired by Pound and Hemingway.

The other Harold was rich. Harold Loeb had a splendid apartment on Charles Street and entertained lavishly. It was there that I met Ford Madox Ford. Every time Ford came, that was the party, for almost everyone went to sit or stand near him, and many sat on the floor so as not to miss anything.

Ford was very blond, with china-blue eyes, his face a pink on the verge of rose. He had become very stout, and had trouble with his breathing. He was not able to sit in a chair in the ordinary way—he sat on its edge, puffing, imbibing Scotches-and-soda like water: gulp, and down the hatch. There was always another glass hovering in mid-air for him, and he hardly had need to stretch out his hand.

Ford was the center of attention, and properly so. He had not only been the collaborator of Joseph Conrad, the friend of Henry James, the mentor of everybody's mentor, Ezra Pound; he was himself the author of a masterpiece, *The Good Soldier*. He was also the greatest story-teller I have ever met. His stories seemed endless, one coming upon the close of another. I was young, I could tell a story or two myself, I wished to share the limelight, and during a pause, while Ford was puffing or downing a drink, I asked him if he had ever heard the story of the man who put mashed potatoes on his head. I had every expectation of telling it, and looked forward to doing so. His response, however, struck me dumb. It was: "Why, yes, I made it up."

He proceeded to tell how.

Long before, when he was editor of the *English Review,* he was invited to speak at a luncheon of the literary society at Oxford or Cambridge—I forget which. As this was in the first decade of the twentieth century, Ford was young, too, and he was nervous. The first course had already been served when he was called on to speak. He stood up, and had spoken only a few words, when his neighbor at the long table nudged him.

"I say," his neighbor upwardly said, "did you know that you are fiddling with the fillet of sole?"

"Oh, so sorry," Ford downwardly replied, he related; "I thought it was the mashed potatoes," and continued talking.

His account was plausible. I remained silent and obscure.

I met him again at the house of a most beautiful lady. Her hair was worn Veronica Lake fashion, a honeyed fall veiling one beautiful blue eye. Glass in hand, puffing on the edge of his chair, Ford talked brilliantly about the English poets, sketching their personal characteristics, hazarding from these how they might have read their poems to friends. This one would have been sonorous, that a whisperer; think, he bade us, what it would have been like to listen to Milton!

Our hostess peered at him with the other beautiful blue eye set like a sparkling jewel on the bare side of the honey-fall hair. She could have listened to Milton—to Wordsworth, too—all day, she said. But if Donne were reading his poems to her, she would have had to stop him—she would have cried out: "To bed! To bed!"

Ford was delighted. So was her husband.

A remarkable woman. A friend of hers told me that she once saw her walking down the street with her lover, the painter Adolf Dehn.

"They were going along," she said, "as though they were lying side by side."

2

Willard Trask returned, and we renewed our friendship.

Hildegarde Dolson once opened her eyes very wide and said to me in an awestruck voice: "Willard knows *mosses!*" He knows birds, too. He is an early riser. He may begin his day with a bird-walk, binoculars slung around his neck. Recently he flew to Iceland for a bird-walk with the Maine Audubon Society. He combines a physically active life with his scholarship. He sounds like Thoreau, and it is a curious fact that he looks like Thoreau. Trask, however, is tall, while Thoreau was short.

There are other resemblances, and several differences. Like his fellow New Englander, Trask eschews politics. But once, during a presidential campaign, he became mildly interested. Herbert Hoover had declared that if he lost, "grass would grow in the streets."

"If that were a promise instead of a threat," Trask told me, "I should be tempted to go in for politics."

Trask, unlike Thoreau, could never settle down—at least voluntarily—to a diet of Indian meal and molasses. He prefers caviar and smoked oysters. His sojourn in Paris with Ford Madox Ford, a notable gourmet, may have helped to form his tastes. Like Thoreau, Trask's life is centered on books.

He has gathered in the course of a long career of book-hunting a library which, if honestly described, must bring pain to fastidious collectors. There are many first editions in it, some of them rare. Alas: hardly a volume is unmarred by a missing back or side, and sometimes even a title page. It is, however, a serviceable library for a scholar—a library to be read, not merely to be admired. Trask holds each decrepit volume as precious as though it were pristine; nay, more precious, for a battered book needs no coddling—it lets itself be read. He has read them all. He works surrounded by waifs and strays of the book world. One of them cost him a nickel.

We have often gone "booking" together on Fourth Avenue, the street of the secondhand book shops. I follow a simple routine; I always go to the poetry shelves inside. Trask, however, has always maintained that if a book is not on the five- or ten-cent stall outside, it is not worth buying. One day I heard the following dialogue in the doorway.

Clerk (Are-you-nuts-or-something voice): "We don't wrap nickel books."

Trask (nettled): "I wasn't asking you to wrap it—I was merely checking on the price."

Clerk (scornfully, after a scornful glance at the book):
"A nickel."

Trask (ending the matter; stiffly): "Very well—here is
a nickel."

At that point, both of us had sizeable bundles, and we
decided to call it a day. We returned to his apartment at 2
Patchin Place and examined our purchases. One of his was a
green-bound volume, *The Holy Grail and Other Poems* by
Tennyson. Although the binding was a little shaken, the book
itself was pristine—in fact, never read. When it was opened
we both observed that the flyleaf was stuck to the endpaper.
Trask inserted a knife and flipped the flyleaf over. There
was an inscription. We both stared—at it, and at each
other. The inscription read: "To my dear wife. Alfred."

It was the nickel purchase.

3

Trask has probably read more poetry than any man alive.
He was even fortunate enough to read some while working
as a proofreader.

"I am the only person in the world," he boasted, "ever
to be paid one dollar an hour for reading *The Faerie Queene.*"

There was an additional relish—Spenser is his favorite
poet.

He has also written a handful of poems which remain,
for the most part, unpublished—they are not *à la mode;*
worse, he won't submit them. (Two of them can be found in
Come Live With Me, an anthology I edited in 1966.) And he

is the author of a little known book which has achieved something of the status of a classic, *Joan of Arc: Self-Portrait;* Lewis Gannett termed it "a little masterpiece," and Ingrid Bergman, rehearsing for the role of Joan, called it "my Bible."

My paperback copy of *Joan of Arc* has the following inscription: "For Charles—For the second time—Twice the only begetter of this in print."

It is a fact that I placed the book twice. The first time was in the thirties. William Soskin, who had been editor of the old New York *Post's* book page, was now the editor of a publishing house called Stackpole Sons. He knew Trask as well as I did, but nothing about the manuscript. I took it to him, he read it, and gave Trask a contract. Exactly twenty-five years later I took *Joan of Arc* to Bruno Fischer, a Collier Books editor, who first thought it too slim for a paperback, but nevertheless put it through.

Trask has six or seven languages at his command, and makes his living translating. His erudition is enormous. Two of his translations bear monumental titles, *Mimesis: The Representation of Reality in Western Literature* by Erich Auerbach, and *European Literature and the Latin Middle Ages* by E. R. Curtius. He has just concluded his translation of *History of My Life,* the memoirs of Casanova; when the first volume appeared, it won him a National Book Award.

I was present when he received it, and so witnessed the bad manners of the intellectuals who walked out when Vice-President Humphrey got up to speak. Mr. Humphrey had come to Philharmonic Hall to honor authors. Dwight Macdonald came to lead a procession of beards to the exit. Marshall Goodman, later tried with Dr. Spock, ran down the aisle to the platform shaking his fist and shouting obscenities. Secret service men came out of the wings, and everyone was in danger.

These are the people who want to make a better world.

Edward Lockspeiser came to New York. To celebrate, we went to the Hotel Lafayette for dinner, then sat in its café, which was as French as any in Paris. As we started to fill our pipes he glanced around and his face lit up.

"I say," he said, "can we buy some Tabac Bleu?"

We jumped up and went to the tobacco counter. In Paris I could not stand Tabac Bleu—I thought it like bitter mattress stuffing. But now the mere sight of that square blue packet on the marble table-top set off a rush of recollections, and the first puffs, which I thought delicious, transported me back to the Deux Magots.

I let him keep the packet.

Lockspeiser, music critic for the B.B.C., had already published his first account of Debussy. Later, never having let go of the subject, he published the monumental *Debussy: His Life and Mind,* in two volumes, a definitive work.

Guy Endore had published the first of his books—*Casanova: His Known and Unknown Life*—the same year that my *Poems* appeared. In 1933 he published three books, including *The Werewolf of Paris.* Hollywood beckoned, and he went to live there. I did not see him again until 1957.

Morris White did not write a life of Frank Harris. He became a teacher in a Brooklyn high school and wrote short stories. He does not appear to have published any. He once told me a story which many men could have written; but now I no longer remember whether he wrote it or merely outlined it to me after an experience he had had. He was calling on a girl he knew, and her phone rang. The phone was on a table next to a big chair where he happened to be sitting, with her in his lap. She said into the phone: "I'm so sorry—I can't see you tonight—I have such a splitting headache." A week or so later, when he called up, he wondered whose lap she was sitting on, for she told him the same thing.

His best story was about one of his classes. He was explaining Keats's *Ode on a Grecian Urn.* He told his students that the Greeks worshipped the human body, and an urn was really a representation of the female form. He drew an urn on the blackboard. A gawky student raised his hand.

"Mr. White," he asked, aquiver with enlightenment; "is that why they call women pots?"

4

Another "find"—once more, not by me.

One afternoon, Francesco Bianco and I entered a second-hand shop on 8th Street. It was a long, narrow sort of place near Sixth Avenue, afterwards a Riker's restaurant. It was run by a man named Kirke who had half a finger missing on one hand, I think the index finger. There was a broad counter down the middle of the shop literally strewn with books, and there Bianco and Kirke lounged and talked while I examined the shelves near the window. I heard Bianco say: "What do you want for this?" Something in the tone of his voice made me turn my head, and I saw that he had taken up an oddly sized book, both thin and flat, and that Kirke was peering at it with a puzzled expression. Perhaps he was thinking: "Why does Bianco want it?"

There was a long pause. Then I heard Kirke say: "What about a dollar and a half?" Bianco appeared to be thinking it over. "I suppose," he finally said, "if it were any smaller it would be only a dollar. But I'll take it." I think he added that rather rapidly. I felt a tenseness in the atmosphere. The two men continued talking. When Bianco said, "Are you ready, Charles?" I actually jumped backward from the poetry shelves. I may even have shouted "Yes!" Bianco paid for the book, put it under his arm, and we said goodbye.

Outside, Bianco whispered tensely: "Come with me."

Those were the last words either of us spoke for the next hour and a half.

We crossed diagonally to the north side of 8th Street and took the bus to the Christopher Street ferry. We got on the ferry and got out at Hoboken. We got on a bus at Hoboken and rode through the flatlands of New Jersey to Jersey City. We got out miles from nowhere. A huge sign read: "American Type Founders Company, Inc."

We entered an office which was paneled and carpeted. Bianco gave his name. In a few moments a man appeared who seemed glad to see him. They shook hands, I was introduced, and the man said: "I suppose you have something to show me?"

"Oh, no," said Bianco. "My friend and I were just passing through, and I thought it a good opportunity to show him the place."

"What is that you have there?" asked the man, whose eyes had never left the flat folio under Bianco's arm.

"That? It's nothing. Have a look if you like."

The man had a look and asked to be excused, taking the folio with him. Bianco and I sank into fat, leather-covered chairs, and sat in them in silence. In a few minutes the man returned without the folio.

"Will $350 dollars be all right?" he asked almost apologetically.

"Oh, whatever you like," said Bianco, as though he had said, "Pish, tosh, what's money?"

"Then excuse me," said the man, "I'll get you the check."

Several months later, over lunch, Bianco laid down his knife and fork and said, apropos of nothing at all: "I could kick myself." I knew at once that he was referring to the spectacular sale he had made.

We were downstairs in the Grand Ticino on Thompson Street. There was a pool table there, not however for young loafers but old paysans; under that table, day in, day out, slumbered two immense dogs, tawny and large as lions, fattened by leftover scallopines and osso buco.

I remarked that I thought he had done very well indeed. He turned on me fiercely, as though I had wronged him in some way.

"I happen to know," he sneered, "that I could have gotten $800 for it from the Columbia Law Library."

I should have remained silent. Instead, I ventured: "In that case, why didn't you offer it to them?"

His anger spilled over. He regarded me scornfully.

"What? And wait for the librarian's decision, and then for the meeting of the syndics to approve the purchase? After that, for the bursar to authorize the check, possibly in the course of the next fiscal year?"

I dropped the subject. He calmed down. We resumed our meal of prosciutto, salad, cheese, and wine. He was quite cheerful when it was over.

The book was an account of the murder of Madame la Duchesse de Praslin by her husband in 1847, as recorded in the Court of Peers. Fourteen copies had been made for the fourteen men who sat in judgment on the Duc de Praslin; a fifteenth, in Latin, on vellum, was struck off for a cardinal in Rome. Bianco's find was the unique fifteenth copy, printed from the types of Didot. It was pristine. Recently, in checking with the American Type Founders Company, I learned that its collection had been sold to Columbia University.

5

I have never found a valuable book, though many desirable ones. The nature of my interests may be deduced from an essay I wrote for the *Colophon,* edited by Elmer Adler. It was called "On Collecting Second, Third and Nth Editions." To me, these were the valuable ones because they contain additional material, sometimes, as in the case of Milton, a poem on which at least part of his fame rests. On the other hand, in the case of Marlowe, I can do without George Chapman's additions to *Hero and Leander.*

My favorite bookshop was that of Alfred F. Goldsmith, who held forth at the "Sign of the Sparrow" on Lexington Avenue near 24th Street. He not only sold books but, like Kling, prints, framed and unframed. As the shop was several steps below street level, and as his apartment was only a block away, he saw little of the light, and his complexion was like bubble-gum. He was also bald, and instead of hair his brow was ornamented by spectacles. On the few occasions that I saw them on his nose, I also saw him push them up when he examined a book or a print.

I was present one day when a shabby man came in, shabby and frightened, for Mr. Goldsmith sometimes made a pretense of staring angrily at unfamiliar clients. The shabby man placed a book by Mark Twain on the counter, and Mr. Goldsmith pushed his glasses up and examined it.

"How much do you want for this?" he asked.

"Would a dollar and a half be all right?" the man asked in a whisper.

Mr. Goldsmith was indignant. He shoved the book toward the man, and pointed to the flyleaf, which was almost entirely covered with writing. The signature read, "Samuel Langhorne Clemens."

"What about this?" he asked, his eyes flashing.

"Aw, a little writin' don't hurt none," the man said. "Give me a dollar."

Mr. Goldsmith snorted. He turned his back and impatiently dialed a number. An immense silence fell on the shop.

"This is Alfred," I heard him say. "Do you still want a copy of . . . ?" He named a Twain first.

After putting the receiver down, Mr. Goldsmith scribbled a name and address on a piece of paper, thrust it at the man, and said: "Go there. Tell him I sent you. He will give you sixty dollars."

The man looked stunned. Then he looked embarrassed.

"Do you have carfare?" Mr. Goldsmith demanded. "No?"

He fished a dime out of his vest.

I, too, was the recipient of many kindnesses from him. He used to put books aside for me, new purchases which he knew I would want to have, without marking up the price.

Marianne Moore told me once, when I visited her in Brooklyn, that she weeded out books she "didn't absolutely have to have" every month; otherwise, she said, she would be swamped by them. I went her one better, one month when I did not have the rent. I had friends, of course, who would have lent me the money, but I had become a borrower, and I decided, in a moment of true desperation, not to borrow another penny from anyone. I called up the Strand or Argosy bookstore; if the Argosy had already moved from Fourth Avenue to 59th Street, it was the Strand. The owner, whoever he was, reacted to my name, and said he would come over himself.

I had told him I wished to sell my entire library, except for a half dozen or so books signed by Cummings. I knew there was no use selecting twenty, thirty or fifty books to sell; books are only valuable when you are buying them. He made an offer, and I accepted. I think he had an assistant with him, and they went up and down the stairs, carting my books away, until the shelves, which I had built myself, were empty. Some of the books were from Goldsmith's shop—a four-volume collected Synge, with the bookplate of John Quinn, his patron; the third edition of Boswell's *Life of Johnson,* on which all modern editions were, until recently, based; his *Journal of a Tour to Corsica,* a second edition with the great folding map; and Langbaine's *History of the English Dramatic Poets,* 1691, a first edition and a perfect copy. Only

Alfred Goldsmith would have put them aside for me, and let me pay him only what he had paid.

I did not, of course, know at the time what I had done. It was many years before I could bring myself to go into a secondhand book store.

6

Most booksellers seem a little mad, a hazard of the trade, for they work surrounded by unmoveable masterpieces, mostly unread, many in sets. I am not speaking of the dealers in rare books and manuscripts. Between them and the second-hand variety there is the gulf that separates the businessman from the romanticist.

Your rare-bookman is more like a banker or corporation counsel. He habitually wears the air of one who knows what there is to know, which is sometimes considerable. He lacks eagerness. He is impeccably dressed, urbane, and receives you, not in a shop, which all may enter, but in a paneled suite.

He is an imperturbable bidder at Sotheby's. My friend, Lew D. Feldman, head of the House of El Dieff, accoutred in his fur-collared coat and silver-knobbed stick, bids the world's record price for a manuscript—Caxton's Ovid—over a quarter of a million dollars—and returns to his hotel, the Westbury, around the corner, unruffled and content, returning another day to outbid all for Robert Herrick's common-place book, full of manuscript material, which happens to be in short supply for this poet.

Precious items do not always make their appearance on

the auction block. The Vinland Map, now at Yale, came "from a private collection in Europe," where it was found by Laurence Witten, the antiquarian book dealer, formerly of New Haven, now of Monroe, Conn.

The Map is officially described as "the oldest surviving map of American lands," and was drawn circa 1440, or fifty-two years before Columbus. The legend on it appears to confirm the fact of a voyage, or voyages, made at the turn of the tenth century to the North American continent, as related in the Icelandic sagas. It reads—in part—as follows: "By God's will, after a long voyage from the island of Greenland to the south toward the most distant remaining parts of the western ocean sea, sailing southward amidst the ice, the companions Bjarni [Herjolfsson] and Leif Eiriksson discovered a new land, extremely fertile and even having vines, the which island they named Vinland" (original in Latin, translation from *The Vinland Map and the Tartar Relation,* Yale University Press).

Mr. Witten kindly presented me with a copy of this valuable book, after one of our meetings at the Ridgefield home of Harrison D. Horblit, the collector mentioned earlier. I have also met that other famous bookman, John F. Fleming, there, sometimes when Mr. Witten was present. Their talk was of ninth century manuscripts, which I had supposed might comprise a scarce handful, but turned out to be plentiful, though not exactly a drug on the market; and of medieval cartographers and portolan maps, which left me a mere listener, coming to life once of an evening at the mention of a printed Caxton, which they thought common. On these occasions I may have felt, and perhaps looked, like an intruder at a board of directors' meeting. Mr. Fleming, head of the Rosenbach Company, is the co-author, with Edwin Wolf 2nd, of an entertaining account of the formidable founder of that firm, *Rosenbach, A Biography.* He stays at the Ritz when in London.

Our host is like the bookmen he deals with and entertains, mainly imperturbable. His country home is a 39-room

COLLEGE OF THE SEQUOIAS
LIBRARY

Georgian town house, and he, too, slummeth not. But once he had dinner with me in my walk-up apartment on 11th Street, and met Francesco M. Bianco, the son of my old friend. It turned out that the Cortlandt Field Bishop collection had been catalogued for the American Art Association-Anderson Galleries by him. Mr. Horblit reacted. Authors were all very well, but here was someone who was knowledgeable about rarissima and provenance; and such were his pleasure and surprise that even I went up in his estimation.

Chapter Eleven

1

The offices of the North American Newspaper Alliance were in the old *World* building on Park Row, now almost entirely empty. The teletype opened at 7 p.m., and it was eerie to arrive for work in a blacked-out building as night was falling. I was assistant night editor.

Although the Alliance had a number of staple features, such as Grantland Rice's sports column, its most important function was to bring to its members the byline stories of the new heroes of that burgeoning age. Men—and women—were flying the Atlantic and Pacific in their own planes; they were flying around the world; they were going to the Arctic and to Antarctica, and one of them went into the stratosphere in a balloon. All wrote for NANA. After a take-off or departure I never knew when their copy would start coming in by cable or from what remote place.

I became an expert transcriber of cablese. The night editor used to stand over me and yank "takes" from my typewriter, sometimes in the middle of a sentence, rush back to his desk and, finding nothing to edit, make spirals with his pencil in the empty air. His name was William C. McCloy, a small thin, wiry man who had been editor of the great New York *Sun* for many years and had hired Richard Harding Davis as a correspondent. Now the *Sun* was dead, too, and the New York *Times* had taken its place as a member; later the NANA offices were moved to the seventh floor of the *Times* building. It was there that a man came, one evening, with a present for Mr. McCloy. He was Fairfax Downey, who had just published a biography of Davis. Mr. McCloy glanced at the inscription and handed the book to me. While they talked I turned to the index and looked him up. I was struck by one of Mr. Downey's characterizations of McCloy: "He lived on wires." It was still true.

It was in the *Times* building that, just after midnight on March 1, 1932, the AP teletype in my office flashed the kidnapping of the Lindbergh baby.

One of Mr. McCloy's responsibilities as editor of the *Sun* was the editorial page, on which a poem always appeared, as in the *Times* today. He explained once how the daily poem was selected from scores already in type. With the page made up, except for a blank space, he would hand the office boy his ruler and send him to the composing room. "Find me a $3\frac{3}{16}$-inch poem"—or whatever the odd measurement was— he would tell the office boy, he told me with an amused twinkle in his eyes.

Mr. McCloy's memories went back beyond his *Sun* years. He sometimes referred to events I had read about only in history books, or the *World Almanac,* but at which it appeared he had been present. Our office boy spent a large part of his time trying to figure out how old Mr. McCloy was, and once asked him point-blank. Mr. McCloy grinned, but did not reply. My guess is that he was around sixty-five, but he may have been younger; he had a teenage daughter, Helen Mc-Cloy, who was to become a renowned author of detective novels. One night he showed me an anniversary issue of *Editor & Publisher;* in it were two pages of *Sun* editors from its founding to its final year.

"See if you can find me," he said.

I looked at the array of Woodburys. There were men with bowler hats, side whiskers, jackets buttoned by one button under celluloid collars, waistcoats and watch-chains showing. I finally found Mr. McCloy and pointed. In his oval frame he was peering up at me from a time before I was born.

"All dead but me," he said cheerfully, and seemed to skip back to his desk.

The event that was outstanding in the old *World* building was Professor Auguste Piccard's story of his ascent into the stratosphere in a black-and-white balloon. He had a companion, whose name eludes me. That night Mr. McCloy held the teletype open for Piccard's story. It failed to come. The night's report started off with Rice's column. Meanwhile, the office boy had gone out and returned with the morning papers—all but the *Times,* which went to bed later. Stretched across the front page of the New York *American* were banner headlines about Piccard's feat, and under them his name in large type and a world copyright. The story began: "We are the first men to conquer the stratosphere! We are the first . . ." etc.

"That's that," said Mr. McCloy. He looked downcast. I asked him if it were not possible—just possible—that AP or UP stories of Piccard's descent might not have inspired the story; it was also possible, of course, that a Hearst correspondent had spoken to Piccard—Europe swarmed with correspondents on the chance. He said it was possible; but now it made no difference.

Around eleven o'clock that night Piccard's story came in. It began: "Experiments with the gamma ray in my laboratory in Brussels had convinced me that ..." And that, dear reader, is how the authentic thing sounds. It made the final edition of the *Times*.

Lincoln Ellsworth signed up for his byline stories from Antarctica. He wrote the first of them before leaving New York. At the top was this quotation:

> my purpose holds
> To sail beyond the sunset, and the baths
> Of all the western stars, until I die. ...

I was reading the first page when a thin, cuffed hand came over my shoulder; a pencil was in the hand, and it changed the "b" of "baths" to "p."

I looked up.

"Mr. McCloy," I said, "the word is 'baths,' not 'paths.' A second-rate poet would have written 'paths,' but Tennyson was not a second-rate poet. 'Baths,' " I repeated.

Mr. McCloy looked startled. He disappeared. Half an hour later he leaned over me once more; this time his pencil was in reverse. He erased the 'p.'

"Right you sometimes are as I always am," he said, and went to his own desk with a happy grin.

He had been upstairs, in the *Times* library, on the tenth floor.

On the night of March 5, 1933, a cabled story arrived from Sweden. It was signed "John Neville," and contained pen portraits of the new leaders of Germany. The portraits were grim: one of them, of Goering, included documentary proof of his drug addiction. I transcribed the dispatch and handed it to Mr. McCloy, who showed instant agitation. Just then, the office boy came over and asked me if I knew who John Neville was. I could tell by his look that he had a surprise for me.

"Mr. Wheeler," he said, proud of his inside knowledge.

John N. Wheeler was head of the North American Newspaper Alliance. I had occasionally sat in on conferences with him and Mr. McCloy. He had gone to Germany for the election that brought Hitler to power, and had left as quickly as possible to be able to transmit, from neutral territory, what he had uncovered.

Mr. McCloy's dilemma was great. On the one hand, the story was a scathing attack on the new heads of the Reich; on the other, the author of the story was his employer. I think he was more worried about the former. He consulted a great deal, on the phone and in person, with the *Times* cable desk, and perhaps with Edwin L. James, the *Times* editor. The story was censored, smoothed over, and appeared the next day, pallid and innocuous.

The same office boy was still with us. His curiosity was as great as ever; but he had found other things to engage his attention. One of them was the hotel across the street from the *Times*. One night, a few minutes before the wire opened up, he came to my desk.

"Mr. Norman," he whispered. "Would you like to see something?"

He did not whisper to Mr. McCloy.

I followed him to an office down the hall. Massed by the windows were *Times* and NANA employees. We joined them.

Directly across was a window in the hotel with a full view of the door, a dresser, a coat rack, and bed. A man and a woman entered. The man still had his finger on the light switch when the woman began to strip off her clothes. She dropped them piece by piece—dress in a heap, a peeled-off stocking, another, shoes flipping in air, slip, and in a startling instant was lying naked on the made-up bed. The man was more methodical. He put his hat on the dresser and hung his jacket on the rack. He stepped out of his trousers and sat down to remove his socks and shoes. Then he came across the room to the bed. The light glared from the ceiling.

He was very methodical.

2

After two years with the North American Newspaper Alliance I went to work for United Press. I was put in charge of a wire that fed news to papers in western Pennsylvania. Anything that mentioned mines, miners or minerals took priority over falls of empires, deaths of kings, elections of presidents.

The UP offices were in the *Daily News* building on East 42nd Street. The first night I reported for work I found the doorway blocked by a scrawny newspaperman with arms outstretched.

"You're Burton Rascoe," he said, and turned to wink at a man standing behind him enjoying the show.

"I know Burton Rascoe," I said.

"You're Burton Rascoe," he repeated.

"Listen," I said, "it's my first night and I'd like to report on time. Are you going to step aside, or must I shove?"

He stepped aside and watched me reporting to Delos Smith, who showed me my desk and the pile of copy on it. For about an hour the office was quiet; then, at 1 a.m., the wires opened up and there was a clatter of teletype machines. Around three there was quiet again; the man who had blocked the doorway came to my desk and asked me to step into the locker room. In the locker room was his companion.

"My name is H. Allen Smith," he said. "And this is Sidney Whipple."

We shook hands. The amenities over, Mr. Whipple took a bottle from his locker and poured. He was the drama critic of the *World-Telegram;* he also wrote a daily syndicated column. Some time later, when he went to the hospital, he asked a number of writer friends to furnish columns for him; one of them was William Saroyan. Mr. Saroyan's column duly appeared in the *World-Telegram* and other Scripps-Howard papers. It began: "Mr. Whipple, who is in the hospital with a bad leg, has asked me to write this column for him. I am happy to comply. I did not ask Mr. Whipple which leg it was; probably the one he writes reviews with."

It was while I was working for United Press that I received a phone call telling me to appear in court the next day. I was considerably startled. What had I done? I had forgotten all about the case against the IRT.

The courthouse was on Chambers Street. The trial took two days. At the end of the first day, as I stood in the corridor with Mr. Sacher, the judge swept by in his robe and said over his shoulder: "A very interesting case." The IRT lawyer came over to learn what the judge had said, and I moved away. He had hurt my feelings.

"Mr. Norman went into the subway looking for a fight," he had told the jury.

Nobody on the jury could have believed this.

"Mr. Norman is a liar. He could not have taken it from two men all the way from 125th Street to 96th Street."

I had taken it: an awesome beating. The police blotter, the intern's report, disposed of that.

"If Mr. Norman stuck his nose into business that didn't concern him, he got what was coming to him."

Mr. Sacher told the jury: "I do not think that when a young man goes to the assistance of an elderly Negro who is being attacked by thugs he is sticking his nose into business that doesn't concern him."

The next day the judge summed up. Sacher was right: the servant of a public carrier must help and defend an inoffensive passenger who is in danger. The jury brought in a verdict of $1,750. Sacher was jubilant. As we descended the steps of the courthouse, a man came running after us. I recognized him. He had stared at me from the jury box with a malevolence which, I was sure, would make the verdict go against me. He grasped Mr. Sacher's hand and shook it, then grasped mine. He was out of breath.

"I held out for the full amount," he gasped.

The IRT promptly went into bankruptcy. I was not paid until five years later, when the city took it over, liabilities and all.

I liked the United Press, I liked the men who worked there, even the one I encountered in the subway on my way to work one night. He said: "Nice hat you got there." I thought so, too; it was a new one. "Make it yourself?" he asked. But when I left the North American Newspaper Alliance I had gone first to the Associated Press to look for work. Suddenly I received a telegram from Wilson Hicks of the AP offering me a job. The salary was higher than the one I was getting. This was a dilemma. I wanted to stay where I was, but could not afford to turn the offer down.

I discussed it with Delos Smith, who was one of the reasons why I wanted to stay on. Smith was an intuitive editor; he could also write. He was from Louisiana, and when a story came out of the South that was just bare bones, he was able to rewrite it with attitudes and details which brought it to life; when it went out again, on the "A" and "B" wires, it got the play it deserved. Smith suggested I present my problem to Mr. Furay, a vice-president. I crossed the sacred threshold and handed him my telegram.

"How long have you worked here?" Mr. Furay asked.

"Two months," I replied.

"And you want a raise?"

"I have a wife and child."

Mr. Furay was a gentleman. He did not think me unreasonable. But I could see that my dilemma was nothing compared with his. How could he put through a raise after two months? It turned out he couldn't. I told Delos Smith I was leaving.

The last night I worked there I noticed that some of the men were congregating near my desk. It was around three in the morning, when the teletypes had stopped clattering. Soon they were standing in a row in front of my desk, staring at me. I became uneasy. I looked from one to the other, and all looked at me. Suddenly one said, in a quasi-quaver: "You'll be sorry." It was like a wail. The others took up the chant. They stared some more before walking back to their desks or into the locker room. I asked Delos Smith what it meant.

"You'll find out," he said.

For the first time I thought him exasperating.

"What will I find out?" I persisted. "Tell me."

A pause.

"They're holier-than-thou," he said.

The following Monday morning I reported to Wilson Hicks, executive editor of the Associated Press Feature Service. I worked for him, and for his successor, William Mc-Cleery, for five years. They were good years for me; they were also the years that broke the hearts of my generation. Everyone saw what was coming—everyone, that is, except those whose business it was to see. The AP was my school and my club. I resigned in May, 1939, to complete my life of Christopher Marlowe, begun ten years before.

Chapter Twelve

1

The Associated Press occupied the sixth and seventh floors of 383 Madison Avenue. The whole of the sixth floor was one vast news room, from the feature service to sports and the foreign desk, with morgue, photo, city, and other departments in between. Ranged along the walls were teletype machines in constant chatter or clatter punctuated by a ringing of bells. On the seventh floor were the executive offices. The great man up there was Kent Cooper, general manager of the Associated Press, of whom all were in awe, including the executives. On the 46th Street corner of Madison was a Childs restaurant, now occupied by a bank. There the men from the various desks met for lunch; occasionally I also had breakfast there.

I never saw any whisky at the AP, possibly because there were no locker rooms. As for being holier-than-thou, I must agree that it was, for a good reason, and it worked fine for the AP and its member papers. Sensationalism was deprecated, and overlooking a whopping error or two due to a bureau chief's or a stringer's zeal, you could count on the AP being right, and it was often first as well. Several staffers won the Pulitzer Prize for reporting while I was there.

Wilson Hicks came from Sedalia, Missouri. It is a curious fact that he had contributed poems to Joseph Kling's *Pagan*. The fact that my poems had been published by Knopf and Morrow, as well as our occasional talks about poetry, in which he still had a keen interest, may have made it easier for him to excuse some of my displays of temper when they came.

My first year under him was far from exciting. I was once more editing copy and writing heads. Some of the copy I found boring, some disagreeable. The health columns by Dr. Iago Galdston, secretary of the New York Academy of Medicine, were well written, but his material disturbed me. Every disease described by him gave me instantaneous symptoms. The further I read the worse I felt. I was a wreck when I got through reading, and there was no balm in Gilead; the next week another batch of his columns stared up at me. The same thing happened to William McCleery when the job devolved on him.

The most attractive copy that passed through my hands was written by Byron Price, chief of the Washington bureau, afterwards assistant secretary-general of the United Nations. I could have sent it on without looking at it, for I never found even a typing error; I read it chiefly for my own pleasure which, as I told Price once, was considerable. James Reston also was to edit his copy, and was afterwards to write as felicitously when he went to the Washington bureau of the New York *Times;* but first McCleery and I broke him in at the Associated Press.

McCleery came from Blue Hill, Nebraska, via the Washington bureau of the AP. He arrived in the New York office about two months after I started work there. Despite the fact that I was seven years older, we became close friends; we still are. He, too, wanted to be a writer; he had written a play at the University of Nebraska, and was to write others, some of which were produced on Broadway. He was bright, attractive, and had an ebullient wit. I once heard him giving instructions to two photographers who were to get pictures of the Easter parade. "Above all," he concluded, "be sure to separate the chic from the gauche." I helped to spread this *mot,* and it has been picked up by others. McCleery was ambitious as well, and in two years was to become the youngest executive in AP history and my boss. He was twenty-three when I met him.

The same year, 1934, Reston came to work. He was twenty-five. He sometimes joined me when, having hung up my hat, I slipped down to Childs for breakfast. He always had oatmeal, and he taught me how to eat it the Scots way—with salt, instead of sugar. I still do. Before coming to the AP he had been publicity director for the Cincinnati Baseball Club. Baseball was his passion and he tried to interest me in it. He never succeeded. One day he asked me if I had ever seen a big league game. I had to admit that I had not. He said: "You'll see—it's different." We went to the Polo Grounds, where the Giants were playing some other team, I forget which. I upset him by my questions and boredom. He gave up. It must have cost him a pang, but he suggested we leave. I was happy to comply.

Late in 1935, Reston asked if he could stay with me for a couple of weeks. His lease was up, he was getting married in December, and he did not want to get another place before moving into an apartment with his wife. I was living alone. He brought a suitcase over and opened it. From it he took a large, unframed photograph of his fiancée and was about to nail it to the wall, when I stopped him. He looked surprised, put the photograph on a chest of drawers, and unpacked. Nothing was said. Years later, in Washington, he told McCleery about it. From the way McCleery told it to me, Reston had thought it very funny; so, obviously, did McCleery. Sally Fulton was as pretty a fiancée as a man could wish, and the photograph of her was of excellent quality; but on my wall, nailed?

Mark Barron, a big, affable Texan with rosy cheeks, was

a fabulous figure at the AP, at least to the staff of the feature service, for which he wrote, but from somewhere at the other end of that vast room. I never learned where he sat. Much of the time he was not in the office at all; presumably he was covering his beat, which was Broadway. Every week, on the appointed day, his six columns appeared on the feature desk, an occurrence which never failed to surprise the copy-editor. About once a month Barron himself appeared, usually a few minutes before five. Starting at one side of the copy desk he made a complete circuit, saying as he went, "Two tickets for every column." He was on his way back to the other end almost before the phrase had been completed.

It meant that he had managed to finish three or four columns, and was in difficulties. The columns did not have to be about Broadway; they could be about Greenwich Village and the literary world. I wrote a great many for him, and saw a great many shows. He also held out the lure of prize fight tickets. I saw Baer knock out Carnera, Louis knock out Baer, but did not see Schmeling knock out Louis because I gave that ticket to Cummings. It was a ringside ticket.

Barron was married to Erin O'Brien-Moore, who played the feminine lead in Cummings' *Him* at the Provincetown Playhouse, so it could have been poetic justice, but it wasn't: I could not spare the tax money on the hundred-dollar ticket.

Another who wrote special columns for the feature service was John Selby, the music and book editor. He was seven years older than I was, and tended to look down on the vulgar newspaper world. He was, in fact, the closest to an aesthete I have ever encountered. Our talk was always about books or music; we lunched often together, and he never once mentioned the office. He was afterwards editor-in-chief of Rinehart & Co., when John Farrar left that firm.

The feature service had an office boy who bore a strong resemblance to the one at the North American Newspaper Alliance (I was to meet a third of the breed at *Time*). If I was not on my feet at five, he would come up behind me—everyone was watching, of course—and whisper, "Mr. Norman,

it's a minute after five," pointing to the clock. It became something of an act, and I something of an actor. I was able to
reach for my hat on the rise and exit hatted in two or three
strides. It proved a temptation to the office boy, who planted
obstacles, like waist-high baskets, in my path until I ordered
him to stop.

This rising and reaching may have been an unconscious
imitation of Mr. Hicks. When the telephone on his desk rang,
everyone turned to watch; it rang only from upstairs. Mr.
Hicks would put down the receiver and start to rise from
his chair; rising, he reached up and pulled the cord on the
electric light which hung above his desk. This saved the
Associated Press about seven and a half mills per week. Then,
straightening his tie, he went to the stair that led to the executive suite. He was photographed rising and putting out the
light on the eve of his departure to become editor of *Life;*
the picture was then blown up life-size, pun or not, and
dominated the banquet hall at his farewell dinner. It was
the office boy's idea. Mr. Hicks was a capable executive, but
perhaps a little more overawed by Kent Cooper than were
some of the others. It made him cautious. He kept salaries
and expenses down.

2

The AP set great store on men who not only did their job
but who "originated" stories. McCleery was the greatest
originator of new material and coverage ever known; the
feature service began to reflect this, and he was watched with

increasing interest from the floor above. He became Hicks's assistant, and his originating powers increased. I, too, benefited; I was given a desk of my own. My originating was not always triumphant.

In 1935, a little more than three years after the Lindbergh baby was kidnapped and murdered, a man was under arrest in the Bronx, and the Treasury Department released three items pertaining to him and the case. One was the suspect's automobile registration card, another a letter he had written to his landlady. The third was one of the ransom notes. It read: "The baby will be found on the boad Nellie next week."

There was no question about the automobile registration card and the letter to the landlady; both bore Hauptmann's signature. The ransom note, of course, was unsigned. Was there a connection?

I called Dr. Samuel A. Tannenbaum, author of a book on Marlowe's death, and of others dealing with Elizabethan handwriting. I asked him if he had seen the items released by the Treasury Department. He had, in the *Times*. Could he come to any conclusion? He thought he could if I supplied him with blow-ups. I delivered them. Several days later he asked me to come to his apartment. He told me that in all his studies of handwriting—which were not confined to the sixteenth and seventeenth centuries—he had never seen an "x" like the "x" in the word "Bronx" on Hauptmann's automobile registration card and the "x" in the ransom note. (The "x" was like two little "e's" entwined.) Dr. Tannenbaum was certain that the "x" and other characteristics, which he pointed out to me, showed that Hauptmann was the author of the ransom note.

I asked Dr. Tannenbaum to write an account of his study of the items released by the Treasury Department. I myself would write an interview with him. His byline story, with a precede telling who he was and naming some of his books, would go to morning papers, my interview to afternoon. His story came; it was well written, closely reasoned, and fascinating. My story began: " 'X' puts Hauptmann on the spot."

I gave the stories to Mr. Hicks, who read them, brought them back and dropped them on my desk. As he was about to walk away, my anger rose.

"Aren't you going to use them?" I asked.

"No," he replied.

"Why not?"

"Hauptmann hasn't been charged with anything yet."

I sat there stunned. I also wondered how I would explain it to Dr. Tannenbaum.

I am convinced if I had been working anywhere but at the AP the stories would have been used. A year and a half later Hauptmann was convicted on the testimony of handwriting experts.

Hicks was more sensitive about words.

The invasion of Ethiopia brought back into prominence a man named Hubert Fauntleroy Julian, "the Black Eagle of Harlem." He had flown Haile Selassie, the Lion of Judah and Emperor of Ethiopia, to the front lines and back. I went to interview him. He was smartly dressed in a uniform of his own assembling, and his boots shone like brown glass. I found him friendly, courteous, and charming. But nothing he told me added to the news stories that had appeared. Finally I asked him how he had managed to get the Emperor safely to the front and back. He replied: "Ah systematized ah system."

I wrote it down. I quickly asked him another question to get him away from that uncut jewel; I have interviewed men, and some women, who have added, "what I really mean is," or "What I want you to say is," and I was afraid if I allowed the pause to stretch he might bring up a substitute. The crisis passed, and I left him with a warm handshake.

Back in the office I found that by paring everything down to essentials, I had a setting for my jewel, slightly polished: "I systematized a system." I wrote about 250 words and saw the story delivered by the office boy to the slot-man on the feature desk, who tossed it to an editor. Having nothing to do, I got up and walked up and down; passing the copy desk I looked over the editor's shoulder, and saw that he had changed the word "systematized" to "formulated."

I went over to Hicks. I told him if he permitted that change to stand I would resign. Hicks looked up at me startled, got up, walked over to the feature desk, and peered down at the story. His eyes found the sentence; a finger came down on the crossed-out word.

"Stet that," he said.

It was now the turn of the copy-editor to look startled.

I have been told by newspapermen that while I was right, they would have resigned had they been in the copy-editor's place. I agreed.

3

I was watching a burlesque show at the Irving Place Theatre when a new star swam into my ken. A stripper appeared who had that electric presence which I had found only at championship prize fights. It is the presence of class. The stripper was very goodlooking. She was also fetchingly dressed, with a frill of lace at the throat, and her hair was swept up and tied in back in a knot. She may not have been the glass of fashion, but she was the mold of form. She did not unzip, whisk or unbutton—she unpinned. She tossed the pins to the men staring up at her from the front rows. There was a rain of dressmaker's pins over the footlights. Her name was Gypsy Rose Lee.

I went backstage during intermission and spoke to her. Intermission in a burlesque house lasts a long time, to give the venders of stockings, popcorn, and soda pop time to ply their wares. It was warm, there was plenty of time for an interview, and I suggested that we go across the street to a bar and have a beer while talking. Miss Lee said: "If you will wait until after the show, I'll give you something better than beer." We were standing in the wings, stared at by show-girls, some of whom raised their eyebrows at this remark.

I returned to my seat.

I had been to this Minsky Brothers production the week before, with McCleery. Miss Lee had not appeared that night, nor did I know of her existence. But there was a girl in the company who was tall and had red hair, of a golden redness, and the face of a Botticelli angel. Although she stripped, or sometimes stood on the stage with other showgirls, statue still and naked to the waist, I could not keep from staring at her face. Her face held all the dreams of fair women from the beginning of time. I wondered how I could meet her. I had not seen her backstage during the intermission, nor did I when I went to pick up Miss Lee.

Miss Lee was waiting for me with a suitcase, which I carried to the sidewalk and then to the curb, where a car waited. In the car were John Farrar and Philip Wylie, one of his authors. We drove two or three blocks to Miss Lee's apartment, which was on Irving Place.

The room we entered was fitted up like a bar room. There was an unpainted upright piano scrawled with autographs, and half a dozen round tables and chairs. Drinks were mixed at once by either Mr. Farrar or Mr. Wylie, and while they chatted with each other by the piano, Miss Lee and I sat at one of the tables, sipped our drinks, and talked. I learned that she not only moved in intellectual circles; she read. Her favorite poet was Cummings. She showed me a brand-new contract, perhaps signed that very evening. She was going to Broadway. Her weekly salary was startling: $1,500. I congratulated her and put my notes away. I asked her who the redhead was. She professed ignorance.

"Miss Lee," I persisted, "this girl is in your show. She is tall, has red hair, last week she was a stripper, tonight she was a showgirl."

"I'm sure I don't know who you mean."

I was fully aware that she did not find my questions about someone else agreeable. I described the girl again, with each description, and additional drinks, waxing more lyrical. At last Miss Lee fixed me with her stern and beautiful eyes under her beautifully trimmed eyebrows and exclaimed: "Oh—you mean Dracula!" She told me her name. We rose together and joined Farrar and Wylie.

The next day I sought out Mark Barron. I told him about the redhead at the Irving Place burlesque.

"What's her name?" he asked. But his manner indicated he already knew. I told him.

"Stay away from her," he warned. "She's poison."

Her angelic Botticelli face peered at me from the gold frame of my mind.

"Why do you say that?" I asked, bewildered.

"She's being kept by two Brooklyn gunmen," said Barron.

Two! Would not one have been enough? I did not pursue my fancy. Not long after, I found myself dallying *à trois*. I cannot say there is much to commend it.

Carl Carmer, author of *Stars Fell on Alabama* and other books, was the greatest host in town, his wife the greatest hostess, their house the most open of any. They had two floors of a brownstone on West 12th Street; on the third lived Joseph Wood Krutch. Their dining room on the parlor floor had an enormous table, and sometimes as many as a dozen young writers and editors sat around it, after dropping in for cocktails. It was in this house that I had the experience just alluded to, followed by another on a more spiritual level.

The hall bedroom on the second floor was rented to a succession of young women, one or two of them Carmer's former students, newly come to the big city to pursue their careers. A friend and I vied for the favors of one of them, and found ourselves bedded down together. That one left, to go on to higher things and a husband or two; and one night, when I rang the Carmers' bell, the door was opened by a new occupant of the hall bedroom. She was waiting for her boy friend.

Propped on the marble mantelpiece in the parlor was a typewritten poem. When I asked her whose it was, she said her boy friend had sent it to her; just then, the doorbell rang, and she rushed off with him. I read the poem. It began:

> Call me not false, beloved,
>   If from thy scarce known breast
> So little time removed
>   In other arms I rest.

There were three more stanzas, of the same excellent quality. I was pretty sure the poem was not the work of her boy friend. I asked the Carmers about it. They told me how excited their lodger had been to receive it. But they did not know the poet's name, and promised to ask her. On another night, they told me what she had told them: "Kipling."

I was dubious, and did not pursue the lead I had been given. The lines stayed with me.

4

One day in the summer of 1936 Wilson Hicks called me to his desk. He told me that he and McCleery had had many serious discussions about whom to send on an important assignment. It was McCleery's idea, he said, to send me; he himself did not appear overjoyed that he had agreed. The staff was full of westerners, but McCleery had felt that a man from New York would have a fresher eye for details. Hicks now told me what the assignment was.

The year 1936 was the year of dust storms and floods. He and McCleery had discussed a series on dust storms, and then had discussed a series on floods. Their conclusion was that the two were so linked together that what was needed was a series on both to wake up America, more or less. He asked me if I would be willing to take the assignment if it was approved upstairs. The feature service had never before sent a man out of town, and it was a grave responsibility. I said I would do my best.

I went first to Washington, where I talked with officials in the Department of Agriculture and the Department of the Interior. All were helpful; I was given printed material and photographs, and lugged them around with me in a suitcase, together with my notes. From Washington I went to St. Louis, where Hal Boyle of the AP bureau was expecting me. He showed me the waterfront, also some waterfront dives, and I left him to go down the Mississippi on a riverboat with a stern paddle-wheel. It tied up that night above Cairo, Illinois, at the confluence of the Mississippi and Ohio rivers, safe behind its sixty-foot wall. The city was like Lyonesse, magical and moving, gleaming with lights thirty or forty feet below the deck of the riverboat.

After Cairo the Mississippi rolled southward in full flood, which was brown from the soil washed into it by rain on denuded land. It was the link between dust storms and floods.

The heart of the "dust bowl" country was Dalhart, in the Texas Panhandle; there the Agricultural Adjustment Administration was experimenting with trees and grasses whose roots would bind the sandy soil together and keep it from blowing away, or being washed away by rain. There was no topsoil left; the air teemed with dust, and there were sand dunes higher than those on Cape Cod. Over the bare fields huge balls of Russian thistle tumbled and rolled weirdly, and came to rest against fence posts or hummocks of sand. In the little hotel where I stayed the windows were sealed with strips of carpet nailed to the window frames, but there were shallows of sand on the floor, and I tasted grit with my food. At night I heard the sand sifting through the strips of carpet.

What had brought this about in a fertile region? Part of the answer was drought; but mostly it was wheat, which had gone to two dollars a bushel in World War I. Two wheat crops a year had depleted the soil. Now the AAA preached rotating crops and contour plowing. But first the land had to be redeemed, and there were rows of little trees like puffs of smoke to the far horizon.

I returned to New York with the suitcase stuffed with material. I soon became bogged down. Mr. Hicks was understandably anxious to see the series completed; but he could not have been more anxious than I was. One day when he asked me how soon he could expect copy, I told him it would not be long—McCleery was helping me. He exclaimed "McCleery!" and walked away from my desk.

Without McCleery I am certain I could not have finished the series that year. One evening, as we worked together, a beautiful young woman came to the office to join us for dinner. She was his fiancée. McCleery cut, and sometimes he rewrote; I was not always happy about that, but to judge by the results it was effective. At last we had five stories with the overall title: "Enemies of the Earth—What Dust Storms and Floods Mean to America." Copies were sent to Secretary of Agriculture Henry A. Wallace, who wrote an introduction.

Many papers published the entire series on the front page. It turned out to be the most widely used story ever distributed by the feature service. I was nominated for the Pulitzer Prize. That was the year the Pulitzer Prize committee decided to split the award among the science writers of the *Times, Tribune,* and AP for their coverage of the Harvard tercentenary. I did not even get a raise.

Chapter Thirteen

1

In the fall of 1936 William McCleery became executive editor. Several innovations followed. One of them was a woman photographer. *Life* had its Margaret Bourke-White; the AP now had Mary Morris. She was assigned to me.

Miss Morris was a goodlooking young socialite from one of the opulent suburbs of Chicago. She had attended Sarah Lawrence, and was full of high spirits. Her usual garb was a sweater and skirt; her sweaters were white and fluffy, with a V-neck. She had studied photography with the famed Ralph Steiner, and afterwards married him.

Miss Morris accompanied me on all my interviews. She had two canvas satchels bulging with equipment, several folding tripods, and an assortment of cameras. I was faced with a decision. How much of this equipment, if any, should I carry? After all, I had my pocket notebook and a pencil or two. I weakened. I took one of the tripods and tried to swing it nonchalantly like a walking stick. On Madison Avenue, before we could get into a taxi, people stared at me and my overburdened companion. I took one of the satchels. It was not long before I was carrying at least half her equipment.

One day, while waiting for the elevator, I heard my name croaked in a hoarse whisper. Al Resch, executive editor of the news photo service, had come up behind me. (His name was Francis Alvin Resch. He was called Al, and liked it, and acted rough-and-tough, but was really a gentleman underneath, and a first-rate newspaperman.)

"There's something I want to talk to you about," he said, speaking out of the side of his mouth in a hoarse whisper.

I waited.

"My men are complaining," he went on accusingly.

"Why don't you give them a raise?" I said.

"It's not that," he retorted, waving my disconcerting remark aside.

"No?" I asked, trying to look incredulous.

"No," he said, hurriedly. "They want somebody to carry their equipment, too."

Looking wise, he slipped into the office.

Miss Morris was bright, and eager to please. Although I had long been an admirer of Aldous Huxley, I did not know he was in New York until she told me and suggested an interview. She had become an originator of stories. I called Mr. Huxley and we went to see him in his midtown hotel.

The presence of a pretty girl when two men are talking can sometimes improve the quality of their talk. She can also be distracting, and I think Mr. Huxley was rather more interested in what Miss Morris was doing than in replying to my questions. He was very tall, and thinner than I had supposed—so thin and so tall that the upper half of him curved and seemed to sway. The curve was toward Miss Morris. In that midtown hotel room, while I asked him questions, and she was busy stringing wires and adjusting lighting fixtures, he seemed hardly to be listening. His good eye found the slope it sought and rolled like a marble into her V-neck.

André Malraux came to the United States to raise money for the Spanish Loyalists. We were eager to help him. The interview was conducted in English, which he spoke extremely well, but with deliberation. He appeared, by his pauses, to be thinking everything out; in French, no doubt, his answers would have flowed swiftly, smoothly, and with the lucidity of his prose. His pauses were helped by the lighting of many cigarettes—he was a chain-smoker. He seemed to have some difficulty with his breathing, and I was struck by the thought that he was smoking too much. He appeared worn out, perhaps not relishing his assignment but acting in obedience to instructions, the very embodiment of the man of action and the dedicated man. Miss Morris captured his strong and solitary self in intimate portraits which were widely used.

2

Miss Morris was a first-rate photographer, and a very good companion. Sometimes, when I thought her occupied with her fixtures, she surprised me by asking a question of her own. At first this rattled me, but never the person being interviewed, who may have thought it part of the procedure. There was only one time when she lost her ebullience and aplomb.

Al Smith had been one of my idols. He was, at the time of which I am writing, president of the Empire State Building corporation. The mayoralty election was approaching and I happened to hear that he intended to back a candidate of his own choosing. There had been nothing about this in the press, and I thought it a good opportunity to pay my respects to the former governor; I might even come back with a scoop. I found that he was unreachable.

Grover Whalen had offices on the same floor. The Goushas knew his secretary. I asked her to use her influence. It worked. A date was set, and Miss Morris and I, loaded down with equipment, took a taxi to 34th Street. Whalen's secretary told me to be sure to address Mr. Smith as "Governor," and showed us in.

Mr. Smith's office was spacious. Near the door was a sofa; Miss Morris sat down to sort out her fixtures and I walked to a desk at the far end. Mr. Smith was behind it, peering out into the room, and then directly at me, with cold, watery blue eyes which never blinked. The amenities were quickly over—there weren't any.

"Governor," I said, "I understand you have a candidate."

I was not given a chance to continue.

"Politics is out," he said brusquely, without change of expression. It was a jolt. I had no other reason for being there.

I said: "Al Smith without politics is like Atlas without his burden."

He stared at me as though I was nuts or something; then, comprehending, he said: "When the time comes, I will have something to say. What else do you want to know?"

There was nothing else. I had my story. I tried not to show my elation. I was in a mood to tell him how much I had admired him in the past; I did not find him admirable at the moment. I said if it was all right with him, Miss Morris would take his picture. He said: "Tell her to make it snappy."

I looked around to signal her, and instantly saw that something was wrong. I excused myself and went over to her.

"What's the matter?" I asked.

"I can't take the picture," she replied.

I glanced at her equipment.

"Why not?" I asked.

"I forgot to bring the female plug."

She sat there, disconsolate. At her feet were arrayed the contents of both bags. An automobile, or at least a motorcycle, could have been assembled from the parts that strewed the carpet like a surrealistic landscape. I walked back to Mr. Smith.

"Governor," I said, "Miss Morris has had an accident. She can't take your picture today. The AP would like to have it, and I hope you will be kind enough to let her come back tomorrow. It won't take long."

He stared coldly at both of us.

I called Grover Whalen's secretary to smooth the way for Miss Morris, who returned alone. She, too, was angry with Mr. Smith. She took along a large box camera. Starting at the door, she walked directly toward the desk until she was in front of it, focusing on his eyes all the way. She caught Smith as he had appeared to me—cold, bitter, and lonely. The picture won first prize at the news photographers' annual exhibition.

3

The first time I ever saw Edna St. Vincent Millay, she was standing in line in front of the Provincetown Playhouse in Greenwich Village. Even without knowing who she was a man would have looked at her a second time. It was 1927, ten years after Vassar, and she still had that lovely, utterly feminine look which her early photographs show. She was wearing a little hat with a little veil, and she looked very slender in a form-fitting suit. Her husband, Eugen Boissevain, was with her, and together they appeared like the newlyweds they were, holding hands, full of delight in each other, and eager as youngsters to see *Patience,* in which her sister, Norma, had a part. Harrison Dowd, another member of the cast, told me that the Boissevains came three or four times to that production.

When I saw her again, ten years later, it was at her farm near Austerlitz, N.Y. She and her husband, now retired from his importing business, received Mary Morris and me in a large, cool, and shadowy room in which two grand pianos loomed like monuments. Miss Millay had been playing tennis up to a few minutes before our arrival, and had just changed into lounging pajamas with a flower pattern; the mandarin-type collar, snug around her neck, was tied with a bow. Her figure was no longer slim, but there was an impression of strength which had come from work and exercise in the open. Her face, which glowed with health, was profusely freckled; it was also criss-crossed with wrinkles. Her blonde hair was bobbed. Her pale green eyes were bright as emeralds, and her voice was warm, ringing, and pleasantly cadenced.

The farm consisted of some eight hundred acres; on a walk with me before lunch she said: "No matter where you stand, you cannot see the end of our land." Lunch, which Mr. Boissevain prepared, consisted of a mushroom omelette, tossed salad, bread, and wine; Miss Millay had picked the mushrooms herself, and termed them "the tiniest ones in the world." We ate in the grape arbor next to the house, and spent the rest of the day there in that pleasant shade. The talk was of poetry, chiefly hers. She laughed good-naturedly over the people—readers as well as critics—who persisted in ident-fying her with the "oh-the-pain-of-it school of writing," as she called it.

"I am a vital person," she said, "not a die-away poet. I

live here because I can work here. You can't live in the city
and not be touched by it—by the tortured faces you see. I am
destroyed by it."

It was the summer of 1937, and the talk in the arbor was
also about politics. Miss Millay's *Conversation at Midnight*
had recently appeared; the reviewers had been about equally
divided between those who praised the book as the fulfillment
of her career and those who wished that she had continued
to write lyrics. She did not mind this, she said, but minded
the inference that she had suddenly become social-conscious.
Speaking with extraordinary earnestness she declared: "No
one has ever read me!"

"It's ridiculous to say that I have suddenly become aware
of the life going on around me," she went on. "I've always
been aware, always writing about it. What was *Renascence*
about? It was about people who were starving, people who
were suffering. And that was my first poem. More than ten
years ago I wrote a play called *Aria da Capo*—that was about
the war [World War I]."

She brushed away, with an impatient gesture, a lock of
hair that had fallen over her brow as she shook her head.

I quoted a sentence of Thomas Mann: "The destiny of
man presents itself to our time in a political guise."

"I agree," she said. She thought about it some more. "Yes,
of course, that's excellent."

She had a way, at such times, of shutting her eyes and
resting her head on her hand; one could almost feel the
intensity with which she was sorting out her thoughts.

"Yes," she continued; "but great poetry has seldom come
out of taking sides, and is not likely to. However, that's a
different matter from having a natural direction from lyrical
toward dramatic poetry, and following it. It would be hard
to look at the destiny of man today with the eyes of a drama-
tist and not find one's self at moments looking into the eyes of
a politician.

"I, for instance, am moving naturally in the direction of
dramatic poetry—by which I don't mean," she threw in

impatiently, "that I've given up writing lyric poetry. Really, the public is very stern with the artist—it looks upon him as an inspired scatterbrain, yet expects him to proceed in more rigidly methodical fashion than any banker! I've given up nothing. But the poet who is both lyrical and dramatic usually turns to drama. Shakespeare did; Shelley would have done so.

"If you don't change and develop between your first book and your tenth," she said after a pause, "then you just keep on rewriting yourself. And it seems to me that life should do more for you than just keep you alive. After all, a child is not merely fed by the food he eats; he is strengthened, and he grows. It's the same with the poet—that is to say, if he has a hearty appetite for life. It's no good nibbling at it." She added with a smile: "He must also, of course, have an excellent digestion."

In all my interviewing only two subjects asked me to show them my stories before they appeared—Edna Millay and Wendell Willkie. In both instances I was the gainer, because each added interesting afterthoughts. Miss Millay wrote me:

"About the photographs: before you can use the one with the hand to the head you'll have to offset the brutality of a clinically probing camera operating in the glare of full sunlight, by the handsomest job of retouching in the history of the AP. Spots, blots, freckles, speckles—everything that the camera is particularly proud of, I want wiped right out. My desire in the matter is very simple: I just want to look as pretty as possible.

"About your story: I liked it so much that I got excited about it, and wanted to be represented as speaking in a way that would merit all the nice things you said about me, so I sort of rewrote the end. I know I didn't say all those things; but they are what I meant to say."

Although Mr. Boissevain had had some perceptive things to say, he was mainly silent, seemingly content to listen to the beautifully modulated voice of his wife, at whom he gazed with admiration. This admiration their visitor shared. I felt—as I was to feel about Willkie—that I had been in the presence of true greatness, not of mere achievement or fame, but greatness of person. Miss Millay had heart, brain, truth, charm; and a vivacity which brought back all her loveliness and added radiance to the summer day.

Her place as a poet has diminished somewhat since her death, although she still has numerous readers and, in Edmund Wilson, one redoubtable champion. Perhaps she wrote too much—she herself was finally aware that such a work as *Lidice* was a disaster; perhaps the posthumous editions of her poems have been too inclusive. She would have been the first to weed out the light and trite if she had lived to do the job herself. But she was another lady whom time had surprised.

4

Charles E. Honce was the executive news editor of the AP. It was from him that I learned Thomas Wolfe was dead when he stopped by my desk to ask for three hundred words "for the wire." He was greatly interested in books and authors, and was an early collector of the works of Edgar Saltus (his book about Saltus is called *The Uplands of Dream,* and includes a bibliography).

Mr. Honce was from Keokuk, Iowa. He was tall, with a ruddy complexion, and wore white linen suits, perhaps because one of his idols, Mark Twain, had; Twain, in fact, had once lived in Keokuk, assisting his brother, Orion Clemens, in the latter's printing shop. Tiring of his job, Twain decided to leave for South America, and arranged with the editor of the Keokuk *Post* to publish his correspondence, under a pseudonym. He got as far as St. Louis and Cincinnati (*vide* Honce, *The Adventures of Thomas Jefferson Snodgrass*).

It was Honce who sent me to interview Masefield, at the home of Thomas S. Lamont on East 72nd Street. What Honce was chiefly interested in was how much a poet laureate got, and whether Masefield had opted for the tun of sherry which had once been a perquisite of the office.

I was in the Lamont library several minutes before Masefield made his appearance, which gave me time to ponder the thoughtfulness of his host in providing masses of daffodils, the poet's favorite, even symbolic, flower. A door opened, and suddenly he was there, looking none too happy about it, in recollection about as shy as anyone I have ever encountered, and strangely tense, alert, almost quivering, like a deer in a thicket, his dark, remarkable eyes peering in all directions.

His replies to my questions were clear and concise. He did not smile when he told me that a teetotaller laureate had asked for the equivalent in money in place of the sack which earlier ones had only been too happy to receive once a year (as a measure, a tun is 252 wine gallons, which appears sufficient for a drinking bout or two). With that money added, the royal salary came to £79. I began my story with the daffodils, but Honce switched paragraphs and led off with the money.

Mr. Masefield, I think, was greatly relieved when the interview was over, and vanished from the library as silently and swiftly as he had entered it. I am certain now that I could have put him at his ease with the following story, if I may be permitted a single flashback after my earlier disclaimer.

Masefield had been my favorite poet when I was in college. Between semesters, one summer, under the spell of his sea poetry, I shipped as an ordinary seaman on a freighter bound for South America. The narrative poem referred to in the Foreword to this book was about that voyage. It was published in 1924 in pamphlet form with the title *The Far Harbour* (not my spelling) and reprinted, with other poems about the sea, in 1925 in a book limited to a hundred numbered and signed copies which S. A. Jacobs designed and printed. Pamphlet and book were dedicated to James Munn, who paid for both publications. The pamphlet cost $110 or $150, I forget which; the book $100.

Chapter Fourteen

1

Marlowe was not my only preoccupation during my working years. From time to time I was able to write a few hundred words on a novel which I afterwards entitled *Dominick Dragon or The Happy Fellow*. The name of my hero was suggested by a fleeting glimpse of a shoemaker's window in some upstate town as I was being driven from the station to a friend's house; the name on it was D. Dragone. The hero himself was inspired by the character of De Hirsh Margules, although I soon found myself drawing on adventures of my own, chiefly of a comic nature. Some were not comic. It was I who stopped the runaway horses on Sixth Avenue. In my book, Dominick is seen by Nina Bramble, whom he loves; in real life, a more beautiful heroine saw me—Dorothy Miller, of the Museum of Modern Art.

The novel was no more than a long story when the first draft was completed; Eric Pinker thought it amusing and sent it around until his agency shut down. I kept on revising it; I also enlarged it. By 1936 it was, if not a full-length work, at least an approximation of one. I had no better luck with it. Very serious works dominated the depression market, and editors seemed very obtuse. They thought my book either whimsy or a satire; it was neither. As it remained unpublished I could only talk about it.

Allan Scott was the co-author of *Goodbye Again,* a Broadway hit which was afterwards made into a movie. I had met him at the home of my old friends, John Gerard and Margaret Linley. When the Gerards went to Stockton for the summer, Scott and his wife took over their Gay Street house; she was an actress. One night Scott said: "Why don't you let me see this book you're always talking about?" I was delighted. I brought it over, and was rewarded by a good dinner.

Scott had been a Rhodes scholar. He had two kegs near the fireplace for his briar pipes; I think he said there were three hundred of them. From time to time he would sit down between the kegs, one of which was full, and taking a pipe at a time scrape it quickly with a knife and toss it into the other one. Smoking the pipes in rotation, he would fill the newly emptied keg, and some months later the process was repeated. Perhaps he had picked up this ritual at Oxford.

The night I brought my novel over was a Saturday night. Sunday morning he called me up. He was very excited about my manuscript and wanted me to come over for breakfast. I went. Over breakfast, he told me that he and his wife had both read the novel in bed. They had read it all. They liked it. Dominick was a wonderful character, and he would like to write a play around him. There was one hitch. He was waiting for a contract from RKO; as soon as it came he would have to go to Hollywood. It might come next week, or the week after; there was no time to start a play; he would be at the beck and call of his employers.

He offered an alternative idea. There was time, if we started at once, to write a short script based on the book. We would work together, and he would take the script along with him and submit it when the time seemed right. I thought it an excellent suggestion. We worked together. By the end of the week we had a ten- or twenty-page script called *The Happy Fellow*. Scott's contract came, and he and his wife left for Hollywood. More than a year passed without a word from him.

On March 25, 1937, I received a telegram. "Have nibble," he had wired. "What do you want for your share?" I wired back: "I'm here, you're there; get what you can for both of us." The next day the AP office boy told me there was a long-distance call. "It's from Hollywood," he said, staring at me with new interest. The call had come through on another desk, and I went over to take it.

"I'm in the producer's office," Scott told me. "They don't want to buy the script. They don't want to buy your novel. They just want to buy an idea in the script. They're willing to give us a thousand dollars apiece. Just a minute—the producer wants to talk to you."

The next voice came through in a rush. It was a harsh, domineering voice.

"What Allan said is absolutely correct," said the rushing voice. "We don't have to buy the idea, but we don't want any trouble. A thousand dollars. Take it or leave it."

I said: "I'll take it."

"Good," said the rushing voice, now slowed down. "In five days you'll receive a call from RKO in New York. They'll have a contract and a check. You sign the contract, they'll give you the check."

My book was full of ideas; I felt I could spare one for a thousand dollars. In five days the call came; I walked over to Rockefeller Center and signed several copies of the contract with RKO. I left with one of the copies and the check.

I put the check in my bank. I began to spend it. It seemed as though it could never be spent. I gave a hundred dollars to my mother, who had always given me money when I needed it; I sent a hundred to my wife; I paid Cummings a hundred for several watercolors, and gave nearly a hundred to Francesco Bianco for books. In six weeks the thousand was all gone. It was a lovely experience to spend all that money. I am glad to have had it. There have not been many others.

2

This slight connection with Hollywood made me look at portions of the New York papers which I had hitherto skipped. I became an avid reader of motion picture news. One day I read that Allan Scott had sold an original to RKO; it was called *The Happy Fellow*.

I wrote Scott and asked him what it meant, and he wrote back that it was due to a slip in the public relations office, which had put out a release without checking the facts. I thought that fine. I relaxed. I might have forgotten all about it if I had not seen another release which announced that a story by Allan Scott was going to be filmed by RKO, with Miriam Hopkins as the star. The new release, and several that followed, made it clear to me that they were not shooting a story by Scott, or even the script he and I wrote together— they were shooting the novel which RKO had never seen. I looked at the contract and my heart sank. I had given away everything—novel, script, characters, incidents, and the right to use Dominick or any other character any time, in any way.

I called Morris L. Ernst, who kindly listened to my side of it. He said he knew the RKO people very well, and that if he asked them for a shooting script they would give it to him. He then asked me to drop off the novel, which I did the next day on my way to work.

About a week later he asked me to come to his office. He told me he had read the novel and the shooting script, and that there was no doubt about it—they were filming the book.

"Now, we can do one of two things," he said. "We can let them go ahead and sue, or we can make them drop it."

"Make them drop it," I said.

He made them drop it. He also got a quit-claim.

I have sometimes thought about what might have happened had I allowed RKO to film my unpublished novel. I would have sued, of course; I might have been rich. But at the time I was angry. All the other things Scott could have done occurred to me. He could have said to the producer: "Listen, there's a guy in New York, works for the AP, probably for peanuts. Let's bring him out here. He and I can do a great film. We've worked together; we'll be a good team. He'll come out for $150 a week, maybe $100. Of course, you'll have to buy his novel."

Scott had started at $1,500 a week.

Word from the New York office reached the coast, and changes followed. My title vanished; in its place was *Wise Girl*. I saw the film; Miriam Hopkins was very attractive as the lead. The credit read: "From an original screen play by Allan Scott based upon a story by Allan Scott and Charles Norman." I was with a friend in a Connecticut theater when I saw it; after a few minutes she turned to me and said: "Wire them to take your name off!"

I did not wire. I continued to regret the fact that Scott preferred his method of operating to the alternative I have suggested.

The following New Year's Eve I went to a party given by the Gerards. Many film and theatrical people were there, among them Scott. An opulent aura radiated from his shining face and glossy dinner jacket. He said: "What the hell did you make all that trouble for?" I could have hit him; he was slower and heavier than in the days of 11 Gay Street.

I walked away. He returned to Hollywood, I to my job at the Associated Press. My salary was $60 a week.

3

Every writer is a born optimist. Still, it was enough to get one down as the years passed and none appeared to say, in effect, "Come—leave your bondage, write for a panting world which will give you whatever your heart wants." I wanted but little, here below.

Bill McCleery had had the same idea—his was to write a play—and vexed me by leaving AP before I could. He had not only made more money than I had, he was married to an heiress from Greer, S.C., the young woman I had met when he and I were working late. Her name was Martha Davenport. They lived on Beekman Place.

With Bill gone, I was "borrowed for a few weeks" by Al Resch, to help AP Wirephoto with literate cutlines. I worked for him for more than a year. In April of 1939 I decided to leave, come what may. I gave Resch four weeks' notice. He smiled like an embarrassed bear, swung around to his typewriter, typed out the resignation, and handed it to me to sign. He was delighted. So was I. Four weeks later, to the day, I left the Associated Press, which was now in Rockefeller Center. The new AP building was adorned by a relief sculpture by Isamu Noguchi, the commission for which he had won in competition. I cannot say I thought much of it.

I had begun my life of Marlowe in 1929, after a brief correspondence with Dr. Leslie Hotson; now, ten years later, the time had come to bring it to a conclusion. I had no money—I had not, of course, saved any; but I had infinite riches in a little room.

I knew Marlowe's work by heart and believed I could distinguish autobiographical passages, as well as the hands of others in his plays. I knew the work of the lesser Elizabethans, an essential sometimes overlooked by writers on the greater. And I knew the London they had inhabited. I had a contemporary map that showed every street and lane, with the buildings on them, the suburbs and Southwark where the first theaters were built, the windmills in Finsbury Fields and the fields stretching to country. I could follow Marlowe and his friends everywhere—to the book shops around St. Paul's, to the Bishop of Winchester's brothels, and to Hog Lane where a three-way duel took place which I believe Shakespeare viewed and used in *Romeo and Juliet*.

The little room was at 9 Patchin Place. When you stood in the doorway you could see the whole of it—white walls, yellow watercolors, brown furniture.

I had been at work on my book about a week when a young lawyer I knew intimated he had a client who might help me. The client wished to know how long it would take to finish the Marlowe, and how much a month I would need. I was past being surprised. I said I was sure I could finish it in six months, and that living alone as I was doing, I could live on a hundred dollars a month (I took into account the fact that I was invited out a great deal). He thought that it might be arranged, but if it was I was not to try to learn the identity of my benefactor.

The lawyer's name was Lewis M. Isaacs. His mother, Edith Isaacs, had been the editor of *Theatre Arts Monthly,* in which all but one of my blank verse poems had appeared. His father had been a patron of Edwin Arlington Robinson. I guessed it was Mrs. Isaacs.

I was still exulting over this piece of good fortune when I received a telegram from the rector of Black Mountain College in North Carolina inviting me to read my poems and give a talk on Marlowe. The telegram was signed by John

Andrew Rice; the true begetter, however, was McCleery, who had preceded me as playwright in residence.

Much has been written about this unorthodox school, with its brilliant faculty and students. Unorthodox is as unorthodox does; Dr. Rice had fallen in love with one of his students, and was living openly with her, to the chagrin and dismay of some faculty members, who shunned his table in the commons, and were barely polite to me because I was his guest. This, to be sure, was not nice; but even at this school the pettiness, meanness, and fatuity to be found in all institutions of learning were present in sufficient measure. At Rice's table there was nothing but laughter, for he was not only a wit himself but the cause of wit in others. Dr. Rice, a Southerner, told country stories with grace and skill. I will repeat one.

A farmer went into town to see his doctor.

"Ezekiel," said the doctor, "what can I do for you?"

"Doctor," said Ezekiel, "I want to get rid of my wife."

"Now look here," said the doctor, "I'm in the business of healing people. You won't get any help from me for something like that."

"Doctor," said Ezekiel, "I can't stand it another minute. You have to help me."

"Very well," said the doctor. "Tell you what to do. Go home, and make love to your wife. Make love to her morning, noon, and night. In three weeks she'll be dead."

About two weeks later, the doctor, driving in his buggy, saw Ezekiel in a rocker on the porch of his house. He was thin, pale, gaunt, almost a skeleton.

"Whoa," said the doctor, stopping his horse. "Is that you, Ezekiel? How are you doin'?"

"Fine, doctor, fine," said Ezekiel in a whisper. Just then, from a hill, above the house, came the voice of a woman. She was singing gaily.

"Who is that singin'?" asked the doctor.

"My wife," said Ezekiel. "Always up there, a-plowin' and a-singin'—damn fool, don't know she'll be dead in a week's time."

The following epigram which occurs in his autobiography, *I Came out of the Nineteenth Century,* may be thought apropos of his story: "Southerners are never so happy as when they are making a last stand."

I was at Black Mountain College ten days. I gave my reading, and another night I gave my talk. After the talk the students of the writing seminar came to me in a body and asked if I would give a Cummings reading. I was delighted. They brought me a copy of the 1938 *Collected Poems,* which was designed by Robert Josephy, afterwards Mrs. McCleery's second husband.

I prefaced the Cummings reading with the remark that he was not difficult, and when read aloud his basic line was as simple as a line of Keats or Shelley. There was a gasp from the faculty area. I also said that what distinguishes one poet from another is the way he breathes, the structure of his line being a reflection of his intensity.

In this conection, it may be interesting to compare my remarks with an excerpt from a famous essay: "And the line comes (I swear it) from the breath, from the breathing of the man who writes, at the moment that he writes" (Charles Olson, *Prospective Verse,* 1950). I do not know why it was necessary for Mr. Olson to swear to this, since I had already affirmed it.

Black Mountain College was not far from Asheville. I saw my wife and child.

4

The life of a writer is solitary, but made bearable by private satisfactions which cannot be communicated. There are also some public ones. I did not mind being alone all day knowing that the nights would find me plunged into company—at the Carmers, the Fillmans, and Christmans, all of whom were apt to let the cocktail hour flow into the dinner hour as though planned that way. Perhaps it was, for it happened over and over. I am grateful to all of them.

Elizabeth Fillman was another South Carolina beauty, from Greer, in fact. Her husband, Jesse, is a tax lawyer whose law classmate, Walter Gellhorn, married one of her sisters. The Fillmans were committed to liberal causes, and they often had as guests leaders in the various civil rights movements, long before this became fashionable. In the forties and fifties it took a certain kind of courage, which was different from marching by the thousands to confrontations. They lived at no. 8 Perry, and now live in Boston. He is the unnamed lawyer in Edmund Wilson's book about his war with the Internal Revenue Service. John Andrew Rice was her cousin.

The Christmans were at 50 West 9th Street, the same building where the Goushas lived when I first knew them. Henry Christman was a former Albany newspaperman. He is also the author of a book entitled *Tin Horns and Calico,* to which Carl Carmer wrote an introduction. The book's subtitle is *An Episode in the Emergence of American Democracy,* and tells about the revolt of upstate farmers against serfdom in the mid-nineteenth century.

At Cornell, Zoë Fales Christman was a member of the Dramatic Club with Franchot Tone, Dan Duryea, and the playwright Sidney Kingsley. But it was not "stage presence" that brought her, throughout her life, the homage of women as well as men. She had beauty, dignity, and grace; she was also self-reliant and capable. Like her husband, she had worked on Albany newspapers, and then for the Division of Employment of the New York State Department of Labor. During World War II she was assigned to the War Manpower Commission, and after her retirement took on special assignments for the U. S. Department of Labor, the National

Council on Aging, and the Manpower Educational Institute. A formidable list—a remarkable woman.

It was at the Christmans that I met Granville Hicks. He was still shaken from the ordeal he had passed through, following his resignation from the Communist Party after the Hitler-Stalin pact of 1939. I also met Raymond Holden, the friend of Robert Frost, and later, Frost himself. I have no reason for mentioning Frost, except that it provides me with an opportunity to comment on his biography: a man's faults are not necessarily greater because he happens to be a great poet.

There was another assemblage of poets at the Christman apartment. The occasion was a party for me. Cummings came, bringing a bouquet of tulips. Padraic Colum came, and went to speak to Cummings, who was standing by the fireplace. Mark Van Doren came, and joined Colum and Cummings, and then Ridgely Torrence came, and joined them. The poets knew who the great one was at that gathering. Cummings, somewhat overwhelmed, basked, and I basked back at him.

It was at the Fillman country house, in Newtown, Connecticut, that I wrote a book about John Muir for younger readers. Knowing that Muir was one of the naturalists—John Burroughs was another—who had gone on the Alaska expedition organized by E. H. Harriman in 1889, I wrote to Governor Averell Harriman to ask him for his recollections, if any, for he too had been on board his father's ship. Governor Harriman wrote back, from Albany:

"The most exciting thing on the whole trip, for a seven-year-old boy, happened on the Bering Sea. We were awakened in the middle of the night—but of course it was light. The ship had struck an uncharted reef. We put on our life preservers but, much to my disappointment, did not have to take to the boats. They pulled the ship off the reef, and we went back to Kodiak, where the ship was repaired and a new propeller obtained.

"We did make one landing in Siberia and saw some

Eskimos. Later, when I was in Russia, I had the rare experience of telling Stalin that I had once made an entry into Russia without a passport. He seemed to think it very extraordinary that I could have gotten into Russia without the proper documents, even in the Czar's time. I explained the occasion to him. He said 'it couldn't be done now.' "

Averell Harriman was our ambassador to Soviet Russia when this conversation took place. Mrs. Fillman worked for him during his campaign for governor.

5

The money offered me by Lewis Isaacs had not been a gift, but a loan. I gave him my claim on the IRT as security. For six months on the first of the month I received a check from him for a hundred dollars. The money was barely enough, the time I had set myself was not enough. It is a curious fact that no sooner had I gone through the final check than the city paid the money owed me by the IRT. Mr. Isaacs joined Mr. Sacher in collecting it; Mr. Sacher took $700, and Mr. Isaacs $600. I was left with $450, and accumulated bills. Years later I learned that my anonymous benefactor was the first Mrs. McCleery.

My fine frenzy was over. I had to get another job. The question was, where?

A former AP man, Richard D. Hippelheuser, was working for *Fortune*. Towering as high as his name was wide, Hippelheuser had won fame for a scoop which, though not made public until after the event, is now, at the least, a footnote in the history books. In November, 1936, at Roosevelt headquarters, on the eve of the presidential election, he asked James A. Farley how Landon would do. Farley asked him for a piece of paper, wrote on it, and told Hippelheuser to place it in a sealed envelope; on it were the words "eight electoral votes," which were what Landon received—hence the quip, "As Maine goes so goes Vermont." With Hippelheuser's encouragement I went to see Russell W. Davenport, managing editor of *Fortune*.

Mr. Davenport wore a hearing aid; I think it made him shy. His body was contorted in his chair, as though withdrawing from the world. Yet he was strangely real, as some people are not, and it did not surprise me when I learned, later, that he had won the Croix de Guerre in France when he was a private with the A.E.F. He offered me a job with the words, "I like to hire poets." (He wrote poetry himself, as it turned out.) But, he quickly added, the job would not be open for two months. I told him I had to have a job immediately. In that case, he said, he would get me a temporary job on *Time*. That is what he did. I never saw him again. When I finally went to work for *Fortune,* he had become the coordinator of the pre-convention campaign to nominate Wendell Willkie for the presidency.

Manfred Gottfried was the executive editor of *Time*. He took me to lunch, and no doubt sized me up. I found him possessed of a quick, sharp mind, not without literary graces.

The *Time, Life,* and *Fortune* building was then in Rockefeller Center. Everyone had his cubicle, and I had mine. How well-dressed everyone was, how well-mannered! How superior, too. The friends I made at *Time* will forgive me a single observation.

Many of those who worked there had, or had had, literary ambitions. For most of them the *Time* style represented something better than anything that could have been achieved or evolved by personal striving. They strove no more. They took that style and out-Heroded Herod, who was Mr. Luce.

I did not find much humor there. The younger men tended to look and act like young fogies.

My first assignment was the world premiere of a Bach fugue, which had recently been discovered. It had been commissioned by Frederick the Great. After the concert I wrote a straight news story. T. S. Matthews, the managing editor, left the story alone, but inserted a phrase: "Said the King of Flutes to the King of Fugues." Mr. Matthews was the best-dressed man I have ever seen, and he had the face—lean and steep—and the figure—long and tapered—to go with it. I found him a great gentleman; recently I read his edition of Lamb's letters, and was delighted to find him a scholar.

After several assorted jobs of rewriting I was given a department, "People in the News." It was not always easy to muster a page of them.

One day a stranger appeared. He was a haunter of newspaper offices, and as soon as he began to speak I recalled some of his feats. He had sold an icebox to an Eskimo, searched for a needle in a haystack, and organized a charge up Bunker Hill to ascertain how close the chargers would come before he saw the whites of their eyes. His new bid for free publicity struck me as funny.

Was California or Florida sunshine more salubrious? He placed on my desk a glossy photograph. In it, he was lying on a beach with half his chest bare. The other half was covered by a sun suit of his own design. It was like half of an oversized brassiere, quite flat, with a scalloped edge. He planned to wear it for an hour in Florida, take it off, hop into a plane, fly to California, don the mate over the Florida sun-tan and expose the other half of his chest. His name was Jim Moran; I saw him recently on the David Frost show.

There was a custom at *Time* which went back to its beginnings. Mr. Luce came around to a different department each week "to keep his hand in." That was the week he came around to see what I had lined up for "People in the News." I began with the sun suit and the copy for it. He looked at the picture of Moran, read the copy, and without change of expression asked: "What else do you have?" I showed him. Exit Moran.

Time had an office boy who, fittingly enough, was the superior of all the office boys I had hitherto known. It was the period when the man-about-the-office wore sports jackets and unmatched trousers. His jacket, from Brooks Brothers or Abercrombie & Fitch, was a many-splendored thing, and probably cost more than any of my suits, even those with two pairs of trousers. A few weeks after Mr. Luce's visit I noticed a new "incoming" box on my desk. It was piled high with newspaper clippings. I phoned the office boy.

"What is that?" I asked him when he deigned to enter my cubicle.

"Don't you know?" he asked.

"No," I answered, almost abashed.

"Them that write 'People in the News' writes 'Animals in the News,'" he said.

I must have looked horrified.

"Two or three times a year," he added, to soften the blow.

"I see."

Looking wise, he left me to my meditations.

Almost without knowing it I reached for the top clipping. It was a news item from the Portland *Oregonian*. I was struck at once by the dateline: "Milwaukie, Oregon." It was not the spelling I had learned at school. I began to read. My recollection of the story follows.

> Deputy Sheriff So-and-so reported today that Mr. So-and-so, the wealthy poultryman of So-and-so, who had been having trouble with chicken thieves, heard a noise in the night and leaped from his bed. As it was full summer he was sleeping in the raw. On a chair beside the bed were his pajamas. Hastily putting them on, he got the trousers on "hind-side to," that is, with the fly in the back. Snatching up a shotgun he left the bedroom, followed by his dog, who had been sleeping under the bed.

Mr. So-and-so crossed the yard to his chicken houses and flung open one of the doors, his finger on the trigger of the shotgun. As he peered in a stooping posture into the dark depths of the chicken house, his dog's cold, wet nose went through the slot of his pajamas, the shotgun went off, and forty chickens were killed.

I began to laugh, and became hysterical. I closed my cubicle door. I took off my jacket, which was far from splendid, and hung it on the back of my chair. I loosened my tie. Nothing helped. Weak and contorted I made my way to the bathroom and washed my face with cold water. I re-tied my tie. I returned to my cubicle.

"Beauty without someone by is like a stab in the back," said Oscar Wilde. Humor without someone to share it is the road to madness. I calmed myself. I put on my jacket. I walked down the long corridor to Mr. Gottfried's office, the clipping in my hand.

Mr. Gottfried's door was always open. He was sitting behind an immense desk with a single piece of copy awash in a shallow of light from a low-hanging lamp; his eyes were fixed on it under a green eyeshade. Without looking up he said: "Come in." I slid the clipping toward him.

All sorts of notions were in my head. He would read it and explode hysterically. He would call someone else in— not, to be sure, Mr. Luce, but someone in the hierarchy. "Read this!" he would exclaim, and wait for the laughter of his colleague as I was now waiting for his.

Mr. Gottfried reached for the clipping and pulled it toward him. He read it through. He shoved it back toward the corner of the desk where I was standing and without looking up uttered one word: "Animals."

I took the clipping and left his office. I walked back crestfallen. The corridor seemed longer and narrower. I vowed I would never again offer to share anything with any- one. I would be a loner, a hermit, a hater of mankind. I would keep all pleasures, all delights, to myself.

I was now back in my cubicle, sitting in my chair, my

head down, the clipping on my desk. My thoughts were bitter. Again, without knowing I was doing so, I took up the clipping. I began to read it. I read it through. I frightened myself by the roar of laughter which leaped from my throat. I rushed to the door and shut it. I removed my jacket, my tie, and laughed until I hurt.

Many years later, at a party given by Frances Mc-Clernan, I told the story of the Oregon poultryman and his dog. A man I had not met before said: "I remember that story." As I never got around to writing an animal column, I could not help asking where he had seen it. "I am the publisher of the Portland *Oregonian*," he replied. His name was Peter Gentenbein.

6

Louis Kronenberger was the drama critic of *Time*. In the dead middle of the theatrical season of 1940 he went on his honeymoon. A musical was produced, and I was given the job of covering it. It was called *Two For the Show,* and I began my review with the phrase, "Tap-happy and tuneful." It was used in advertisements. I saw myself as a drama critic. Perhaps Mr. Kronenberger wouldn't have a job when he got back. I looked forward to my next assignment. It was *My Dear Children,* with John Barrymore. It was not much of a play. I thought it pathetic to see Barrymore playing a parody of himself and hamming through a soliloquy from *Hamlet*.

No one left when the curtain came down on the third act. The curtain rose, and there was Barrymore, alone on the stage. A hush fell over the theater.

At that moment a man raced down the right-hand aisle from the rear of the theater, leaped over the orchestra pit onto the stage, and grasped Barrymore around the neck. He had on a dirty sweatshirt and his face looked as though it had been pressed into a flour barrel. Photographers' bulbs popped from all parts of the theater; there was a *Life* photographer in the seat next to mine, and he popped away, too. A mass nightmare was being shared. The theater was very still. The bizarre figure on the stage, still panting from his exertions, began to speak.

"Mr. Barrymore," he croaked and wheezed. "I've always wanted to be on the same stage with you, I've always wanted to play *Hamlet* with you."

Barrymore twisted his head inside the armlock that held him. Facing the man, he said: "My dear fellow, you must have had a hard winter."

Still hooked by that grubby arm Barrymore took a sideways step toward the rear of the stage, the man perforce following. The curtain descended with a rush. A gasp of relief came from the audience.

Once more the curtain went up, once more Barrymore stood alone in the center of the stage.

"You will be happy to learn, I am sure," he said calmly, "that the heaviest electrician in New York is now sitting on my late friend."

The pent-up emotions of the audience broke forth in applause, stamping of feet and whistling. Still no one moved. The moment all had been waiting for was at hand—Barrymore's curtain speech.

"It has been eighteen years since I last appeared on a New York stage," he began. "As you know, I have been in Hollywood, and I have appeared in theaters elsewhere." A trace of emotion began to be evident. "But I want to tell you one thing—nothing counts except appearing here, on Broadway, before a New York audience."

The curtain descended for the final time. The audience

began to leave. I went to bed that night pillowed on phrases of my projected review.

The next morning I arrived for work at a quarter to eleven. The office boy was waiting for me. A thick thumb jerked backward from an elegant sleeve.

"You're wanted in there," he said, indicating the managing editor's office.

I wondered if the morning headlines had anything to do with it. Pictures of the man running down the aisle and leaping on the stage were on every front page. The *Journal-American* had his byline story. Other things, too, had happened—after the show.

Present in Mr. Matthews' office were Mr. Gottfried, John McManus, who had succeeded Whittaker Chambers as the movie critic, several senior editors and researchers. Mr. Matthews said: "In view of what happened last night, we think a running story of events would be more appropriate than a review." I agreed. "It may prove a lot to handle," he went on, "and McManus has offered to help."

The story appeared in the next issue. Carefully spliced together by McManus and myself it was, following the debut of the flour-faced man, as follows.

After his curtain speech, Barrymore went to his dressing room. His estranged wife, Elaine Barry, an actress, appeared backstage. Diana Barrymore was there. She placed herself against the door of the dressing room and screamed: "You can't see my father!" Barrymore opened the door, gave his daughter a shove that ended in a pratfall, and yanked Miss Barry in. He then explained that, much as he wanted to, he could not leave with her—he had promised to attend the traditional first-night supper with the cast. He proposed, instead, a rendezvous afterwards, and implored her not to show herself at the supper party, which was to be in a nightclub.

Miss Barry showed up wearing a low-cut gown. As she started toward Barrymore's table, the band began to play. He gallantly met her, they danced, and then left, pursued by reporters. The chase ended at the Hotel Novarro. Several reporters hung around on the floor of their suite until Barrymore popped his tousled head out of the door and uttered the words: "Consummatum est."

7

Mr. Kronenberger returned from his honeymoon. I continued to write "People in the News" and was glad when the call came to go upstairs to *Fortune*. Richardson Wood was the editor, and I wrote two stories for him. One, about pulp, took me to Canada. The Nazis had interdicted the Kattegat and the Skaggerat, and there was a growing shortage of pulp for paper.

The other story was about La Guardia Field, which was nearing completion. I went to City Hall to interview Mayor La Guardia. When I asked him how much the city had put into the project he looked around wildly and exclaimed in his high, piping, squeaky voice: "Don't ask me that! All the cockroaches, all the cut-throats, all the sons-of-bitches, will jump on me!"

I told him I had been to the airlines involved and that I could arrive at a conclusion without his answer. It would be better if it came from him—it would at least be accurate. He saw my point. I got the answer. It was a pretty penny.

The writers on *Fortune*, who wrote very well indeed, differed from those on newspapers and the wire services, even from those on *Time*, in that they were more like big businessmen than writers. I found myself out of my depth; Mr. Wood

was the second to observe this. He fired me so politely that if
he had been a woman and the situation somewhat different,
these lines of Shenstone would have fitted the occasion:

> So sweetly she bade me adieu,
> I thought that she bade me return.

I cannot take my leave of *Time* and *Fortune* without another observation about our small world. Mr. Matthews, who
had been married before, married Walter Gellhorn's sister;
she, too, had been married before, to Ernest Hemingway. His
son, Paul Matthews, a painter, married a cousin of Willard
Trask.

In 1952, when *Time* launched a feature similar to the
New Yorker profile, but consisting of only one page, I did
the one on Cummings. Payment for the page was a thousand
dollars, just short of a dollar a word, and the easiest money
I ever earned. The piece in *Time* is *The Magic-Maker* in
little, as readers of both can ascertain. Cummings was apprehensive about it, and as it turned out, correctly. I showed him
proofs, which he approved; then a young fogy cut out one or
two of my lines to make room for a disparaging remark about
the poet's painting. I had to live with it.

It was all the more embarrassing because I had become
a painter myself.

Chapter Fifteen

1

"Two and a half years ago, Charles Norman, a newpaperman who never had painted before, decided to try his hand at watercolors. So he started painting pictures of objects and scenes in his Greenwich Village apartment. The first art dealer to see his work took him on for a one-man show. Today, the sign at the Julien Levy Gallery, one of the nation's important galleries, reads: 'Watercolors by Charles Norman.'"

"Today" was January 9, 1940. The writer was Mary Elizabeth Plummer of the Associated Press. Her story continues: "Levy, the dealer who handles Dali and Eugene Berman, said that when he saw the pictures he thought they were extraordinary for the shortness of time Norman had been painting. 'A young man like Norman who sits down to paint what he wants to,' he said, 'is more likely in his approach and method to have the fundamental chemicals of an American painting than a man who has been spoiled by too much education.'"

I should like to relate the events that led up to the show which Miss Plummer (now Mrs. Davidson Taylor) covered.

I began to paint in 1937, perhaps in the spring of that year, since I recall bright, tingling days on my trips to and from the art shop on Greenwich Avenue where I purchased my supplies. The whites and yellows of that year are still white and yellow; I ascribe it to my lucky choice of Winsor & Newton watercolors. They came in tubes, and I used them like oils.

The first pictures I painted were not much to look at. There were too many pencil lines showing; the very first one, which I gave to Marion and Estlin Cummings, was hardly more than a drawing with some color brushed in. But soon I was intoxicated by my new *métier* and began to paint instead of draw, and my papers and cardboards grew larger and brighter. By the summer of 1939 I had fourteen watercolors—not counting some I had given away—all from a palette consisting of white, lemon yellow, viridian, rose madder, and burnt umber. De Hirsh Margules was the first painter to tell me white was not a color; nevertheless, I continued to use it as though it were.

My technique was simple. I left out everything except the objects to be painted, but painted the space around them as carefully as the objects themselves. Just as white was a color, so space was part of my design; yellow, however, was more predominant in my backgrounds than white. Once I used rose madder both for the object—in this case flowers—and the space behind and around it: rose on rose.

I found great satisfaction in ordinary cardboard of varying thicknesses. Each took paint in an individual way. The thin ones sucked the paint in and permitted me to build unusual surfaces. I wrote in the catalogue of the Levy show: "On one occasion, when pity for my old cardboards brought me a present of what I presume was wonderful Dutch paper,

I learned, at one stroke, so to speak, why most watercolors look alike; to paraphrase Buffon, in the art of watercolor, *le style, c'est le papier."*

No useful purpose will be served by modesty. I knew my watercolors were good. Good or not, I liked them. They hung in narrow raw wood frames on the white walls of my small living room. I left them with regret in the morning, and saw them again in the evening with admiring eyes. So did the painters who came to call. The thought struck me: I would have a show. But where?

Julien Levy occupied a position in the art world somewhat analogous to that of Alfred A. Knopf in publishing. His gallery at 15 East 57th Street was internationally famous, not only because of the artists he handled, but because he himself was knowledgeable, and spoke and wrote on contemporary art with authority. He was a dark, slender, and vibrantly handsome man who had played a bit part in a movie made by his friend, Jean Cocteau.

The gallery was posh, with a surrealist aura. In addition to painting by Dali, Berman, and Tchelitchew, there were magic boxes on the walls, made of mirrors and velvet, in which dwelt tiniest fairylands. Beautiful women were also to be seen there, fluttering the draperies: Levy's wife at the time, Goiela, daughter of the poet Mina Loy, and Muriel Streeter, a young painter and his future wife.

I wrote to Mr. Levy. I told him that I was a writer who had taken up painting; that all the painters I knew, whether abstract, representational or surrealist, liked my work; that I liked it even more than they did, and that in deciding on a gallery in which to show it I had concluded only the best one would do, and—carried away—quoted Dr. Johnson. Like him, I said, I "could not forbear to wish that I might boast myself *le vainqueur du vainqueur de la terre"* (letter to the Earl of Chesterfield).

Mr. Levy responded. He came to 9 Patchin Place. It was a bright Sunday afternoon. A bottle of Scotch was in plain view. I opened the door. He did not enter. Standing on the threshold, taking in all the walls with flashing eyes, he exclaimed:

"What would you like me to do for you? I will do anything for you. I will give you a one-man show."

I said: "Come in—have a drink."

I do not now recollect that he took me up on the drink. It was still early in the day. I recall, however, the sobering effect his final words had on me.

"You must paint between now and the show," he said. "You must paint a great deal."

I promised. He left. I rushed either to the bottle or the phone; but perhaps I merely sank back in my upholstered chair.

2

I was unable to keep my promise. It was as if his words had cast a spell over me—or, at least, over my painting hand. It was not his intention. Days, and then weeks passed. In desperation, I went to Connecticut—there, surely, I thought, I would be able to start afresh, I would even do landscapes.

Croswell Bowen had kindly offered to let me use his cottage. Nothing really came of it, except a love of nature which has never left me. Today, more than a quarter century later, I can still see in my mind the sumac turning red in Hidden Hollow—that red which has no counterpart for me—and breathe again, in memory, the sharp caesuras of the air. I found that I could not paint still lifes there, either, and in addition that I was not ready for outdoor painting. Fall winds buffeted my easel, and scattered my cardboards. I managed, however, in terror of Mr. Levy, to finish a tiny land-scape—indoors—and brought it back. It is called *Trees, Sherman, Conn.* in the catalogue, and now hangs in the Fillman home in Boston.

Mrs. Addie Turner's house was up the road a piece, and I used to see it on my walks. Malcolm Cowley and Peter Blume, who lived in Gaylordsville, drove over to see me, and a neighbor drove me to William Slater Brown's house in Patterson, where I spent the night. Looking in on him before breakfast to see if he was up, I saw his dog, a terrier, curled around his head, asleep. It opened one vexed eye, and was instantly transformed into a tam-o'-shanter with an oddly placed hatpin. Then they both rose, the dog first, and we had breakfast together.

The show consisted of fifteen pictures. Mr. Levy raised a sophisticated eyebrow when I told him those were all I could muster, and went right ahead with his plans. (There was, in fact, a sixteenth, which I did not show him, and still possess —a self-portrait, the only portrait I have ever painted.)

Mr. Levy thought that, as I was a writer, I ought to write something for the catalogue. Here are some additional paragraphs:

"I paint furniture and pitchers and common household objects because I see beauty in them, as others see beauty in sky and trees; everything in a room has form and being—even a spiritual appendage, a shadow. Shadows are the spirits of objects."

Of my use of white, I wrote: "Some mystery beyond the comprehension of a beginner seems to be attached to this color, for painters who have gone to school apparently have been taught to be wary of it. They have generously passed this proscription on to me, but without elucidation. What can it all mean?"

And in conclusion: "I hope eventually to add variety to my work by painting outdoor scenes, but thus far such efforts have led me only to this rueful reflection, which I pass on: if trees grew in pots, I would be a landscape painter."

The opening was a gala event, like a first night. The gallery was thronged. There were flowers and telegrams, handshakes and drinks. How beautiful the women were, and in particular one, who came from afar. She had on a mink coat and a mink hat, and was more admired than painter or paintings. I did not mind. Many of the men present were distinguished; writers or painters themselves, they showed only goodwill.

Mr. Levy beamed. Someone asked him if I were not just another primitive. His retort was memorable, and I give it here: "On the contrary, a more sophisticated painter would be hard to find." I agreed completely, but said nothing, which best becomes an eavesdropper.

I returned to the gallery only once during the course of the exhibition. I tried hard to look like a connoisseur on his rounds; nevertheless, a woman approached me and asked: "Aren't you the painter?" I admitted it, then asked her: "How did you know?" She said: "You look like your pictures."

The exhibition closed on January 22. Mr. Levy sold one painting, no. 1 in the catalogue, entitled *Flowers, Red Pitcher*. I never learned who purchased it, and have not seen it again. But no sooner was the show over than several clients appeared at my "studio." They all had had the same idea, and one of them expressed it this way: "I wanted you to have all the purchase money." The truth, so far as I was concerned, was otherwise; I would have preferred to have Mr. Levy do the selling.

He came to see me in 1941, after I had turned to oils. He appeared quite impressed, and told me he would give me a second show. But it was not to be; the army got him, and the gallery shut down. After the war he retired to Connecticut, where he lives the life of a country gentleman with another wife.

It is curious to reflect that oils have given me more trouble than watercolors (painters usually find it the other way around). I once had a picture measuring three feet by four feet which had to be destroyed because I tried to improve a corner of it. From the corner I was led upward, then inward, until the time came when I saw that it could not be saved no matter what I did.

I also destroyed a smaller oil in the same way, having been unable to leave it alone. One night, when I had a guest for dinner, I sat facing this picture. It was not where I usually sat. The more I looked at it, the more I believed I could improve it. The next day I took it down, removed it from its frame, and fell to. One stroke led to another, and before I knew it I was inches away from the spot I was going to improve, and working to save the spot I had reached. It turned out to be impossible. I have often thought of this picture with regret. There was an effect of light in it which I had striven hard to capture. I have not recaptured it.

From time to time, the lure of another one-man show has been held out to me. Over the years I have painted by fits and starts—an apt phrase. I have filled a shelf with my books, and have had little time left over for anything else. Perhaps I will resume painting when this book is out of the way. It is a recurrent reverie. Sometimes, at night, it is still with me, and I lie awake embellishing it. I am in a cottage in the country. Behind the cottage is a barn which has been converted to a studio. At one end of the studio is a table by a window (old Norse: *vindauga*, an eye on the wind or air), a place for writing poems. Painting or writing, and possibly doing neither, I would mark the seasons instead of measuring the passing years.

3

Many painters have expressed their views about art, particularly their own (see *their* catalogues). Some of their sentences are weighty, like slugs of linotype. I have difficulty understanding them. I see no reason why I should not express my own views. All of them may be considered as exegesis on a sentence by Yeats: "A work of art can have but one subject."

What is a work of art?

It is something that gives the beholder (or reader or listener) a new experience, one which he could not have had *without the work of the artist.*

A painting is an arrangement of colors which, in turn, create line and movement.

The subject of a painting is never what it appears to be, but is almost always color, line, and movement.

Color is important; but more important are line and movement.

There is no such thing as modern art.

There is no such thing as ancient art.

There is only art—that is, work which is entirely itself, belonging unquestionably to its own time, but which is seen to have an affinity with works which have preceded it, and will prove to have an affinity with works of the future. Its common denominator is beauty whose metaphor is timelessness.

All artists belong to the same generation.

There is no folk art.

There are only artists.

Critics are extraordinarily preoccupied with ideas which can be brought to bear upon a given work. They have little boxes, or little drawers—or little boxes in little drawers—which they open without perceptible effort, although some straining may be evident in the result. Were it really a work of art, and if they recognized it as such, all their ideas would have to be discarded, for nothing could be brought to it, and only something taken away which the artist has generously provided.

The first artist who saved or destroyed his work was also the first critic, the indispensable one.

When people say they know what they like, what they really mean is: they know what they don't like.

What I have said may apply to literature: stories for children, but sentences for men.

I agree with Cummings, who held that all you can say about a work of art is "thank you"—to the artist.

Some artists, to be sure, are a little rough and it might be difficult to bring it off. One night, as I was sitting with Barbara Perkins at the old Cedar Tavern, I became aware of a man staring at me. He finally made it to our table, and standing there, staring, said: "You look like a painter," quickly adding with pleased discernment: "You must be a painter."

I said: "No, I'm a writer."

That set the tone of the ensuing conversation.

It was apparent that he wanted company and I asked him to join us. I told him my name and introduced Miss Perkins. His head fairly sank to the table, and looking down, as though what he was about to say was too much for him, us, and the world in general, said: "My name is Jackson Pollock."

"Have a drink," I said.

At this he raised his head and smiled. He had a nice smile. It did not last overlong. He had already had several drinks on his own, and after several with us he became aggressive.

"I'm the best goddamn painter in the world, did you know that?" he asked. I felt the same way I had when I was accused by Bodenheim's wife of not showing sufficient respect to "America's greatest poet." I did not think Pollock was the "best goddamn painter in the world" either. Perhaps I said so, or showed it somehow, for he offered to fight, and we might have, but Miss Perkins, with charm and skill, dissuaded us, and we had another drink instead.

Chapter Sixteen

1

Before Pearl Harbor, the population of the United States was divided between those who wanted to be in the war on the side of Britain, those who foresaw we would be in it, those who did not believe we would be, and those who were against the prospect. It was the period of the America Firsters; it was also a period of affection and admiration for the British people, standing alone against Hitler as their forebears had stood against Napoleon:

> Another year!—Another deadly blow!
> Another mighty Empire overthrown!
> And We are left, or shall be left, alone;
> The last that dare to struggle with the Foe,

as Wordsworth wrote.

A great deal of time was spent listening to the radio and looking at maps as the Nazi tanks streaked through France

to the Channel ports. One of my friends had a map with little
flags stuck in it; as the flags moved inexorably to the coast the
eye left the land and fixed itself on the embattled island:

> Night takes day in her arms,
> But the valiant swan is awake;
> Her breast is to the shore
> Of the perilous lake.
>
> Fear ripples the deep,
> And terror throngs the air;
> The solitary swan
> Keeps her voyage there.

It was in this atmosphere of foreboding that I went to
work for Brewster Morgan, a producer at the Columbia
Broadcasting System, which was about to sponsor a show
called "Proudly We Hail," intended to speed up armaments
production by dramatizing the sweat and skills of workers in
defense plants. The subject was not always easy to dramatize,
but we tried; I worked nights as well as days, and devised a
desk motto: "Meet Morgan and Never Sleep." I wrote the
show for eleven weeks. John Daly was the announcer. Guy
della Chioppa was a handsome, cheerful, and inventive
young man when there was trouble.

The show was not supposed to "take sides." We could
not praise the British or attack the Germans. The script went
to the State Department by teletype several hours before
showtime.

We had a different star each week. Morgan told me that
we would either have to pay a thousand dollars each for their
appearances, or nothing; we paid nothing. All were eager to
help. The eighth week was coming up, and the star was to
be Gertrude Lawrence. Morgan came into my office.

"You know a lot of poems," he began. "Isn't there some
poem about England that doesn't mention England? I'd like
Miss Lawrence to speak one at the end of the show."

"Brewster," I said, "I know a lot of poems about England.
They all mention England."

He went away with a disappointed look, but returned to ask the question again. It was like an obsession. He had a vision of Gertrude Lawrence standing at the mike in the final moments of the broadcast, reading a poem about England in her beautifully modulated English voice. I agreed it would be effective; we were both Anglophiles.

One day that week I was at the British Library of Information in Rockefeller Center. On the wall was a broadside poem by T. S. Eliot; its title was *Defense of the Islands*. It was the perfect answer to Morgan's quest—except for one thing. It mentioned England; worse, there was a line about "British bone on the sea floor." Nevertheless, I told Morgan about it. He asked eagerly if we could get a copy. It came by messenger. Morgan read it and shook his head. But in half an hour he was back.

"Why can't we omit that line?" he asked.

I was indignant.

"What—edit Eliot?"

He went away, and came back. He seemed to be pleading with me. But I would have nothing to do with it. At last I said: "I won't take the line out. But you could cable Eliot."

His eyes lit up, he looked the very picture of gratitude, and snatched the broadside from my desk.

I do not know whether Morgan cabled Eliot. Perhaps he did. I do know that tacked on to my script was *Defense of the Islands*, with a line of dots where the offending line had been. That Friday night Gertrude Lawrence read the poem, and it seemed while she read that a hush had fallen not only over the studio but over the entire CBS building on Madison Avenue. Morgan was exultant.

Seven years passed. I had new friends. One of them was Mrs. Mary Bass, executive editor of the *Ladies Home Journal*, who gave splendid dinners in her Park Avenue apartment, one of the walls of which was adorned by a portrait of herself by Vertès, in which surrounding Cupids on the wing guarded her fashionably veiled and handsome head. Many distinguished men and women were always to be found there, be the season what it might. On a winter evening in 1948 there were fourteen at the table, among them Robert S. Kintner, the new vice-president of the American Broadcasting Company. I was in a good mood, and wished to contribute my mite to the lionizing he was getting. I brought up the subject of radio by saying: "Don't you think it was silly of CBS and NBC to have a self-imposed censorship before we got into the war?" ABC was a newcomer to broadcasting.

His reply startled me.

"You don't know what you're talking about," said Mr. Kintner, the man of the hour.

I said: "I don't know you, and don't know what right you have to speak to me that way."

He brushed that aside.

"Want to bet?" he asked.

"Why, yes," I said.

"A hundred dollars?"

"A hundred dollars."

"Want to make it five hundred?"

"When I'm that cocky I offer odds."

"Even money," he countered.

I considered. If I lost the bet, a hundred would be awkward, but five hundred would be catastrophic.

"Make it a hundred," I said.

Mrs. Clarence Day interposed.

"If even a single instance of censorship can be shown," she said, "that is the bet, gentlemen."

Mrs. Bass seconded Mrs. Day, Kintner and I agreed, and the conversation turned to other things.

It was a Saturday night. On Monday I called Guy della Chioppa, now a vice-president of CBS. He was delighted to hear from me and wanted me to come right up. I told him my problem and asked if the "Proudly We Hail" scripts were still in existence. They were in a warehouse. My heart beat faster. He remembered the show in which Gertrude Lawrence was the star; if I came up tomorrow he would have a copy for me.

I went to see him on Tuesday. He handed me the script. Across the top of the first page was the legend: "This is an exact copy of the original in the CBS files." Under his signature was his title. I turned to the last page; the dots were there. We exulted together.

I returned to my apartment and wrote a covering note to send Mr. Kintner with the script. On Thursday I received his reply; pinned to it was a check for one hundred dollars.

Mr. Eliot never included *Defense of the Islands* in any of his collections. As a matter of fact, he did not even have a copy of it until I sent him one in 1957. I used it in my biography of Ezra Pound, contrasting his contribution to the war effort with Yeats's "silence" poem in World War I, and both of them with Pound's broadcasts in World War II.

2

Between CBS and the army I worked on *PM,* a new afternoon tabloid with typographical innovations, no advertising, and of a liberal cast. It was financed by Marshall Field and edited by a former *Fortune* executive, Ralph Ingersoll. Mr. Ingersoll brought Louis Kronenberger and John McManus from *Time* and Margaret Bourke-White from *Life*; William McCleery, who became editor of its Sunday magazine, brought Mary Morris and, some time later, myself. Willy Ley wrote about the marvels of science, and married a girl on the staff who wrote about beauty and wellbeing. The man who had revised my "systematized a system," and one or two other colleagues from the AP, were on the copy desk. Among the staffers whom I now met for the first time was a tall, goodlooking young woman who lived in the Village. I used to walk home with her after work. Her name was Chandonette Norris.

The trial runs of *PM* were superb examples of a new species of journalism. Unfortunately, when the press runs began, it was found that all the brilliant writers from the magazines, who were used to days or weeks in which to polish a story, were incapable of getting out a daily newspaper. Gotten out it had to be, and the hacks did it. Such are my conclusions; dissents can be expected. *PM* alumni still meet annually.

I had occasion to discuss the paper with Mr. Ingersoll once. I called him up to present an idea, and he said: "You want to see the boss?" He could see me from where he sat, and when I said "Yes," he waved me into his office. First I told him I sometimes blushed to see *PM*'s headlines on the stands—they were neither news nor feature, merely emotional. Mr. Ingersoll bowed his head. Only afterwards did I learn that he had written most of them. I hurriedly explained my idea. I said that in a period of crisis, many people wanted to know the news at a glance. *PM*, with its tabloid-size page, was perfectly geared to give it to them, by running a page of bulletins—a bulletin being a paragraph with a dateline. All the important cities of the world would have their paragraph; if background material was needed, a line in parenthesis would tell what page had it.

For a long time *PM* published a page of bulletins. Inevitably, the single paragraph became two, then three.

The best of *PM* was the Sunday magazine section. The answer is simple: it had a good editor. When I was in the army, and somewhat idle, I took it upon myself to write Mr. Field. I urged him to make McCleery editor of the paper— under Ingersoll, of course. Mr. Field replied. He appreciated McCleery's qualities, but had complete confidence in the managing editor chosen by Mr. Ingersoll. I myself thought him not up to the mark; the public appears to have agreed.

I worked for *PM* twice—before I enlisted, and after the

war. In February, 1942, I went to interview Wendell L. Will-kie. It was McCleery's idea. What had Mr. Willkie been doing since his defeat in 1940?

Mr. Willkie was practicing law. I went to see him in his downtown office accompanied by a male photographer, Leo Lieb, a husky chap who not only carried his own equipment —he could have carried me. I had been talking with Mr. Willkie about three-quarters of an hour when his secretary came in and reminded him of an appointment. Mr. Willkie stared hard at me. He asked me if I would come to see him at his home the following Sunday; he would like to continue our talk.

This one, he told me when I arrived, would be "off the record." It took place in his apartment on upper Fifth Avenue and lasted about four hours. His wife never entered the room; I glimpsed her once peering at us or at me from a doorway, and left without meeting her. Her behavior was consistent with certain stories, but these were not any concern of mine. For the second time I was face to face with the man who had won the Republican nomination for President by acclamation.

Mr. Willkie was strikingly handsome. He spoke quietly; much of the time I had the feeling that he was unburdening himself. Many of his views were similar to my own—that is, they had a liberal cast or slant. When I asked him what a man with such views was doing as a corporation counsel and Republican standard-bearer, he replied that he was "a Newton D. Baker Democrat." It was an astonishing statement, but consistent with Mr. Willkie's character. Baker had supported President Wilson's war policies; Willkie, though opposed to President Roosevelt's New Deal, supported him on his foreign policies and broke with the Republican party as a result.

He had already told me that he would accept the Republican nomination again if it was offered, which was the way my story for *PM* ended. I sent it to him at his request, and he called me up. He said he would not think of changing a single word; he would merely like to add ten at the end, first turning my period into a semicolon. The words he added were: "but I would not trim my sails to get it."

I left his apartment at nightfall saying to myself that if he ran again, I would not only vote for him—I would work for him. The opportunity never came. I felt, as I had after my talk with Edna Millay, that I had been in the presence of true greatness.

3

Reflections on the war came from another source. Accompanied by Leo Lieb I went to interview Wayne Forrest, a hairdresser aged twenty-three with Antoine of Saks Fifth Avenue. Why Mr. Forrest? He had flown to Nassau to do the Duchess of Windsor's hair.

I interviewed him in the luxurious three-room suite he shared with Antoine at the Waldorf-Astoria. Antoine was there, too. Their apartment was full of flowers—massive branches of apple blossom, clusters of carnations, stalks of lilies, heather, snapdragon, and palms in pots. The air was heavy with the scent of flowers.

First I asked Mr. Forrest whether it did not seem extravagant in such times for anyone to have a hairdresser fly all the way to Nassau.

"I don't know how you'd feel about it," he said, "but there was no one in Nassau who could do even a housemaid's hair."

He told me he had been a "designer of coiffures," as he described himself, for about two and a half years. He was born in San Francisco. He wanted to be an actor, and had appeared in "a few movies." Then he got a job as an interior decorator. "I found it amusing rather than lucrative," he explained.

He began his career as a "designer of coiffures" at a School of Beauty Culture in Philadelphia. He met Antoine there. Mr. Forrest had brown eyes, dark, wavy hair with a three-pointed widow's peak—not that I noticed it, but he called my attention to it—and a cupid-bow mouth. Antoine offered him a course in his own school.

It was Lady Mendl, the former Elsie de Wolfe and the first woman to have her white hair blued, who recommended Mr. Forrest to the Duchess of Windsor.

"He has ze beautiful destiny," Antoine told me, "ze beautiful future—if he follows the right way. He must study. He must go to Greece, to Egypt, to the museums of Europe, to learn ze people and ze coiffure. When he comes back, he will be ze greatest hairdresser from world."

Mr. Forrest overheard, and exclaimed: "He has been no end of an inspiration to me."

I brought the conversation back to the Nassau visit. The Duchess's woman secretary met him at the airport and drove him to a hotel "to freshen up." His hotel bill and all other expenses were paid by the Duchess. He stayed eight weeks, "long enough," he explained, "to train someone to do the Duchess's hair." From the hotel he was driven to Government House, the official residence of the Windsors.

"The Duchess herself came out and found me sitting in the hall," Forrest said. "She introduced herself graciously. Then, while I was dressing her hair, the Duke came in. He said he was very glad to meet me. I cut his hair, after arranging the Duchess's."

The Duchess wore blue a lot.

"Even when she is wearing black there seems to be a blue sheen to it. The most startling thing about her is her coloring. Her eyes are Delft blue, while her skin seems so transparent that all the tones show through. Her hair is light brown with a cap of red. The red is real. I was there long enough to find out."

I asked Forrest if the assignment in Nassau had not been the outstanding event of his career.

"Not really," he said, "because I have been treating people of that sort both here and in Paris."

He had been working in Antoine's Paris salon when the war started.

"Mr. Antoine," he explained, "thought I was a bit on the young side to be around all those falling bombs, and he brought me back. It has always been my aim to study more, and I would like to go back. I have had a Hollywood offer—it's from 20th Century-Fox—to become a studio stylist. Right now I'm thinking it over."

Antoine interrupted.

"Don't forget you have to go to Egypt, Greece, Syria, to complete your education!"

This came from the other side of the room, where Mr. Lieb was photographing Antoine and his sculptures.

"Sculpture has ze great connection with hairdressing," Antoine explained, "if done artistically. I make them plas-tic. We do for each person ze individual coiffure. We are surgeons. We are not interested if woman is princess or shop girl if she have ze interesting head."

I asked Mr. Lieb to start shooting Mr. Forrest, who was sitting on a sofa, one leg under him, his right profile to the camera.

"I'm glad I'm sitting this way," he said. "I've got a filthy left profile."

"No such thing," I said.

I looked admiringly at him, and Antoine looked admiringly at Mr. Lieb, stooped over tripods and lights.

In conclusion, I asked Antoine a question similar to the one I had asked his protégé at the start of the interview: were not salons like his something like a luxury in a time like this? I liked his answer, and pass it on.

"Beauty," he said, "always bring you to be better. Beauty bring you to be good. Why Europe so craz-ee now? Because they neglect ze art, because they forget ze artistic life. A man doing beauty forgets about ze fighting."

Chapter Seventeen

1

Christmas, 1941, after Pearl Harbor.

Between the windows facing Patchin Place, at no. 4, there is a small but gaily adorned tree full of brightly colored birds; three or four of them have real tail-feathers. Beneath the tree are unopened presents, including a hamper or two from which beribboned necks of bottles protrude. On the bookcases and mantelpiece miniature elephants throng the dusk which is beginning to flood the room beyond the lightfalls of the lamps.

The furniture is old, familiar, and serviceable. One piece, now covered with a cloth, is merely a card table brought out for the occasion. There is also a kind of Queen Anne, straight-backed chair where my host will sit when he appears, while the rocker, which I habitually take, is now next to the tree. The cloth-covered table is to my right.

Everything being ready—tea in a copper pot, sugar, cream, buttered bread, jam, crackers and cheese, cookies, cups, spoons, napkins in serving array—my hostess takes an elephant bell from the mantelpiece, steps into the hall, rings it two or three times, and returns, leaving the door slightly ajar.

A minute or two later my host descends from the upstairs room where we first met, enters the apartment, and closes the door, grinning happily. He has on a soiled sweater and unpressed trousers—his painting costume. What with work done, tea, and a guest for tea, he is very cheerful—his grins are from ear to ear. Everyone is smiling, I with affection, his wife with affection and something else—a mock deprecatory look for a child who has been acting up. He catches that look, and makes faces like a child who has been acting up. Still, he is forty-six, and when I give him an opening the conversation quickly turns serious.

"You ask me what I think about this war. Well, let's see. The word 'war' reminds me of a poet named Hart Crane. He said there had always been three kinds of people—warriors, priests, merchants. Not just one kind; not just merchants. And I think he was right.

"As for this particular war, I think that if the totalitarians think they can destroy our culture, they're crazy. Do you know why? Because we have no culture.

"To be accurate, we have nothing even remotely approaching culture. Quite the contrary. What we have is a very expensive system for compelling things to mean whatever they aren't.

"Take anything. Labor, for example.

"What is labor?

"Labor is a miracle. When this miracle happens, a girl or an earth or a poet begins to sing. That's labor. That's not what labor means, that's what labor is.

"But what does labor mean, according to the idiotic system of compulsions which we playfully call ours? Labor means this—ever so many people do what they don't want to do in order to be compensated for the loss of their self-respect. I refer to money.

"In other words, a laborer and a slave both do what they don't want to do; but a laborer gets paid for doing it, whereas a slave does it freely.

"What a fine specimen of our heap-big sub-moronic supermechanized hyper-unworld's non-mind!"

Another day he said: "Call this a free country? Compulsory education!"

2

There was talk that the army might raise the age limit for enlistment. I rowed in Central Park. I was already a great walker; I became a greater one. I was in good shape when it happened. On May 7, 1942, two days before my thirty-eighth birthday, I was sworn in on Governor's Island. That afternoon I reported to Penn Station, where a train full of civilians took me to Fort Dix, New Jersey. For the first time since my Boy Scout days I slept in a tent. Five days later I went to Camp Shelby, Mississippi, on a troop train.

There was a great deal of martial music blaring from every quarter when I arrived. The base was immense, with sixty thousand men on it, the training was arduous, there were few women to be seen except officer nurses and PX attendants, and the world of books, poetry, and Greenwich Village seemed far away. It was therefore pleasant to learn, one day, that someone had been asking for me, another soldier who had seen my name posted among the new arrivals. We became friends. We met at night and wandered far from our company, battalion and regimental areas, eating an occasional steak in distant recreation centers and seeing all the movies on the base.

One night, we saw a war movie. It was called *In Which We Serve*, starring Noel Coward, who had also written it. It begins with a ship moving through fog. Rain begins to fall. On the bridge are several officers making small talk about the weather. One of them said: "As the poet says, 'Teeth of the rain nibble the night.'"

I dug my elbow into my companion's ribs and whispered exultantly: "I wrote that!"

It was my good fortune to be with him. Another soldier would have said: "And I'm Napoleon," or something equally devastating. But my friend knew. I was safe and happy. The quoted phrase was from the first line of *Saint in Modern Dress*. If recollection serves, there was also a variation of it. The men are in the water, clinging to a life raft in a downpour. One of them says, ironically or sarcastically: "And the poet speaks of the little teeth of the rain!"

There was another pleasant incident connected with Camp Shelby. Dwight Fiske, on whom I had pressed a copy of *Poems*, and who was a friend of Coward's, was playing in a nightclub in New Orleans. He invited me down. I went, accompanied by two other NCOs who had earned weekend passes. The nightclub was in the French quarter; years afterward I was told it was owned or run by the man whom Marjorie Spencer married. A table was waiting for us; Scotches reached the table as soon as we did. Our drinking took on an aspect of close-order drill. No sooner were we started on a fresh round when the back-up, or follow-up round, reached our table; at least once that evening there were nine glasses, those in our hands and the rest ranged before us. As for Fiske, he seemed to be playing only for his uniformed guests. He leered and flashed eyes and teeth at us, his fingers dripping or dragging notes. Between performances he sat with us.

3

My first furlough coincided with that of John Cheever. A party was given for us by Dorothey Dudley, registrar of the Museum of Modern Art. Present were Dorothy Miller, one of the curators there; Dawn Powell, Niles Spencer, other writers, other painters. One of the other writers was Loyd Collins, author of a single book, *Call Me Ishmael,* a novel I greatly admired. Although it appeared in the thirties, it is non-political. Hemingway's *To Have and To Have Not,* published later, bears a strange resemblance to it. One of the other painters may have been Arshile Gorky. I recollect picking him up for lunch one day. He pointed proudly to a canvas on the floor, which sagged with sand and paint, and exclaimed: "Is my best picture!" It was he who ran back into his studio to snatch up a brush and apply another stroke to a canvas on the wall, as I have recounted in *Dominick Dragon;* I should add, however, that in the book Gorky has been combined with another painter, Myron Lechay, and I am no longer able to separate one from the other, although their work, being distinctive, cannot be confused.

Miss Dudley's party took place in the fall of 1942. Cheever and I were the first of our circle to show up in uniform, and much was made of us. Everyone, of course, was eager to hear what life in the army was like. We told them. We must have concentrated on the bizarre, because the entire evening is enveloped, in recollection, in a cloud of laughter as well as smoke.

Cheever was particularly effective because of his soft, well-bred manner of speech; although his eyes flashed the astonishment he felt, his speech was in low key. He told about the marvels of policing the grounds, which had nothing to do with police duties or even those of MPs, but consisted of picking up butts and odd bits of paper under the stern direction of an NCO. Perhaps he told the story of the old lady who saw a policing operation in progress and was so touched by the spectacle of poor soldiers scrounging for cigarette butts that she returned with an armful of cartons and tried to distribute them.

I started to talk about mess hall etiquette, but hesitated; Cheever saw what was coming and helped out by making it a duet.

"Pass the fuckin' bread."

"Pass the fuckin' meat."

"What's the fuckin' dessert?"

"Give me a fuckin' light."

Those astonished, flashing eyes, that well-bred, low-keyed voice, now rushing rapidly with mine to a fuckin' crescendo, convulsed our audience, and ourselves as well.

In line outfits, these exuberances passed, the petty thievery and jealous bickerings ceased. The men began to see each other in a new light, the light of combat. The transformation was impressive and moving.

> Solitary the man
> Who, serving under arms,
> No longer knows his own,
> But a host's, alarms.
>
> He has a secret self;
> But neither friend nor foe,
> By his dark deeds of faith,
> That self can know.
>
> Such is the soldier, such
> The man in uniform;

The heights long held from him
His secret self shall storm.

By the end of 1943 I had a collection of poems to which
I gave the title *A Soldier's Diary*. I sent it to my agent, and
Scribner's published it in 1944. Francesco Bianco saw it
through the press for me; William McCleery, seeing the
Scribner ad in the *Times,* wrote me: "It took a war." The
blurb on the jacket was notable; it was written by John Hall
Wheelock.

4

I was in New York that year on a ten-day leave. One day,
while talking about my poetry with Bianco at the Lafayette,
I saw a strange, almost anguished look come over his face.
Addressing no one in particular, he exclaimed: "I am an
exile—I can have no audience!"

What did he mean? I learned, to my astonishment, that
he himself wrote poetry. He had written poetry all his life;
some years before, critically, or in a fit of depression—I
never learned which—he had destroyed the bulk of his work.
But he was still writing poems; Willard Trask, to whom
I showed them, characterized the Italian originals as "a
unique blend of symbolism with classicism, marked by an
extraordinarily subtle music and the utmost purity of dic-
tion." I give one of them here, called *Feather,* in Bianco's own
translation:

Time consumes each word:
time, and poor usage, and a negligent style;

but the Poet invests with grace
noble and base alike, and he gives weight to a feather.

Every word reveals to him its sweetness
as does a woman to her lover in close joy,
who trembles, and smiles, and whispers, 'Ah, never,
for you my youth, my youth must never die.'

Ravished, he notes; and one day, if the Dark
Muse demands it, remembering all, he recalls
those sounds to life; and in an airy frame
of flowers, and marbles, heartbeats and green boughs,

Builds he a garden paradisial,
shining in never-ending spring;
but in that garden none but the desperate may enter—
none but he who has drunk, Dionysius! thy wine.

Ah, why did I not know these things
in my mad April days, my mad, my fleeting April,
which I wasted wandering without rest,
and exiled from the laurel and the rose?

Now that I am become slow at the fierce game of love,
and I lack the poet's craft,
I cannot tell which it is—more cruel,
or more useless—the fire that burns me up.

But steadfast against all hazards, good or bad,
you, Poet, stand! outlasting the long years;
and you smile to the sorry pupil, who is searching for you,
with wet eyes, in the Anthology;

And you call to him, you invite him to that garden,
which he glimpsed once, and hardly hopes to enter.
Let your spring blossom for him, too—
let happiness sing to him in your language.

His light verse does not read as though a foreigner had
written it. An example is the now famous clerihew which
won first prize in a contest in *PM* (the announced subject

was the New York Park Commissioner's arbitrary removal of
the Aquarium from the Battery):

> No one opposes
> Commissioner Moses;
> Even the fishes
> Must do as he wishes.

A poet should be described as well as quoted. Francesco
Bianco was short and spare, with a neat figure. He had blue
eyes and sandy hair which had once been a bright red. He
must have been very handsome as a young man; a photograph
of him which his daughter showed me recently is strikingly
like the Joseph Severn portrait of Keats. There is the same
prominent nose, the same luminous and intellectual quality in
his face, and he shared with Keats a passionate concern for the
craft of verse.

There was a mysterious affinity between them, of affection as well as poetry, for he often mentioned Keats, and
always with tenderness. He was puzzled by the rage of the
reviewers who had dealt Keats such dreadful blows. It was a
recurrent theme with him. In a mixture of astonishment and
indignation he would say: "Why, anyone who read only one
line in his first book—'I stood tip-toe upon a little hill'—
should have known he was a poet." Presumably he did not
know, or had forgotten, the political nature of most of the
attacks.

Surprisingly for a poet, he knew Euclid by heart, and
his son, now my friend in his stead, says there was no
classical problem in geometry which his father could not
solve. He was a skillful chess and card player. And he could
cook. A world of vanished delights is compressed in these
four words. He cooked without fuss—with his left hand, as it
were; and aromatic dishes appeared almost without a break
in the conversation. The shopkeepers of Bleecker Street welcomed him, for he brought not only pleasant Northern
Italian speech into their shops, but a discerning eye.

His last years were lonely and full of frustrations. The

disasters to Italy in World War II oppressed him. His children were married. The death of his wife in 1944 left him the sole occupant of an apartment thronged with memories. I think it also left him without the will to live.

He complained that Margery's Pomeranian, now aged and decrepit, had made him a slave to its whims and needs. One day, he took it to be destroyed. He came to see me after it was done; he looked stricken. He died in 1946, aged sixty-eight. He left a manuscript consisting of twenty-nine poems, fourteen of which he had himself translated into English (I used four of these in *Come Live With Me*). Of the remainder, one was translated by Margery Williams Bianco, and the rest by Willard Trask. I have tried in vain to interest a publisher in a bilingual edition.

5

The leave I have mentioned took place several months after my book appeared. I was able to see a rehearsal of McCleery's first play, *Hope For the Best,* which was produced by Jean Dalrymple, with Franchot Tone in the lead. I met Tone, and his new red-haired wife, who was beautiful and radiant, but who seemed less attractive when she triumphantly exclaimed that he had given her two dozen pairs of nylon stockings as a wedding present. I could not help thinking that other women were unable to get even one pair in that year of shortages and rationing.

I had let John Hall Wheelock know I was in New York, and he invited me to lunch. After introductions to the other editors, he led me into the little library on the fifth floor of Scribner's—a closet really, a word which the producers of *Hamlet* seem not to know the meaning of; they think it means bedroom. The walls were shelves of books; on a table by one of the walls were heaped the reviews of *A Soldier's Diary*. Mr. Wheelock looked in on me once; I had glanced at the books, mostly sets of James, Stevenson, and other noted Scribner authors, and I said, pointing: "A bit overwhelming, don't you think?" He said: "You're one of them now," and left me to my reading. One of the syndicated reviews was, in part, as follows:

"It is not a soldier's diary, or even a diary at all, but it is something more important. It is a collection of 38 short lyrics and one longer poem which seems to me to establish its author as an authentic American poet—not a fake British poet and not a latter-day Heine. Underneath every line there is a feeling of solidarity with the upward social current of the world, but never a hint of propaganda. And there is one great poem. It is called 'Ask Not Where the Townsmen Are,' and it comes close to being the perfect picture of America at war —12 lines of beauty."

I feel I should give them here:

> Ask not where the townsmen are;
> The trains will answer in the night;
> The trains will answer from afar—
> The men are here, but not in flight.
>
> The land unfolds from light to light;
> Between, the land lies dark with dreams;
> The towns troop to the tracks at night—
> America strings out in gleams.
>
> The towns stand silent in the night,
> And lovely, lit by lamp and star;
> The townsmen have gone forth to fight—
> Ask not where the townsmen are.

The review was written by John Selby, who was still the

book editor of the Associated Press. It was one of the last he wrote; when I met him the following year, he was editor-in-chief of Farrar & Rinehart, which shortly after became Rinehart & Company. Mr. Farrar has told me what happened while he was serving with the Office of War Information abroad, but I am not at liberty to disclose it. Perhaps he has written his own memoirs.

I was working for *PM* again when Selby asked me to lunch with him at the Players Club. There had been favorable reports on my life of Marlowe, which my agent had submitted, and while he talked enthusiastically about my poetry, his ambition being, he said, to publish my collected poems, it was his thought that the Marlowe would be best to begin with. I had no sooner signed the contract for the Marlowe than I was asked if I had ever considered writing a life of Shakespeare; after all, he had been born the same year as Marlowe, and their careers were parallel up to their twenty-ninth years. I decided to do it, and resigned from *PM*.

The last story I wrote there, and the last for any news medium except my "profile" of Cummings for *Time,* was entitled "The Case For and Against Ezra Pound." Pound had just been brought back to face a charge of treason. McCleery thought I ought to ask other writers for their views, and there were contributions by Cummings, William Carlos Williams, Louis Zukofsky, Conrad Aiken, F. O. Matthiessen, Karl Shapiro, and Louis Untermeyer. In addition to stating his views, Mr. Aiken called my attention to a matter which, as I wrote in my article, transcended the case of Pound in importance. It was censorship.

Mr. Aiken was editor, with William Rose Benét, of *An Anthology of Famous English and American Poetry,* a Modern Library book. Random House had flatly refused to let him include poems by Pound in a new edition.

I called Mr. Bennett Cerf, who referred me to his editor-in-chief, Saxe Commins. Mr. Commins told me: "Random House is not going to publish any Fascist." He was one of those greatly renowned "great editors" with which the publishing world swarms, and he added: "As a matter of fact, we don't think Ezra Pound is good enough, or important enough, to include. If we thought he was, we might have carried him anyway. We just don't think he is."

I printed his statement. It contrasted powerfully with Mr. Aiken's: "It seemed to me that a burning of the books was a kind of intellectual and moral suicide which we might more wisely leave to our enemies."

There was an immediate uproar. Mr. Cerf took his problem to the readers of the *Saturday Review*. In the end, he backed down; Pound's poems were included.

6

"The Case For and Against Ezra Pound" appeared in a Sunday issue of *PM,* which sold out, I have been told, for the first and only time. The following day, Julien Cornell, Pound's counsel, appended the story to his affidavit in support of an application for bail. He told Chief Judge Bolitha J. Laws of the United States District Court for the District of Columbia:

"In order to furnish the Court with further information about the defendant, if desired, I have appended as Exhibit A, a copy of the only material concerning him which has been published currently, namely an article which appeared in the newspaper *PM* (New York) for November 25, 1945."

Mr. Cornell afterwards wrote me: "My purpose in using your material was to supply the Court with biographical and literary data concerning the defendant which I believe helped the Court to reach a decision."

I should like to end this chapter, as I began it, with Cummings. This was his contribution to the *PM* symposium:

Re Ezra Pound—poetry happens to be an art; and artists happen to be human beings.

An artist doesn't live in some geographical abstraction, superimposed on a part of this beautiful earth by the nonimagination of unanimals and dedicated to the proposition that massacre is a social virtue because murder is an individual vice. Nor does an artist live in some soi-disant world, nor does he live in some socalled universe, nor does he live in any number of 'worlds' or in any number of 'universes.' As for a few trifling delusions like the 'past' and 'present' and 'future' of quote mankind unquote, they may be big enough for a couple of billion supermechanized submorons but they're much too small for one human being.

Every artist's strictly illimitable country is himself.

An artist who plays that country false has committed suicide; and even a good lawyer cannot kill the dead. But a human being who's true to himself—whoever himself may be—is immortal; and all the atomic bombs of all the anti-artists in spacetime will never civilize immortality.

On November 30 Mr. Cornell called at 4 Patchin Place. He explained that he was trying to raise money in order to obtain psychiatric and medical help for Pound. Cummings looked at his wife; she nodded, and he endorsed and handed over a check for a thousand dollars which he had received that morning from Rochester for a large canvas. I happen to know he had no other money. It was before any of those national awards which afterwards made his life easier, as did the Charles Eliot Norton professorship at Harvard and the publication of *Poems 1923-1954.*

Chapter Eighteen

1

John Lamont was the editor at Rinehart whose enthusiasm for my Marlowe had been decisive. He "worked" with me on both the Marlowe and Shakespeare; the said work consisted of taking me to lunch at the Yale Club on Vanderbilt Avenue, where many martinis and Scotches were consumed, so that I barely made it downtown afterward without be-pissing myself, and lost the rest of the day in fog or sleep. Lunches with editors are one of the hazards of authorship.

Mr. Lamont was a kinsman—a second cousin, I think—of Thomas S. Lamont. He was well-read and good company. It was he who suggested that the apostrophe in my title should come after the "s," instead of before it, and while it is true that Marlowe wrote lyric as well as dramatic poetry, singular "muse" would have sufficed. Better still, the title should have been *Christopher Marlowe,* and it now is.

The Muses' Darling was published in 1946. Its title is

from George Peele's *The Honour of the Garter,* 1593, the year Marlowe was killed:

> vnhappy in thine end,
> *Marley,* the Muses darling.

It was a beautifully designed book, with superb illustrations, some of them generously lent me by John Bakeless, who had done a major scholarly work on Marlowe. He and his wife drove me to their country house, which had been closed for the winter, and from it I returned with a box full of cuts and engravings. Mr. Bakeless had also offered to read the galleys with the remark, "I must read the book some time and may as well do it when I can still be of use."

One day, when I appeared at the Rinehart offices to consult Mr. Lamont about the Shakespeare—in reality, to pick him up to go to the Yale Club for lunch—Stanley Rinehart rushed over to me and pumped my hand up and down. He was glad I had come in, he said; he had something to tell me. It was this: "The greatest review ever received by a Farrar & Rinehart or Rinehart & Company book was the review of *The Muses' Darling* in the *Saturday Review.*"

Mr. Rinehart continued: "Of course, we don't expect a book of this sort to have a spectacular sale. But we look for a slow but steady demand for at least twenty or thirty years."

Perhaps at the time he said this he meant it.

"This is the book that I shall give to anyone whose mind I wish to turn toward Christopher Marlowe," Ben Ray Redman had written at the end of his full-page review of *The Muses' Darling.* Someone else had had the same idea and gave it to William Styron. I met him shortly after the publication of *Lie Down in Darkness* at a party given by Elizabeth and Jesse Fillman in their Connecticut country house. It was an immense party, and many of those present were strangers to me. Suddenly I saw Mrs. Fillman, all smiles, coming toward me with a handsome young man in tow.

"Someone wants to meet you," she announced cheerfully, and introduced Mr. Styron. We shook hands. Even if he had only said "hello!" I would have been pleased. What he said was: "I have always wanted to meet you. Your life of Marlowe sustained me in college."

My life of Shakespeare appeared in 1947. Its title was taken from the dedication of the First Folio to the Earl of Pembroke and his brother by the actors Heminge and Condell who had collected the plays, "without ambition either of selfe-profit, or fame: onely to keepe the memory of so worthy a Friend, & Fellow aliue, as was our SHAKESPEARE."

Several months after my book appeared I received a letter sent in care of Rinehart & Company. It was from a professor at Dartmouth College. All that I knew about him was that he was the friend and an early biographer of Robert Frost. He wrote:

> Dear Sir,
> You have written the first biography of Shakespeare that has something akin to the spirit of its subject in the writing. You have demonstrated that research and accuracy need not sterilize the power of being personally affected by what one reads, and that scrupulous regard for authenticity need not destroy the capacity either to make good guesses or to contemplate data and phenomena with amusement. It is a great achievement to write a life of Shakespeare that is not utterly incompatible with the playfulness and profundity of Shakespeare. Seldom does a well placed word and imaginative sentence accomplish more than either of these often accomplish in *So Worthy a Friend*. I feel a gratitude that demands utterance.
> Yours sincerely,
> Sidney Cox.

Although the custom is fast disappearing, in the years when my Marlowe and Shakespeare were published it was still possible to see, over the cash register, or upon the wall, the framed first dollar taken in by a greengrocer, bartender, or other species of merchant. Had I been Stanley Rinehart I would have kept the Redman review and Professor Cox's letter handy, and the books thus noticed in print. I have not observed that the two bestselling novels for which he hoarded his paper are still around. *The Muses' Darling* was remaindered a year after publication, *So Worthy a Friend* ditto.

William McFee reviewed both books in the New York *Sun*. He took me sternly to task for believing that Shakespeare had ever existed; he himself was either a Baconian or Oxfordian, I could not make out which. As for Marlowe, he declared flatly that nothing was known about him. In this review, he let his readers know what kind of nut he was dealing with:

"Norman has published three volumes of verse and he has lived in Greenwich Village for twenty-two years, which shows true fortitude."

I have lived in it twenty more, and perhaps some fortitude is becoming necessary.

2

So Worthy a Friend brought me the offer of a job from Dean Warren Bower of New York University, and a quarter century after I had left it I returned to its classrooms on Washington Square to teach Shakespeare. I taught for three years. The classes were at night; I recall with pleasure that no one ever got up to go when the bell rang, not even the teacher. How young everyone was, how eager, how talented in the reading and acting parts! Many of the students were there under the G.I. Bill.

Antony and Cleopatra was being shown on Broadway, and I took my class to see it. Katharine Cornell had not only invited me to her dressing room after the show, but generously agreed to let me bring a small group of students along.

Perhaps the greatest single act that Shakespeare ever wrote is the last one of this play, the last moving scene of which had its genesis in the death of a queen in Marlowe's *Tamburlaine:*

> Make ready my couch, my chair, my jewels,
> I come, I come, I come.

I had just heard what Shakespeare had made of this, and could not help asking Miss Cornell how she, or any actress, could bear to speak the lines beginning

> Give me my robe, put on my crown,

without being overcome by them.

She laughed as she wiped greasepaint from her face. Her own beauty emerged.

"I'm two hundred years American," she replied; "there's not enough gypsy in me."

The subject of Marlowe's influence on Shakespeare brought me an unusual compliment—with a little persistence. It happened at the MacDowell Colony in Peterborough, N.H., where literary discussions begun at the dinner table sometimes continued into the night. They were most animated when Padraic Colum was at the center of them.

In addition to his own considerable reputation, Padraic —as I reminded him recently—has a unique distinction: he appears to have been the only writer in contemporary annals who was liked by James Joyce and praised by Ezra Pound, who between them have flayed about everyone else. When I first met him, and the talk turned to Joyce, I could not resist quoting a sentence near the end of *A Portrait of the Artist as a Young Man:* "I go to to encounter for the millionth time the reality of experience and to forge in the smithy of my soul the uncreated conscience of my race."

Padraic grinned an Irish grin.

"And to think, Charl-ess," he said, his blue eyes shining, "that I once drank ale, with the man who wrote that, in a pub in Dublin!"

Night after night, as we talked, I observed his seemingly ritualistic way of putting sugar in his coffee. It was a long time before the ritual dawned on me. Elbow on table, staring straight ahead, occasionally glancing down, but with no interruption to the flow of his talk, he dipped his spoon in the sugar bowl. From a heaping spoonful he sprinkled some of the sugar into the left side of his cup, then the right, then the side of the cup farthest from him, and finally the side that was closest. He was making the sign of the Cross.

One night, surrounded by writers and painters—composers seldom took part in literary discussions; they had their own coteries—he began to talk about "a won-derr-full book." He and his wife had not only read it with pleasure—they were using it in their classes at Columbia. It was "the firr-st book" that showed the great hold Marlowe had had on Shakespeare. Some of my fellow "colonists" looked at me.

"What is the name of this wonderful book?" I asked.

"Ah, Charl-ess, you wouldn't know it," he said patronizingly. "It was published in England and has not come out here yet."

So Worthy a Friend had not been published in England; *The Muses' Darling* had. But the more he went into detail the more I was certain he was talking about my life of Shakespeare, and not some other book, unless it was based on mine.

"Is it *So Worthy a Friend* by any chance?" I asked.

"It is that!" he exclaimed. "How did you know?"

"I wrote it," I replied as modestly as possible.

Padraic stared at me as though stunned, then gave his forehead a resounding thwack with the heel of his hand.

"Bejabbers, Charl-ess," he cried, flushed and happy, "if I

had wanted to praise you, I couldn't have done it any better, could I now?"

He could not. The group around us basked in the pleasure of two writers beaming at each other. Molly Colum told me later that Padraic could never remember titles or authors' names. She, too, called me "Charl-ess."

3

I began to go to the MacDowell Colony in 1946, and have spent ten or eleven summers there. The first summer I read proofs of the Marlowe biography and wrote part of the Shakespeare in the Mansfield studio, a cottage in the woods. In the years that followed, most of my books were begun, continued or completed in that studio, and it was there that I wrote almost all of my recent poetry.

The Colony has had a notable history, often told. The grounds consist of some seven hundred acres; scattered over these acres are thirty or more studios which have sheltered numberless writers, painters, and composers, some of them great, many who strove hard to achieve greatness, and the usual percentage of mediocrities. It was there that Edwin Arlington Robinson did all his writing, there that DuBose Heyward met—and afterwards married—Dorothy Kuhns in a romance that was still talked about a quarter century later. The ghost of Elinor Wylie hovered at dusk near her studio door, a psychic poetess assured me; I peered hard to please her, but was not psychic enough to see anything.

The driving force behind this unique establishment was

the widow of the composer for whom the Colony was named. It is a curious fact that I interviewed Mrs. Edward MacDowell for the Associated Press when she was in New York City on one of her concert tours to raise money for the Colony. She was then almost eighty years old, and indefatigable in the cause to which she had devoted her talent and her life. I met her again in the house on the hill which was the subject of one of Robinson's poems. In her nineties, even when blind, she recognized callers by their voices. She was, and remains in memory, a great lady from the American past.

Another curious fact: William McCleery was at the Colony the first summer I spent there. So was Carl Carmer.

Bill was making revisions on his second play, *Parlor Story*. On the side he was writing a story for his young son. He showed it to me in manuscript; I thought it one of the most enchanting, as well as hilarious, children's stories I had ever read. Carl thought so, too. When he left, he took the manuscript with him and showed it to Knopf. Knopf accepted it. Meanwhile, Bill's producer, Paul Streger, came to the Colony to see how the play was coming along and Bill also showed him the story. Back in New York, Mr. Streger mentioned it to Basil Bass, who told his wife, Mary, with the result that the story appeared in the *Ladies Home Journal*. Mr. Bass was Bill's lawyer, and as Bill did not have an agent, he took over that role.

The following year, shortly after *Wolf Story* appeared, Bill and I were once more at the Colony. He showed me, one day, a letter he had received from Mr. Bass. In it was a royalty check for several hundred dollars. Bill was exultant. He let me read the letter, which quoted a communication from Knopf. The gist of it was this:

Mr. Knopf was forwarding the money due on publication day from advance sales, as required by the contract; but, he pointed out, in all his years as a publisher this was the only contract in which the phrase "after deduction of the advance," paid when it was signed, had been omitted. Mr. Bass told Bill that that was Mr. Knopf's lookout.

Some months later, Nancy Wilson Ross had dinner with the Knopfs. She told me that Bill's name had come up in conversation, and Mr. Knopf had said: "His lawyer thinks he's smart, but I can outsmart him. I'm going to drop the book."

Years passed. I did not think *Wolf Story* should be out of print. I showed it around, and finally took it to Jeanne Hale, an agent who specialized in children's books and was, in addition, an executive of the E. M. Hale Company, a giant Midwest publishing concern, which included Cadmus. Cadmus reprinted *Wolf Story*. A few years after that, Simon and Schuster reissued it.

Nancy Wilson Ross was married to Stanley Young, a good poet as well as a playwright. I once went to Philadelphia to see his play, *The Big People,* on what turned out to be its last night. There was a moment—perhaps more than one— when I heard the echo of loud, hysterical laughter, only to realize by swarming silence it was mine; the rest of the audience was mum, like Philadelphia cream cheese. I think New Yorkers would have liked the play, being quick on the uptake; when I saw it, it was not only entertaining but timely. Perhaps it still is.

I rode back on the train with Stanley. I tried to cheer him up, and suggested he stay over on Perry Street and not continue, it being late, to Old Westbury, Long Island, as he intended to do. His response surprised me.

"Listen," he said, speaking unemotionally. "The director has a wife in the hospital with meningitis. Do you think I have troubles?"

He was a pro. So was Nancy.

It was in their house in Old Westbury that I met Elizabeth Bowen, for which I am grateful to them. How gentle, how unassuming, she was, how gentle, how unassuming the truly great are.

4

I found at the Colony, as elsewhere, that those with most talent were also the least pretentious, and that the simplicity of their behavior was matched by generous instincts. I see in this a parallel with really beautiful women, who as a rule are not self-conscious, and are neither surprised nor hysterical when confronted or pursued.

Thornton Wilder had, in extraordinary measure, the non-competitive aura of which I have already spoken, and it was a great pleasure to me to observe how he managed, so effortlessly, to mingle and even merge with twenty or thirty obscure but ambitious younger men and women, some of whom always made it plain that they looked down on everyone else.

One summer there was an elderly woman—I no longer remember what she wrote—who seemed to me to be shunned by the other "colonists." Perhaps she was not witty at the dinner table; perhaps it was her age. But perhaps she wrote intelligible prose or verse. Toward the end of one dinner the cook came out of the kitchen bearing before him a birthday cake. He went directly to the table where she sat. I learned later that Mr. Wilder had quietly made all the arrangements.

I had some interesting conversations with him. His passion was the prose of Gertrude Stein; it was not mine. Still, a woman who could write "Before the flowers of friendship faded friendship faded" cannot be all bad.

Some of the remarks at table were silly enough. One young man who appeared more concerned with his person than his product twittered at dinner: "I couldn't write a single word today!" He looked both pleased and proud. Whether he ever wrote anything I cannot tell; he was neither seen nor heard from again. The self-importance, self-centeredness of some writers interfered with their critical judgment, supposing they had any.

At a cocktail party given by Mrs. George Kendall, wife of the manager, she told us she had been taking a course in poetry at Harvard, driving to Cambridge several times a week. The instructor liked to pass out mimeographed poems which were unsigned. She had one there; perhaps the group would like to have it read. A "colonist" was chosen to read it; perhaps it was I, which gave me an advantage.

Comments came from the audience. They were mainly negative. A poetess who could boast of formidable sponsorship for her own work was vehement against it. Then Mrs. Kendall asked me what I thought. I said that the poem was obviously the work of a very young poet. I could not tell whether the poet was male or female. Nevertheless, if I was correct about the poet's youth, and the poet had gone on writing, he or she would be famous.

Mrs. Kendall smiled. She told us that the poem was by Stephen Spender, and had been copied from one of his early notebooks.

I was fortunate to be at the Colony several times when George Milburn was there. He lived on West 8th Street, and we saw each other in New York as well. He was two years younger than I, and it came as a surprise that he had been born in Coweta, Indian Territory (afterwards Oklahoma, the locale of many of his stories). To praise his work—his clean style and inimitable ear for American speech—is probably superfluous for readers who know it.

I should like to pay tribute to another writer I met at the Colony, and then knew for many years. His name is James Vincent McGee. I thought him the most poetic, the most original contemporary playwright; I read, or had read to me, all of his plays, and even went to Boston to see one of them.

It failed to come to New York, but I do not think it was Mc-Gee's fault. The name of the play was *The Temptation of Maggy Haggerty*. It was—if anything can be compressed into a phrase—an American *Playboy of the Western World*. His wife, Phyllis Love, had a leading role in it. After the show, I took them to call on Cummings and his wife, who were living in a little house in Cambridge; it was when Cummings was giving his famous non-lectures at Harvard as the Charles Eliot Norton professor of poetry.

I remember staying up with Jimmy and Phyllis, and some other members of the cast, to read the Boston reviews. They were all negative, some abusive as well. Again, all I can say is, New York audiences are different, and I think they would have reacted differently to his play.

Phyllis Love was the understudy for Julie Harris in *A Member of the Wedding*. Miss Harris became ill, and Phyllis took her place.

To understand what happened, I must describe Phyllis; but perhaps that isn't necessary, since millions of moviegoers saw her in *The Gentle Persuasion*. I think of Yeats:

> She carries in the dishes,
> And lays them in a row.
> To an isle in the water
> With her would I go.
>
> ... shy as a rabbit,
> Helpful and shy.
> To an isle in the water
> With her would I fly.

There was also her voice, which was soft, musical, and clear.

When Miss Harris put her dukes up and shadow-boxed around the stage, she was the perfect tomboy trying to be tough, and almost succeeding; but when Miss Love played this scene, she was so obviously Yeats's rabbit that a new element entered, of adolescent beauty and vulnerability. The word spread, and the word appeared in print; Miss Harris, after five days and nights of this, rose from her sick bed and declared she would never be sick again. She resumed her triumphant role.

5

Although no one was supposed to return to his studio after dinner—a regulation which was dropped when Mrs. Mac-Dowell died—many "colonists" did, in fact, return to their studios after dark, some to work; and there were occasional parties.

Miss Margaret Widdemer was the soul of rectitude. She was also sociable. From time to time she invited her friends to drop in at night, and one by one they slipped out of Colony Hall to wander down a wooded path to her studio. It was a composer's studio, and there was a stately grand piano in it. We sat on the floor in its shadow, candles alight in the middle, talking like Indians in a pow-wow. Like Indians, we smoked; we also drank.

On one such evening it was suggested by someone, perhaps our hostess, that we recite favorite poems. When my turn came I quoted the poem I had read a decade before in the Carmers' parlor on 12th Street, adding that I did not know who had written it, although I had looked hard and long. Miss Widdemer's voice came from the shadow of the piano, against one stout leg of which she was magnificently propped.

"Why, you damn fool," came her cultivated voice, now a little on the shrill side, "don't you know who wrote that?"

"No," I replied feebly.

"Kipling!"

It was a snort, edged with scorn. Every face I could see in the candlelight seemed to glow brighter at my discomfiture.

Kipling it was; Miss Widdemer told me that he had written a number of poems in the classic manner, all of them good; and so it proved when I went to the Peterborough library the following day. He rose considerably in my estimation. So did Miss Widdemer. I resumed my work in the Mansfield chastened, but wiser.

The window at which I typed framed the woods; it was a large window, and often when I looked out I saw deer in stately procession, sometimes a fox. A brook of birdsong flowed continually over and around the cottage, and once, in a winter month I spent there, a flock of rose-breasted grosbeaks alighted on the snow where I had scattered seed. It was like a descent of paper flowers.

There was a sunken forest, the entrance to which, between two bushes, was not always easy to find. It began as a gently descending trail which turned into a ravine. A landscape of decaying trees bordered either side, but overhead there were green glades and hovering spears of sunlight. Once when I was walking there an enormous owl drifted silently past me, perhaps a great horned owl. Its claws were like grappling hooks. It had descended without sound behind me and now, in an eerier silence, sailed slowly upward with short strokes of its wings, like a rower in air.

6

The Mansfield had a screened porch in the back, and it was there, one summer day, that I observed nature truly in the raw. My eyes went to a web that hung in a corner, about five feet from the floor. That day, there were several heavy strands under it which had not been there the day before. They were like flying buttresses protecting the web, which had sagged under the weight of the spider in its center.

The spider was black and hairy. From its upraised end there protruded a round white object like a ball. The white ball was almost as big as the body of the spider. The spider's eyes held terror in a fixed stare. A fly that had blundered into the screened area of the porch buzzed and bumped its way from one end to the other, seeking an exit; but even when it came close to the web the spider did not stir. It seemed to be in a kind of stupor. It seemed to be waiting. And the terror never grew less in the fixed stare of its glowing eyes.

Suddenly something dropped through a hole in the center of the web and hung suspended three or four inches beneath it. It was a newborn spider. Naked and helpless, but shielded by the flying buttress strands, it dangled, spinning at the end of a silken cord which it grasped tightly with one upward extended limb like a miniature parachutist, tiniest acrobat. At first water-pale, then with a pinkish cast, with the passing seconds it assumed more and more the shape and appearance of a foetus.

Around and around it spun, five or six times; then, as the spinning stopped, it gathered its strength and ascended the cord with swift, nimble, overhead reaches of its needle-thin limbs to where the mother spider waited, crouched on the floor of the web beside the hole. The mother spider's eyes were a blaze of terror. It was as if she knew that through this hole which she had made for its convenience, her offspring would return to her—and why.

Like a tiny mechanical toy the newborn spider entered the web and embraced her. At the same moment it began to take its first nourishment in this world. Less than a minute had elapsed between the birth and the feast when, through the hole so opportunely there, it dropped what remained of the body which had borne it. A gossamer shell, from which the flesh had been gnawed, the marrow sucked, floated down, insubstantial as a shadow, in slow motion. The next moment the new possessor of the web closed up the hole with swift, precise stitches, then crouched over it with bright, suspicious eyes to await new prey.

7

A final Marlowe-Shakespeare story.

One day I received a phone call from a young man who told me that he was a great admirer of *So Worthy a Friend*. He had a project in mind; could he see me to talk about it? I invited him down. He said that he had long dreamed of putting on Shakespeare's plays; now, at last, he had a theater on East 6th Street at his disposal. Would I give a talk on Shakespeare to launch the project?

I told him I would do better than that if he would provide actors and actresses. With some on my left, some on my right, I would talk not only about Shakespeare, but about Marlowe's influence on him. When I called attention to passages and scenes in Marlowe which Shakespeare appropriated and enlarged, the two groups would read alternately from marked copies of the plays. It would not be necessary to memorize lines.

He was enthusiastic. The talk and "dramatizations" were given to an appreciative audience. The young man's name was Joseph Papp.

I did not see him again until January 10, 1967, at a reception of the Mayor's Committee for the New York Shakespeare Festival in Gracie Mansion. We shook hands. When

I told him I could not remember the year of my talk he offered to send me the Festival's "chronology and producing history." Under 1954 I read:

"Workshop presents first production at Emmanuel Presbyterian Church, 729 East 6th Street: An Evening With Shakespeare and Marlowe."

Chapter Nineteen

1

Yaddo was another writers' colony, located near Saratoga Springs. It was a region I knew fairly well, since I had friends in nearby Burnt Hills—Martha and Claude Bailey, aesthetes and apple-growers. Martha was another sister of Elizabeth Fillman.

At the first of my two sojourns at Yaddo I became aware of a man watching my reception, from the handing over of the keys to my room and studio, to the occupation of my room. Finally, he caught me alone. He had apparently been sizing me up all this time; and introducing himself—he was a writer from upstate—he pumped my hand up and down and behaved in general like a welcoming committee of one, although I was already ensconced.

I assumed that he, like the others in residence, knew of my expected arrival. Still, it was overdone; I was not all that important, though not without ability. I soon learned why he had singled me out. My appearance at that juncture, he told me, was particularly agreeable to him, for by my arrival I had evened the opposing sides—or camps, I should say—into which the colony had divided, the homosexual contingent having had a majority of one until that lucky moment. Later, I also learned that his behavior was due, in part, to his own bitterness; he was not very prepossessing, being on the short and sullen side, and he had been left out of the parties forever going on in mansion rooms and studios.

I wrote Cummings about the occasionally glimpsed spectacle of young men in ardent pursuit of the arts and each other, and he replied: "Let me suggest that you purchase (don't rent) a *made-to-measure* chastity girdle from your local blacksmith; & be sure to throw away the key when same arrives."

My recollections of Yaddo in 1952 and 1955 tend to merge. I do not even remember what I wrote, if anything; I have some watercolors I painted there. The recollections range from snow on the ground to a flight of bees; a thunderous roar brought me to my studio porch in time to see that black cloud pass with the noise of a hundred planes.

As for the snow, I was having a ritual tea of official welcome with Elizabeth Ames, the director, in her charming cottage. Sunlight came through the open door, and as I delicately balanced my cup and saucer on my knee, in strolled her cat, dragging a dead grouse by the neck. The cat laid the grouse at her feet, then gave her an upward and sidelong glance of modest pride. Miss Ames was only slightly embarrassed. She may have said "Naughty," but without conviction. She placed the grouse outside her door, and received a reproachful glance from her cat. I had seen a brace of grouse perambulating in the snow; and now there was one.

The only event I can fix with certainty in 1952 is a reading, at nearby Skidmore College by Dylan Thomas. He seemed very pleased when I conveyed Cummings's greetings to him, and spoke with enthusiasm about their meeting in Patchin Place. We stood in the center of an admiring circle of intense and goodlooking young women, Skidmore students, including one who, I was told, "was looking after him." He was neatly dressed, earnest, and sober. He began his reading with a prose passage about poetry in one of his notebooks; it was just as melodious as the poem that followed, made so by that most extraordinary of reading voices.

A year later, he was dead. Cummings remarked when returning a book he had borrowed from me called *The Great Migrations*, which has a chapter on the strange and immense stampede of lemmings: "I knew a couple of lemmings once. Nobody could stop them. On they rushed—straight ahead—and plunged in. Hart Crane and Dylan Thomas."

2

William Slater Brown was at Yaddo one of the times I was there. He was the original sideburns man, having worn his long, wide, and luxuriant from the twenties on, at least. He had a great shock of hair, too, which always looked slept on, on one side. He was remarkably goodlooking in a shaggy sort of way, with very expressive eyes which were a help in his story-telling. He was a good story-teller. To a certain extent, he told stories the way John Cheever did, pitched in low key; but when he was through, and saw the effect his final line or word had produced, a single, surprised, almost apologetic ghost of a chuckle fluttered away from him, his attractive eyes having rolled upward and somewhat sideways to peer from beneath shaggy brows at the company.

One night, over coffee in the dining room, Brown, who

had said little, lowered his head almost to the table; or so it seemed, for the first thing I knew, his head was coming up, and his eyes were peering sideways. "Imagine," I heard him say, "Coleridge sinking slowly down into one of his opium trances, and then coming up with the word *eftsoons!*" The final word, on which his voice expired, reached all with extraordinary force, and as our laughter subsided, from across the table came the single, ghostly, deprecatory chuckle. "Eftsoons" occurs before Coleridge, however; I have come across it in Chaucer, Holinshed, and, the other day, in Spenser.

Each time, there were about twenty writers and artists in residence. I remember one composer; at least, he was there in that capacity: Leonard Bernstein, who created a stir on his arrival by going straight to the phone in the West House and calling Shelley Winters in Hollywood. "Shelley dear!" Oh, those theatrical conversations! There were several. He simply had to have her in something or other he was staging at Brandeis. Later, he charmed everyone, including me. Of the writers I recall only three in addition to Brown and the up-state one, all women: Dawn Powell, the poetess Jean Starr Untermeyer—who then or later, on learning I admired George Moore, presented me with a first edition of *Memoirs of My Dead Life*—and Mary Britton Miller, author (as Isabel Bolton) of several remarkable novels.

As at MacDowell, there were long and intense discussions about art and literature, in a vast Gothic Victorian room where hung full-length portraits of the founders in massive gold-leafed plaster frames. I remember that one of the "new critics," as they were then called, held forth at great length, to the assembled company, about the role of critics in relation to the work of T. S. Eliot; they were priests, he said. When I could stand it no longer, I remarked, loud and clear: "Well, if they are priests, let them go frock themselves." The women in the room were the first to laugh, after a stunned silence; and then the others joined in, not least myself.

Dawn and I were glad of the opportunity to get away when the Baileys asked us to dinner. They came for us in a

Jaguar sedan, in which they also brought us back. One morning, after a late night at the Baileys, I failed to see Dawn at breakfast, and wondered if she was all right; finally, that evening, when I asked her what she had been up to, she replied: "Oh, I took a good, long, hard, brisk nap!"

3

Yet another writers' colony.

In the spring of 1957 I flew to Los Angeles to meet Betty and Carl Carmer in order to drive back with them and see the country. They were staying at the Huntington Hartford Foundation on Rustic Canyon Road, a scatter of houses like a little village at the bottom of the canyon. Each house was a studio, complete with bedroom and kitchen. I was given one. The refrigerator was stocked so full each day that it was almost impossible to get an ice tray out for a drink. There were canned hams, curled bacon in tins, chickens, cheeses, pâtés, frozen vegetables, frozen desserts, containers of milk, oranges in heaps, and bananas in clusters. It was all like a miniature supermarket. Yet these provisions were only for lunch or snacks; breakfast and dinner were served by the management.

I called Norman Perry's daughter, Joyce, who was living in Hollywood with two beautiful daughters of her own, a divorcée trying to make a living writing for the screen. I told her to bring a big paper bag. They make them big in California—she brought one that stood three feet high. We filled it; the next day my refrigerator was restocked, and the process was repeated.

I called Guy Endore. Guy didn't need the food, but we loaded his car anyway.

The passing years, and in particular those of the witch hunts in the entertainment world, had not passed him lightly. But when he became animated it was as though time had stood still, and we were back in the villa in Golfe Juan. He was critical of *The Genteel Murderer*, my biography of Thomas Griffiths Wainewright. He thought that I had passed up wonderful opportunities to fictionalize. I was overjoyed when, a few years later, the Book-of-the-Month Club took his fictionalized biography of Dumas, *King of Paris*. It is a brilliant *tour de force*.

Twelve years after our meeting at the Foundation, Guy and Henrietta Endore came to dinner on East 11th Street. We talked about Morris White, who had died. Both said they were grateful to him, for it was White who had introduced them. After they left, my wife and I sat there with the same thought. We had had so many literary guests, so many discussions! That evening with the Endores was unique—we had conversed. I said I would write a thank-you letter to them for a lovely evening! This was in the fall of 1969; less than a year later, Guy was dead.

The Foundation was set in an idyllic spot. Deer, smaller than the eastern variety, nibbled contentedly even when cars approached; mockingbirds sang tirelessly. The flora was as unlike the East as could be imagined. Every time I stopped to admire a flower like an enamelled gem, I saw that it had a rubbery stalk. I used to walk up and down the winding canyon road; one morning, near the top, I came face to face with a man and a dog. I stared at the man, and the dog stared at me. The man was elegantly dressed for walking. He was bareheaded, with a foulard scarf in his open collar. I could tell by his expression that he was used to stares; he knew that I knew who he was. He was David Niven. We said "Good morning" to each other, and went our opposite ways.

While I was able to walk about the grounds, it was impossible to walk into town. People without cars are arrested.

One day I drove with the Carmers to the Henry E. Huntington Library at San Marino; Carl had some research to do on the Mormons for the book he was writing. The library was a repository of original Americana; it also had other things. We inscribed our names in the register, and a librarian asked me if I would like to see some of the treasures; I could pick my period.

I was escorted below; steel gates were unlocked. For several minutes I held in my hands three little notebooks that had belonged to Shelley. I have described my sensations in a poem, and will not repeat them here.

I was a guest of the Foundation for three weeks. Two good writers I met there stand out in my mind: Wright Morris, a man of natural and unlimited charm; and another who was the vainest and most temperamental of the whole ilk, and whom, unfortunately, I was to meet again at the MacDowell Colony, where an innocent remark by me sent him from the table in a rage; afterwards, his dinners were delivered to him in his room.

There was a third writer about whom I will now tell. This one gave me a quizzical, then searching glance when we were introduced; later, I learned why. He not only knew who I was; he also knew that I was the friend of a man whose current wife had once been his. He appeared anxious to get me alone.

"Would you like to know why I'm no longer married to her?" he asked. He was eager to tell. I let him.

There had been many arguments between them; one day, exasperated beyond measure, he attempted to strike her. She beat him to the punch with a right cross which landed squarely on his chin. It knocked him cold.

"That was the end," he concluded with a nervous laugh.

I could have told him a thing or two about her, but refrained.

Why certain men marry certain women—and vice versa, if the truth be told—will always remain a mystery. My friend was the gentlest of men; with a few drinks in him, he was one of the most entertaining. His wife was humorless. She was stocky and stolid; had she been a man she would have fought as a welterweight. She had the build for it; also, apparently, the punch. What every virtue, every grace women are supposed to have, she lacked or hid from view.

I once brought her flowers. An impartial observer—there was one with me, Barbara Perkins, who afterwards married George Gamow—might have thought I had slipped her a hand grenade. My friend's wife stripped the paper from the bouquet like an assault, and looked around frantically for a receptacle. In a corner, on top of a cabinet, stood a dusty vase. Clutching the bouquet, she got up on a chair and thrust it, waterless—with the rubber band still around it—into the vase.

Her second marriage proved durable, all the same.

4

At last the Carmers were packed. But we did not head east. We drove north along the Pacific to San Francisco. We stayed at the Palace in that most beautiful of all American cities for five days. From San Francisco we drove to Virginia City, Nevada, where Carl had an appointment with Lucius Beebe. Beebe had a dog that was bigger than the dogs at the Grand Ticino. He was too big to get off the floor, which he covered like a mountain range. Perhaps he was hand-fed. He gave us a dull-eyed look without raising his head; if he had, all of us would have jumped, for he would have been like a lion rousing himself. When lunch was over, Beebe poured from a bottle of cognac that had a neck a yard long, an impressive sight.

Virginia City was a ghost town which Beebe owned and ran. San Francisco was built by those who had struck it rich there. The houses, fallen into ruin, once had silver doorknobs; now the only silver to be seen was silver dollars, the currency of the town. For a while it was a pleasure to tote them around, but they soon became a nuisance. Saloons and shops were run by men in the costumes of the Old West, and women wandered around dressed to appear no better than they once were. A man with a shoe fetish would have been happy there: shoes were laced or buttoned high, under trailing skirts.

Beebe stood us to martinis in one of the bars, plunking down silver dollars like pennies. The glasses were goblets, filled to the brim. We emerged to become spectators at a wedding on horseback; the minister was a woman. The bride was a wistful-looking girl; someone whispered she was an heiress. The bridegroom worked on the dude ranch where they had met. He looked ornery. The ceremony did not take long. The wedded couple turned their horses' heads and galloped down the dusty main street to whatever awaited them together. It may not have been much for that wistful girl.

We drove to Salt Lake City where Carl did some research in the Mormon museum and library. We stayed at the home of Sam Weller, owner of the Zion Book Store, and his pretty wife. I received a special dispensation to smoke; we gave ourselves dispensations to drink. Carl took me to the hill where Brigham Young had pointed to the future site of Salt Lake City and called a halt to the long trek from Nauvoo, Illinois, where the Mormons had built a beautiful town of stone houses before being driven out. I saw Nauvoo about two weeks later; I also saw the jail at Carthage, Missouri, where Joseph Smith and his brother were shot. Brown stains were still visible on the cell floor.

From Salt Lake City we headed for the Grand Canyon

whose days, after millions of years, appear to be numbered. At a place called Parry's, in Kanab, Utah, as we were buying box lunches, we saw a movie company making a western, whose reign seems endless. We ate in an airy lodge on the southern rim of the canyon; afterwards we walked around and peered down, marveling at the corrugation of mountain and air. But engineers shall inherit the earth.

We drove to Santa Fe, where the Carmers had friends, and where I made some, but it did me no good at the time. The altitude—eight thousand feet—and three martinis for lunch when we arrived knocked me on the head. I became lethargic, lost interest in everything, and missed all the parties because I did not wish to, or could not, rouse myself to go out. The opposite phenomenon happened to Carl. Usually calm, unruffled and deliberate, in that rarefied atmosphere he fairly zoomed about, saw everyone, and ate and drank everything. All I wanted was to get out of there, and awaited his pleasure, which turned out to be calm, unruffled, deliberate, and slow.

One afternoon, our hostess, Mrs. Lippincott, the wife of the curator of the Indian Museum, took pity on me. While everyone else was at a party, she came into her guest house, where I sat forlorn, expressed sympathy, but insisted I get up; she would take me on a field expedition if I did. She was handsome and forceful; I did as I was told. We drove in her station wagon to the outskirts. I felt weaker than ever in the open air. She pointed to a wall; it was all that remained of a stone fort the Indians had built against the Spaniards—to no avail; all had been massacred. Strewn everywhere, if one had the patience and strength to probe the soil, were Indian artifacts, of stone, quartz, and jade.

Even in my lethargic state I could not help finding them. I unearthed half a dozen tiny quartz arrowheads, used by the Indians to bring down birds; in New York, I gave them to the children of my friends. I repaid Mrs. Lippincott's kindness. I found a piece of jade about four inches long, smooth to the touch. Jade had been sacred to the Pueblo Indians, and she said she knew an old chief who would cherish such a specimen. I gave it to her.

There were two poets living in Santa Fe, with whom I later corresponded. Winfield Townley Scott told me he had made some remarks about Cummings as a New England poet when introducing him at a reading at Brown University that Cummings had liked. He promised to send them to me, which he did, and I used them in *The Magic-Maker*.

Witter Bynner, who appeared to me to be as handsome as his early portraits on Knopf jackets, had met Ezra Pound as a young man; two years later, when I was working on Pound's biography, I wrote to Mr. Bynner, who supplied me with important information about Pound's earliest publications in this country, in the placing of which he had had a hand. He also sent me his recollections.

So some good came of my visit to Santa Fe. Shortly after we left that beautiful city of adobe houses, I recovered. Suddenly we were all very gay. A sign read: "Tucumcari, N.M." Betty, pointing, said: "Tucumcari enough for three."

Dark skies over Texas, and tornado warnings, made us take a diagonal route; even so, it took us all of one day to get through the Lone Star State. I saw Dalhart again, with a green haze over it. On we rushed, north and east, through flatlands, deserts, marching forests, and prairies. The vastness of the country as well as its beauty was awesome.

The Carmers had a guide book full of stars. We advanced upon the states like a friendly patrol, one at the wheel, one on lookout, the third poring over the pages. Our routine never varied. We stopped around five and took adjoining rooms. From his room Carl ordered a bucket of ice. Everyone showered and we drank until it was time to eat. It was always steak. Carl's friendly smile and distinguished air helped when he gave our orders.

"May I tell you," he would say, "how we like our steaks done? Just run around the stove with them!"

One morning, in an ill-starred motel, I joined the Carmers in their room. I was packed and ready; Betty was packed and ready; but Carl was still standing before the mirror in his calm, unruffled, unhurried way. Betty became impatient. She stamped her foot and said:

"Carl! Have you your wits about you?"

Carl turned his head slightly.

"You mean you and Charles?" he asked.

Chapter Twenty

1

That fall, I went once more to the MacDowell Colony, to work on my biography of Cummings. I remember the October morning when the first Soviet sputnik began to weave the net in which our globe is snared. I thought then, and think now, that if I had been President Eisenhower, I would have congratulated the Russians—but added that consultations were in order before other satellites were launched. In the light of events, I believe my conclusions on a leafy New Hampshire road are as good as those which afterwards prevailed, and which have filled the sky with tin cans stamped "U.S." and "U.S.S.R.," not all of them innocuous.

Cummings believed there were other objects in the sky, but approved of those. On one of my visits to his farm he suddenly appeared in the doorway of my room, where I was reading by the light of a kerosene lamp. It was two o'clock in the morning; I had retired perhaps an hour before. He said quietly: "Would you like to see a flying saucer?" I leaped up and in pajamas and flopping sandals followed him to the roof.

It was a flat roof with a railing around it, like a captain's walk. Mrs. Cummings was peering through a telescope. Cummings pointed to a bright point in the sky and handed me a pair of binoculars. Another pair was in his hands, and for several minutes we all stood in silence while the dews of the night and the fog that comes on little cat feet crept over my sandals.

It took me some time to adjust the binoculars and find the object at which I was to peer. I saw in the sky, perhaps five or fifteen miles distant, a bright light cradled in a shallow arc shaped like a cigar-end. In the August night thronged with stars the light blazed like a planet; from time to time it whipped downwards a few feet, then soared to its former position. It not only whipped to the right, but sometimes to the left, and this gave me the idea it was some kind of balloon, perhaps a meteorological balloon. I was foolish enough to suggest this, and received for my pains incredulous, star-lit looks from both Cummings and his wife, who thereupon returned to their saucer-gazing, disregarding me. After a while, the dews and the damp had gone above my sandals, and I decided to call it a night.

I did not know until the next morning that I had gone to bed disgraced. The subject came up at breakfast, and I stuck to my view: it was a meteorological balloon.

Did I agree it did not look like any balloon I had hitherto seen?

Yes—I had to agree to that.

"There you are," Cummings said.

I had the feeling that he and his wife were seeing me in a new light—Charles obtuse, Charles a little slow on the uptake. And this unnerved me. I said: "What do *you* think it was, if not meteorological instruments?" Cummings replied: "Little men from another planet."

He looked at me pityingly, she scornfully.

"They've come to see about all the mischief we're hatching, and to make their own plans."

Over the eggs, over the marmalade, over the coffee, so delicious in the morning air of New Hampshire, the discussion went on, or rather, discourse; I no longer dared to comment, and merely listened. I did not know what to make of it then, and know even less now.

In 1957, I had known Edward Estlin Cummings thirty-two years. That year, Mr. R. L. De Wilton, my editor at the Macmillan Company, asked me what I planned to do next. Mr. De Wilton was tall and bore an extraordinary resemblance to the portrait of Yeats which hung in the Macmillan reception room at 60 Fifth Avenue; he was also the best-read man I had met in the publishing industry. I wanted to please him, but I had made up my mind—or so I supposed—to write no more biographies. I told him I had done enough of them; and anyway, there was no one else I cared to write about, with the exception of Cummings.

The name slipped out without premeditation. Mr. De Wilton asked me if he could present the idea to the Macmillan book council, and I asked for time to think it over. I also had to know if Cummings would cooperate.

I called Marion and told her there was something I wanted to ask Estlin, and she invited me to tea. In the course of the next hour or so, after we had talked of everything else, she said: "I thought you had something to ask. Now what can it be?"

Cummings said: "Perhaps Charles wishes to write a book about me."

Quite startled, I exclaimed: "That is it—if your Highness will permit!"

He replied, with a bow: "My lowness will be honored."

It was Marion's turn to exclaim: "But, Estlin, what about your privacy?"

Turning to me, Estlin said: "Go ahead."

This was the genesis of *The Magic-Maker*, published in 1958. The frontispiece, in color, was a self-portrait by Cummings. It is now at the University of Texas. The book no sooner appeared than the Macmillan Company received a violent attack on it, which Mr. De Wilton showed me. It was written by Mrs. Cummings.

2

The book about Cummings was followed, in 1960, by a biography of Ezra Pound.

All my biographies have been about writers. In the case of Cummings, it was about a poet who was also a painter. *The Genteel Murderer* was about a painter who was also a writer—and poisoner. My first step in writing these and the other biographies was to read or reread the works of the writer who was my subject. In the case of Pound, the task was formidable: from predilection or necessity, he had published a great many things in "little magazines," of which there were at one time a great many. There were also some obscure books.

I learned that Professor John H. Edwards, of the University of California at Berkeley, had done a "preliminary checklist" and set out to find it; I was going to the MacDowell Colony to work on my book, and wished to have it with me. There were no copies to be had. I wrote to Professor Edwards; he replied that he had only one, and could not spare it. Two booksellers whom I had consulted came up with a copy each; I bought both and sent one to Professor Edwards so he could have an extra copy of his book. He thanked me. In the same letter he asked if I was planning to write a biography of

Pound (I had been told he was planning one, too). I replied I was; I also told him that I understood he knew where Mary Moore was to be found; I would be grateful if he told me, but would understand if he did not. He did not; but he knew. She is the lady of Pound's durable dedication.

From 1909 to the present day, Pound's *Personae* has borne the following inscription:

> This Book Is For
> MARY MOORE
> Of Trenton, If She
> Wants It.

I do not know why I did not ask Pound if he had her address, for he not only had it, but hundreds of letters, as I afterwards learned, had passed between them from the time their engagement was broken in 1907 to the very year of my book. It may have been because of the reply he sent to one of my queries, an effort on my part to pin down the source—two sources, really—of a line in his most beautiful poem, *Envoi (1919)*—"Tell her that sang me once that song of Lawes."

Lawes was easy enough—he was Henry Lawes, who had set Waller's *Song* to music in the seventeenth century. What I innocently asked him was, "Who sang you once that song of Lawes?" Pound replied from Rapallo, "Your question is the kind of damn fool enquiry into what is nobody's damn business," which bore out what William Carlos Williams told me about his former schoolmate and friend: "One trait I always held against Ezra was that he'd never let you in on his personal affairs." This, to be sure, may be admirable; but I was dealing with a text, and exegesis could have been useful.

I set out to find Mary Moore in a roundabout way. I went to Trenton, believing that I would be able to spot her name in the files of that city's newspapers. Surely, I thought, starting out, even if she had married, her maiden name would be cross-indexed (a pun of sorts, as it turned out). I did not find her name listed, and wrote my book without meeting her. Considering how much I was able to get in about other people, other matters, this was a source of regret. One day, while visiting my friend Charles Woolley on Jones Street, I regretted it aloud. Woolley, a plain speaker—like Miss Widdemer, in fact—exclaimed:

"Why, you damn fool, you've known her nephew for ten years!"

"Who is that?" I asked, startled.

"Sam Moore."

It was worse than that—I had known his wife almost twenty. The reader is not likely to have forgotten her maiden name: Chandonette Norris, my colleague on *PM*.

I called Sam Moore. He sounded amused. I did not ask him why he had not spoken up: I asked him for his aunt's address. She was now Mary Moore Cross, and a widow. I wrote to her; she replied the same day and invited me to her home in Montclair. Thus it was that I met another lady from the American past, who has become a cherished friend.

Mrs. Cross showed me her copy of *Personae*, sent her from Kensington while she was still Mary Moore of Trenton. Under the dedication Pound had written: "In attestation whereof I do set my hand and sign." The sign was Pound's "dragonfly" signature, formed by the letters "E" and "P" intertwined. I must confess that as I held the little brown and gold volume, Pound's first published book of poems, sent in 1909 to his first and lifelong love, I was greatly moved. It was not only because I was sitting with Mary Moore in the parlor of her frame house, under the amused gaze of her bright, gray-green eyes; it was also because I felt reverence for the man who had written that book, and many of the books that followed it.

I had brought with me a copy of my *Ezra Pound*, and I now inscribed it in her presence "To Mary Moore Cross of Montclair," with appropriate sentiments; later, I sent her the revised edition, in which I tell of her first meeting with Pound, of the young poet as suitor, their engagement made and broken, her marriage, and his, and of the letters that flowed from him to her through the years.

One of the letters, written in 1908 when he came back from Spain, or 1910, when he made a brief visit here before returning to his long exile abroad, assures her she is "a great comfort in this foreign land where no one else speaks anything intelligible." He is trying to confirm a date: "Tell me where I'm to meet you to do what on Wednesday if it is Wednesday." And he chides her for being critical of a poem he had sent her. "Your asking 'What if there isn't any last verse' is very like asking a painter 'But what if there isn't anything to go in the lower left-hand corner of the picture?' It's really more a matter of what nine out of eight things one won't put in."

Recently, Mrs. Cross and I were at the Whitney to see the Eakins exhibition. She said, apropos of this letter: "Maybe if I had not been so critical something would have happened."

3

Between my last-named books—the last one hopefully my last biography—I began to have long talks about the happenings in the sky with George Gamow.

"Will spaceships be of any military use?" I asked him.

"Spaceships with or without men? The Intercontinental Ballistics Missile is a spaceship. But now they talk about sending men up to gather information, and I think it is nonsensical, because instruments can do it better."

I said: "But a man in a spaceship would not only control and observe the instruments, he would bring something else to bear—his own perceptions, for example."

He did not agree.

"No," he said, "instruments can do it much better than man. Suppose there is a satellite or moon rocket, and you have the instruments in it, then we can balance it so the flight is very smooth. And the photographic camera will photograph stars, moon, and what not. You can have the instrument space only as big as this table, dozens of very fine instruments which photograph and register everything we want to know, and will not mind being burned when entering the atmosphere; whereas a man would mind being burned. So that you have a lot of trouble to put a man on, without any advantages, because the instruments can do it much better, and all the observations made by instruments can be sent by radio."

"Instruments really do that?" I could not help asking, for I had never really thought about it.

"Why, sure," he said. "Well, look; I'm going for a trip to Japan, and suppose you've never been there and you're interested about how it looks. So you wait for me to return to tell you about all the things I have seen. But it is not necessary because I can write it. And I don't have to return—I can phone you. By instrument. When Marco Polo traveled in China, then it was essential he should return to Italy to tell the tale, because there was no mail at this time and no long-distance telephones. When Columbus sailed to discover India and discovered America instead, he had to return to Spain to tell the tale. But if he had had the radio he could have stayed over there and given the information in a broadcast. You see, return is really only important if you have no other means of communication. But we have."

"All the same, they are planning to send a man up and bring him back."

"Oh, sure. But this is just from the point of view of a strict adventure. Look—suppose you want to investigate the top of Everest. Well, you know, you finally climb to the top; but these two people, the Englishman and the native, were so exhausted they could barely get back. But if you really want to know the information about the top of Everest, well, send the airplanes, fly by and take all the photographs, make all the measurements, do anything you want. The ascent of Everest was not a scientific achievement—it was just a sport. And in the same way, I am sure, people will fly in space and land on the moon."

"But surely some of the people who fly to the moon will be scientists?"

"If they're foolish enough."

"You mean scientists will be satisfied with the photographs, measurements, and so forth, without going there?"

"Yes, because they would know all that would be accurate. You remember Piccard. [I remembered him well.] Piccard flew in his gondola in the stratosphere and made some measurements of cosmic rays. Nobody ever does this now. They send rockets and balloons with instruments. The same situation goes for the moon. I would love to land at the moon and make a walk around and pick up some rocks and come home and say to my friends, 'Last week I was walking on the surface of the moon.'" He paused to chuckle, then added: "I would like the trip as a person, but not as a scientist."

Three years later I found that Dr. Gamow still did not set much store on the manned satellite race; he was, in fact, quite contemptuous of it. To emphasize his contempt, he asked for a sheet of paper and put it into writing for me:

"It is my opinion that all of today's hysteria about SPACE-race, SPACE-agency, SPACE-men, SPACE-chimpanzee, etc., has no scientific or practical value. It is just an expensive political football. I hope that U.S. government, press and citizens will get soberer about it, or else it will cost many billions of thrown-out dollars. George Gamow. June 10, 1961."

Chapter Twenty-One

1

George Gamow was an amiable Russian-American with sun-tanned face and square, earth-colored hands. Six foot three, and weighing 220 pounds, he could make ordinary furniture appear Lilliputian; my wide upholstered chair was all but lost to view by his bulk, and creaked whenever he made a gesture or reached for a cigarette or a drink. He spoke with an accent, breathing heavily between phrases, and though very earnest was never far from humor. When I asked him the color of his eyes, he replied "Dair-r-ty green," and a huge smile expanded slowly from behind his bifocals. His hair was a yellowy blond and of a silken softness. "Russians don't get gray hair," he told me. No, I thought; they just give it to us. It was a warm day, and he had left his jacket in the hotel where he was staying. A checked sports shirt was wide open at the neck and a cowboy belt with a silver buckle encircled his ample waist.

"I got the belt at Los Alamos when working on the H-bomb," he said.

Dr. Gamow (pronounced "Gahm-ov") was the originator of the quantum theory of radioactivity which led to the hydrogen bomb. He was born in Odessa in 1904 and was graduated from the University of Leningrad in 1926. A talk he gave in the U.S.S.R. Academy of Sciences in 1932, on the apparently inexhaustible energy radiated by the sun and other stars, brought him an offer from Bukharin—at that time a high Soviet official—to direct a controlled thermonuclear reaction project. Bukharin wanted to know if nuclear processes could be given direct application; Gamow thought it would be extremely difficult and declined. Other reasons may have influenced his decision. He came to the United States in 1934, and the following year joined the faculty of George Washington University, where he taught theoretical physics for twenty-two years. He became an American citizen in 1939.

Although he is best known as a physicist, there are those who maintain that he was just as great a biologist, mathematician, and astrophysicist. When I asked him once if he had any hobbies, he exclaimed: "Hobbies! Writing books. During the last twenty years I wrote more books than I read." Among his better-known titles are: *Birth and Death of the Sun, Biography of the Earth, Atomic Energy in Cosmic and Human Life* (which bears the dedication "To the hope of lasting peace"); the famous *Mr. Tompkins* series, science made simple—or fairly simple—for the layman; and *One, Two, Three . . . Infinity, Biography of Physics, Gravity, A Star Called the Sun,* and *A Planet Called the Earth.* He has also written such learned papers as "Theory of Radioactivity and the Structure of the Atomic Nucleus," "Relativistic Cosmology and the Origin of Chemical Elements," "Theory of the Synthesis of Proteins and the Transmission of Information by Nucleic Acids," and "Theory of Thermonuclear Reactions in Stars."

At the home of William McCleery in Princeton I met a

young professor of astrophysical sciences. His name is Edward A. Frieman. Before dinner, as we talked together in a corner with cocktails in our hands, I mentioned Gamow's name. Dr. Frieman's eyes lit up. "You know him?" he asked, making no effort to hide his excitement. "When I was a student," he went on, "reading Gamow's papers was like," he fished for an apt illustration and came up with it, "like your reading Keats and Shelley!" he exclaimed.

2

I knew George Gamow for more than a decade, or ever since his marriage to Barbara Perkins, whom he met at the New York branch of Cambridge University Press, one of his American publishers. Year after year, beginning in 1958, whenever the Gamows came to New York from Boulder, Colorado—which took place once, sometimes twice, a year—I sought to get from him answers to some of the anxious questions of this atomic age. He spoke, as a rule, with calm detachment. For him, it went without saying that "This is how things are," or better still, "This is what we know." Purely metaphysical speculations did not seem to interest him; at least, whenever a question tended in that direction, he looked blank or lit a cigarette to cover a deprecatory silence. Yet always lurking was his sense of humor, expressed by sudden twin gleams behind his bifocals; by grins, groans, chuckles, words drawn out, and gestures.

Like a good many others, I had been wondering of late what all the new discoveries were leading to.

"From a scientific point of view," Gamow said, "to a better understanding of the world around us. From a practical point of view, to better living."

"But won't certain values disappear which the race has always considered as of some importance?" I asked.

"No," he replied. "Take the value of good music. Now we have hi-fi development of electronics, which permits you to play high-fidelity records; the value doesn't disappear. The primary thing is increase of knowledge, and there are two secondary ones. One is the peaceful use of scientific discoveries, another is military uses.

"The discovery of atomic energy is very interesting purely scientifically, but it has a lot of peaceful applications—cheaper power, and things like that. As for the military applications, they always went together. When Nobel discovered nitroglycerine, then it was interesting from the chemical point of view to see what came from metastable molecules. It was useful practically, to blow up rocks, to bore tunnels. And it was used militarily. Every discovery has these three things: scientific, peaceful-practical, and warful. Engineers look at it, businessmen look at it, and see it as improving the way of life; and the military look at it."

"I'd like to know how the scientist feels when he sees the knowledge he has gathered taken over by the military," I said. "Or doesn't he care?"

"Oh, I don't think that has anything to do with science. It is a purely political thing. I mean, this is a question how the scientist is placed as a politician, and so on."

"But, isn't that a contradiction?"

"Well, during the war, the physicist and the engineer were building the atomic bomb. Now they build hydrogen bombs. Okay—let's not call it political; let's call it patriotic. If it's necessary to do it, it's necessary to do it. The evil is in the fact that different nations have economic or political contradictions and they fight it out, and one has to develop weapons to fight with. The weapons are developed from scientific discoveries. These discoveries have gone far ahead of man's ability to deal with himself. But that has nothing to do with the people who make the discoveries, although they may help to convert them to military use."

I said, "Some atomic scientists believe there is present danger of annihilation from radioactivity, but others say no. For example, Teller says no, Urey says yes."

He replied: "Well, Teller says no in respect to the tests of the bomb, our exploding one or two hydrogen bombs during the year. But if you ask Edward if all the bombs now in storage would be exploded, certainly the answer would be if it does not destroy life it will affect it harmfully very essentially all over the globe. If war starts, hundreds of bombs, thousands of bombs, would be exploded within the first few days, and this is certainly the case. And this is the only hope, that both governments realize it is the case. Because certainly we know that if you use all the arsenal bombs on Russia, the fallout in the atmosphere drifting back will cripple the United States; and Russians know—I don't know what their stocks are, but they are now about the same—it will come back to them if they use theirs on us. But, logically, if you are sure you're not going to use the bombs, don't make them! Suppose you are afraid a burglar will come into your house or apartment when you are asleep, and you arrange a high explosive trap and have the button near your bed, and you know if you push the button, if you hear somebody, it blows up and kills the burglar; but you also know it kills you. So there's no point in pushing the button, no point in building the whole arrangement. And it's being built. But on the other hand, of course, if *we* did not have the bombs, *they* would have attacked. So you have the overpowering possibility on one side—and you have the possibility of defending yourself here even if it costs you your life."

Did he really think war was possible?

"It has happened before, may happen again. Probably will."

This particular conversation with Gamow took place before the test-ban treaty, which has not prevented China and France from testing in the atmosphere, and the Soviet Union and the United States from testing underground.

Did he think the so-called secrets of the universe would be largely explained through instruments before men went all over space?

"Oh, sure—certainly."

"What do you think will be found in the end?"

"Well, we know the universe pretty well now."

"Do you think we'll find out in this infinite universe where the stars are streaming?"

"Oh, no, you don't go beyond your planetary system—there is not power to go beyond it. You can explore the system of planets—Mars, Jupiter, Saturn; one can fly by Saturn and make some pictures of the ring, etcetera; but I don't think one will ever fly to a nearby star."

"You mean that we will always be barred from the galaxies?"

"I think so. You see, it takes to the nearest galaxy, if you travel with the maximum possible velocity, velocity of light, it takes two million years. So if you want to go to Andromeda, the nearest galaxy, and come back, it will take four million years for the round trip." His high-pitched, cultivated Russian voice rose. "The travelers should take wives and breed children for the two million years, which is a much longer time than humanity has existed, have a supply of food for this time—ah, it is fantastic!"

"Well, isn't it possible that if men discover how to fly to a galaxy they will discover how a man will not age during such a flight?"

"Sure, one can deep-freeze a man probably, and send him up frozen, and after a couple of million years in time defreeze him."

Now my voice rose.

"But whom will he talk to when he gets back—the language will change in all that time!" I exclaimed.

"Certainly, that's the point."

"Well," I commented, "in a way, I'm glad to hear there's a limit."

Gamow made no comment, but I thought I detected a perplexed stare through his bifocals.

I tried another angle.

"What is the scientist really interested in so far as the moon or Mars is concerned?"

He thought a moment.

"Well, lots of things. First, it will be nice to get photographs of the opposite side of the moon. Then it will be interesting to measure the magnetic field of the moon, and to analyze the material from which the moon is made, to see if it is closer to granite or basalt or other rocks. In the case of Mars, it would be interesting to collect some of its vegetation and see if it is built from the same proteins, the same chemicals, as ours."

I knew that this subject was a specialty of his, so I asked him to explain it further.

"Proteins are made from twenty amino acids—I should say, a selected twenty. Yes. Chemists can make hundreds of amino acids, but there are only twenty which form the proteins. So the question is whether the vegetation on Mars is made from the same twenty amino acids as on the earth, or maybe different ones."

"In all life on earth you find these same twenty amino acids?"

"In all life—plant life, human life, everything—the same amino acids out of thousands which could exist or that could be synthesized. And the question is, whether the vegetation on Mars has the same twenty. Or maybe a different fifteen or a different forty. But if it is the same twenty, the same building blocks from which terrestrial life is formed, this would throw interesting light on the origin of life. But there is one very sharp problem in all this.

"You see, amino acids have the so-called mirror property or symmetry. The same amino acid can be left-handed and right-handed. Now, all life on earth is built from left-handed amino acids. You and an oak tree and amoebas are all left-handed. Now, when chemists produce amino acids in a lab, fifty percent are left-handed and fifty percent are right-handed. So if life originated chemically, there should be two kinds of lives—left-handed and right-handed—and each would be poisonous to the other in the sense that they would be acting against each other."

Here, he began to laugh at the thought which had struck him.

"In the sense," he went on, "that if you eat a steak from a right-hoofed cow, it will poison you! And if a right-hoofed cow eats left-bladed grass, it will be poisoned! Actually, however, all plants and animals have left-handed symmetry, because everything is left-handed in life. So that maybe in the beginning there existed two kinds of life, left-handed and right-handed, and they kind of fought a battle, and what we call left-handed won, and right-handed was destroyed."

I brought him back to Mars.

"Do you really expect to find plant life there?" I asked.

"Well," he replied, "according to the observation of Mars, there are some green patches which show the same color as mosses do. They are probably mosses. In the summer on Mars it is greener, in the winter on Mars it looks brownish. This shows seasonal change of color."

I asked: "If some of that plant life is plucked off from Mars and examined in a laboratory would it show amino acid structure?"

"Oh, sure," he replied.

"And you'd be able to determine if it is left-handed or right-handed?"

"Yes."

"Is there a possibility that the vegetation on Mars was somehow transferred from the earth?"

"Or the other way around—it doesn't matter."

"But from some common source?"

"This would not be excluded. But most probably life on Mars originated independently from life on earth. And for the Mars mosses, you see, one question is: is the development from the amoeba, from the early forms of life to you and me, is it more or less a random process? If you repeat it, you may get something entirely different. Suppose man, *homo sapiens,* were to develop independently on Mars. Would he also have two hands and two legs, and a head where it is supposed to be, and so on? Or would it perhaps be entirely different?"

"Didn't some scientist say that if man developed on another planet, the chances are that he would have legs and arms, and a head on his shoulders, and eyes in the head so that he can see out?"

He did not reply as expected.

"You can imagine—you can construct engineeringly— quite a lot of differences," he said. "For example, the automobile has four wheels, but it's not necessary—bicycles have two wheels, tricycles have three wheels, and locomotives and tanks have even more wheels, plus treads on tanks. So the fact that automobiles have four wheels is just a product of Ford or General Motors. If you think hard, you can imagine other forms.

"Suppose we have another race—another human race, I mean—on some planet, and it developed airplanes; would those airplanes look like ours? Maybe they'd look entirely different. Is the present form of airplane, with cigar cabin, two wings and a tail, the only type of flying machine? For example, the Convair firm built the Delta plane triangular, without tail. This is different. So maybe we can do still more different things. The question is how much the development is forced by necessity and how much it is just mere chance."

"Still," I ventured, "it does seem to me that the best place for a head is on the shoulders."

"I don't think so," he said. "Probably better in the middle —it would be more symmetrical."

He pointed to his silver buckle.

"You could stand on your head without difficulty."

There were two little gleams of pleasure behind his bifocals.

3

On September 14, 1966, in the Penguin restaurant on West 9th Street, between the cocktails and the hors d'oeuvres, I handed him four questions, expecting him to pocket the slip of paper and answer at his leisure from Boulder. To my surprise, he insisted on answering them at once and took out his fountain pen. The questions and answers follow:

"Do you still think space race is nonsense?"

Between "think" and "space" he inserted the words "man in," then wrote "Yes" at the end of the line.

"What is the real meaning of the race to the moon?"

"Political competition."

"Is there a military objective involved in the moon race? The other planets?"

"No!" [In conversation afterwards, he modified this by pointing out there were military gains involved in perfecting more powerful rockets.]

"Has anything been learned that instruments alone could not have told us?"

"No!"

He was never happier than when he was reciting Russian poetry. The following is his own translation of a favorite poem, *Cadet's Prayer*, by Lermontov, which he sent me from Boulder:

King of Heaven!
Save me
From tight uniforms
As from fire.

From drilling
Excuse me,
In parades
Don't put me.

And let, in the riding ring,
The voice of Alec
As rarely as possible
Disturb us.

One more prayer
I ask you to accept:
Next Sunday
Give me permission
To be late.

I, Almighty King,
Am good if only because
By excessive asking
I will not trouble you.

(Gamow's note: *Alec*, riding master; *late*, to church.)

That night, in my apartment on East 11th, Gamow cheerfully recited—it was a ritual with us—hundreds of lines from Pushkin and Lermontov. But soon cheerfulness vanished. Abruptly, he protested that writers, and humanists generally, were not interested in the scientific disciplines—were, in fact, hostile; scientists, on the other hand, were often well-versed in the humanities.

I said that if I wrote a poem, it made no difference whether anyone liked it or not, except perhaps to me. But when a nuclear physicist made a nuclear bomb, the end result could be that scientists and humanists alike—and everyone else—might be blown to bits. He looked very thoughtful as he reached for another cigarette.

Perhaps he was sad over a division which was not even the scientists' fault, but a result of the use to which scientific discoveries are put. He was also, as it turned out, seriously ill. He did not live to see Borman, Lovell, and Anders reach the moon and send back to earth's inhabitants the pictures of a tiny ball rolling nowhere until time must have a stop. I think he would have liked that particular combination of instruments and men. Just before he died he had the following dream, which he dictated to his wife with whose permission I use it:

> This is a dream that is really quite serious and is based on brain work I have been doing for decades. In the dream I am the Hero, the man who supposedly has died and who has had a revelation about the hidden problems of cosmology, particle physics, topology, basic mathematics, etc.; at the same time I am the Spectator.
>
> The setting is somewhat oriental—not a part of a pagoda or temple, but a very beautiful room with glass doors opening on a pond or pool with water lilies, reminding me a bit of the hotel in Marrakesh which gave on a pool at the back. The man who is living there and who is I (or I, Sir Arthur Eddington, my image) has long been trying to find out the connections between the unproved theories of mathematics.
>
> This Hero, apparently dead and dressed in a grayish robe of some sort, whose funeral I have been watching and who has joined the spirits of such great scientists as Newton, Galileo, Einstein, etc. (who after they died learned the ultimate truth of all this) has found out that the Truth is really very trivial, of the type of the Klein bottle solution, the Mobius surface, the left hand returning from far out in space as the right hand, etc. And yet at the same time he has come to the realization that this is complete science.

(In *Mr. Tompkins Inside Himself,* Gamow has described a Mobius surface, made by pasting the two ends of a strip of paper together after giving one of the ends a half turn or twist. "Unlike other rings," he wrote, "which have two sides, an inner and an outer one, it has only side. You cannot paint this ring white on the inside and black on the outside . . . if you begin painting it, starting from some point on either side, and go all the way around, you will find that the entire ring becomes the same color." As for the Klein bottle, it, too, is a one-sided surface, being entirely closed, and lacking an inside or outside.)

It is curious to reflect that while poets see the metaphor in all things, physicists likewise see the universe in metaphorical terms: for what are their formulations but scientific metaphors? If they remain apart, perhaps it is because poets are content to leave things alone.

At the McCleery dinner in Princeton, which took place in 1962, Professor Frieman, the young astrophysicist previously mentioned, defended the decision of the United States to explode a hydrogen bomb in the Van Allen Belt, despite protests from scientists abroad, notably British ones. I added my indignant voice. "Leave the universe alone," I declared, perhaps with more warmth than was called for; perhaps not.

Professor Frieman was one of a number of physicists who served as advisers to President Kennedy. He assured me, and all those at the table, that in their view no harm could come of the explosion in space. The Van Allen Belt was merely dislocated, and is now somewhere else, and something quite different.

There was another warm discussion at the dinner. When I stated, quite simply, that I wished Russian and American scientists would leave the moon alone, Dr. Frieman could not understand it. I said that the moon ought not to be turned into a scientific laboratory. It belonged to the peoples of the earth, to whom it was an immemorial symbol. I do not know what the other guests thought; Dr. Frieman's look was like Gamow's perplexed stare. I invoked Cummings, who wrote:

> I'd rather learn from one bird how to sing
> than teach ten thousand stars how not to dance.

Chapter Twenty-Two

1

Marion Morehouse Cummings was warm, hospitable, generous—like her husband, in fact. One day, at their farm, she said to me: "We happen to have a complete set of Johnson's *Lives of the Poets,* and Estlin and I have talked it over and decided that you would most appreciate having those books, and so we are going to make you a present of them."

I stood transfixed. The word "set" can hardly convey the magnitude of the gift, for it was a first edition in sixty-eight calf-bound volumes, and included the works of the poets whose lives Johnson had written. The next thing I knew, both she and Cummings had begun to wrap the individual volumes in old newspapers; it was a present, they said, and I was not to help.

Together, they once went to my bank; I had gone to the hospital for an operation. But first Cummings had set out by himself, to deposit $550 to my account. He had difficulty with the forms, and had to enlist her aid. Why $550? He had intended to deposit $500, but raised the ante on the way.

Mrs. Cummings had long been known as a skillful portrait photographer. Her studio was on the floor over her apartment. What was not so generally known was that she had also mastered a species of still-life photography of extraordinary sharpness and beauty. Cummings finally prevailed on her to publish an album, and it was he who made the selection. It was called *Adventures in Value—Fifty Photographs by Marion Morehouse, Text by E. E. Cummings*. She told me that he also had written an introduction, but that she had suppressed it; "too much praise in the family," she said.

He did not live to see the beautiful book on which he had worked with his wife. But he saw the proofs at the farm, and made final corrections in his text; and there, that last summer of his life, he had painted, and added to the poems which he habitually put in a folder for inclusion in future collections. He had also "done his chores," like Sam Ward, who had been the overseer of his farm, and is the hero of "rain or hail" in *1 x 1*. He asked me once if I would like to help with one of them, but that I didn't have to do it—in fact, he advised me against it. I said, I was there, I would be glad to be useful, and so we set out, first picking up a shovel and pickaxe in the barn.

He needed another swill-hole.

Shouldering the tools, we marched several hundred feet downhill from the house, and came to a clearing. First, he scratched a large circle in the bare ground with the pickaxe. Then he began to swing it. He worked for about ten minutes, without very perceptible results, then asked me if I would like to try it. I leaped up from my squatting position and seized the pickaxe, raised it high, and brought it down hard. It made a slight dent, but mostly it bounced. Cummings, who was watching me closely, said not to do too much at one time —it was better that way. At the end of ten minutes I was glad to resume my squatting position and watch him.

We took turns throughout the afternoon. Little by little, the pickaxe did its work, followed by the shovel, and at last there was a depression in the earth of perhaps a foot. Then we heard Marion calling us; it was time for tea.

"Now you know why we call it the Granite State?" Cummings asked cheerfully as we trudged back.

2

Over the years a custom had grown up whereby I came to sit with them when they were going to the farm. Surrounded by suitcases and boxes of books and manuscripts, we drank coffee and waited for the car that would take them to the airport. They usually left early in May and stayed until October. In May, 1961, when I arrived, he was having a hot cereal as well.

"I am trying to fatten him up," Marion said.

She went to the kitchen to bring me a cup, and Cummings, bending toward me, whispered: "All I ask is one more year."

He was sixty-six. The years which had brought him honors and awards no longer sat lightly on him, for they had also brought illness. He looked, and felt, unwell.

Something else was making him uneasy. He asked me if I thought he had done the right thing by including everything previously published in *Poems 1923-1954*. I gave the answer that was best for him. I said that he had solved the problem of a collected volume in the best way possible for a poet. His smile was radiant.

Mrs. Cummings returned. He became cheerful with talk

about the farm and the prospect before him of writing and painting through the summer and autumn. The city he had loved and celebrated so often in his poems had become for him, as for others, increasingly harsh and discordant. He said to me: "We were lucky—we both knew New York when it was enchanting."

In 1962, on the eve of another departure for the farm, when he and his wife were dining with me, he said: "I need at least another hundred years to finish my work." My wife told me afterwards that he said it twice. He seemed better, and ate heartily: roast beef, Yorkshire pudding, roast potatoes and asparagus, with a good Châteauneuf du Pape (he had brought an even better wine); and for dessert, trifle. Once, when he began to refill the glasses as I was busy carving, Marion said mockingly: "Aren't you making yourself rather too much at home?" He smiled at everyone with a far from abashed look in his hazel eyes, and said: "My blush is one of pleasure, not embarrassment."

He came alone to another dinner; Marion was visiting her mother in Connecticut and had asked us to see that he was properly fed. He was. He seemed delighted to renew acquaintance with acorn squash, which he remembered from his boyhood in Cambridge as "Indian" squash. The plate was hot; when he put butter on it for the squash, it began to ooze away from him, and he remarked that trying to get at it was like pursuing peas. We had as fourth a young woman of considerable charm. In his note of thanks to my wife he asked: "Who was *la belle dame avec merci?*" She was Karen Termohlen, now Mrs. Thomas Meehan.

That cold spring the Cummings left later than usual for the farm. The last time I saw him was on May 23, when he and his wife came to tea. His last note to me—perhaps the last he ever wrote—reached me on Saturday, September 1. It was an urgent request for a dozen canvas boards. He enclosed twice as much money as was necessary. All that day, after mailing them, I thought of phoning him to say they were on the way. On Sunday he had the cerebral hemorrhage from which he died.

3

A few minutes after nine on the morning of September 3, Willard Trask called me. He had just heard a news broadcast. Cummings was dead. Other friends called. Silent crowds had begun to form at the entrance to Patchin Place.

I called the farm; Mrs. Cummings answered. She was surprised that the news had reached the world so quickly. She told me that on Sunday he had been chopping wood. It was very hot, and she suggested that he stop. He took the axe to the barn, sharpened it, then put it away, "like the good woodsman he was." Then they returned to the house, and he went upstairs to change. Waiting for him, she heard what she thought may have been a call for help, followed by a fall. Later that day he was taken to Memorial Hospital in North Conway, New Hampshire. He died at 1:15 a.m. Monday without regaining consciousness. His ashes were buried near his father and mother in Forest Hills Cemetery, Boston, after a private service. He would have been sixty-eight years old in October.

Anne Barton was in Maine, visiting her son, Peter Girsdansky. She wrote me: "The day Cummings died was a beautiful early fall day. For some reason I had a strong compulsion to go to Madison, N. H., and had Pete drive me over. I stopped in to see Mrs. Sam Ward, who was, and is, a dear friend of mine. She was crying. I said 'Cummings has died!' She told me it was so."

Mrs. Cummings did not ask me to the service. When she returned to New York, my wife and I went several times to Patchin Place, and we had her to dinner, with Padraic Colum as a fourth. I observed again his ritual with coffee spoons.

One night, among people who had known Cummings, Trask said: "Everyone is talking about what a great poet we have lost; but I have lost a dear friend."

A curious thing happened around this time.

My wife and I were spending a weekend in Connecticut with Harold Loeb and his wife, Barbara. Loeb told us there was a program in honor of Cummings on Camera Three, a CBS Sunday feature. We watched it.

The man who presided sat behind a table on which reposed a copy of *The Magic-Maker*. There were two others present: William Slater Brown, who had been imprisoned with Cummings in France, as related in *The Enormous Room,* and Glenway Wescott. Brown and Wescott had copies of *The Magic-Maker* in their laps.

Loeb said: "Very strange." I let it go. But my wife said: "She hates you."

I looked at her in astonishment. She was referring to Mrs. Cummings. I refused to believe it. The truth is painful. CBS had asked her whom she would like to have on the program, and she had suggested Brown and Wescott. She afterwards told me that she was furious with Wescott for criticizing *The Enormous Room*. Perhaps she was also furious because he had praised *The Magic-Maker*.

4

Despite some coolness between us, in April of 1963 she asked me to edit the poems Cummings had been putting together before he died. Her own title was *74 Poems;* it turned out there were only seventy-three when I went through the manuscript and found a duplicate. She now agreed with my suggestion that *Last Poems* would be better as a title, the more so since many of Cummings's collections had been designated by the number of poems they contained.

I worked on the manuscript from April 19 to April 24. It was arranged in a manner Cummings himself might have followed: three sections comprising "Portraits," "Impressions," and "Sonnets." Mrs. Cummings sent the manuscript to Harcourt, Brace & World.

During this period we were constantly on the phone. I told her, one day, that I was revising *The Magic-Maker* and had written a new last chapter. She asked: "Are you going to let me see it?" I said: "Of course." Nevertheless, I was uneasy.

I went to see her, and left the new chapter. She read it. She called me up. She was furious. She objected violently to it. She objected most of all to the confidential remark Cummings had made to me in 1961 while waiting for the car that was to take them to the airport.

I tried to explain it was the kind of remark a man would make to his friend, but not to his wife, who might understandably be upset. I also said that I had not given her the chapter for her editorial judgment or advice, but as a courtesy.

I went to Patchin Place to pick it up. She said that Cummings had not made the remark attributed to him in my chapter, and that I was a liar. I stood up to go and asked her for the manuscript. She wished to keep it a few more days. "You must have another copy," she said. She added that if I persisted in publishing the chapter as it stood, she would withdraw all permissions on quotations from his work and letters.

I said: "Marion, would you really do that?"

She replied, coldly: "Yes."

I told her I would not change my chapter, and left the

apartment I had known for thirty-five years, where I had lived with my first wife, and Cummings with his third. A few days later I received from her, in addition to my manuscript, a note in her own hand: Harcourt, Brace & World had found it "too difficult" to set up *Last Poems* in my arrangement, and the book had been given another format, with the original title restored (minus one digit).

A year or two later, when I learned of Mrs. Cummings's illness, which proved to be fatal, I tried several times to make up. I was not successful. The presents, including pictures, I had given her and Cummings over the years were sold to strangers by her administratrix, as were the inscribed copies of my books. I saw some of these at the Gotham Book Mart; it was a disheartening experience.

5

Number 28 of *73 Poems* is about me. I am happily able to supply complete exegesis on Cummings's text.

Over the years I reported three incidents to him. The time span between the first and third is approximately twenty-five years. In writing the poem he merged all three into one. It is curious—to me, at least—that he concentrated on the third, while making use of the site of the second, for he had not only been told the incident of the overcoat, he had read it in the manuscript of *Dominick Dragon*.

When I came to Greenwich Village, apartments were plentiful. Landlords would paint an apartment and give a tenant the first three months free. Rental agents handed prospective tenants lists of addresses and great bunches of keys. I found myself, one summer day, on the top floor of a building on 8th Street. As I tried to fit a key into the lock, another door opened and a man in a rustling dressing gown emerged. He assumed that I was going to be his neighbor, and after a few exchanges, while I continued to fumble with the lock, he asked me what I did. I replied that I wrote poetry. "Just think!" he exclaimed. "A real poet!" His voice now came from below, for he was on his knees kissing the palm of my hand. I fled, leaving a dangle of keys in the unopened door.

On 9th Street, on a day in fall, a man approached me to ask—as I supposed—for a dime. As I began to reach into my pocket, he asked me instead if I had an overcoat to spare. Yes, I had; I took off the one I had on and offered it to him. He took a step back. He looked at me suspiciously. Was I making fun of him? I said: "Try it on; if it fits, it's yours." He permitted me to help him on with the coat. It fit. It was an old Brooks Brothers coat; we stood there admiring its cut. "Good luck," I said, and walked away. Then I turned to look at him. He was peering at the way it hung, front and back, as though before a triple mirror in a Madison Avenue shop.

One winter night, on Seventh Avenue near 13th Street, a well-dressed man asked me for a quarter. It was bitter cold. I said I did not have any change and handed him a dollar. He stared at me in the light of the street lamp; then tears filled his eyes, and I hurried on.

> "right here the other night something
> odd occurred" charlie confessed
> (halting)"a tall strong young
> finelooking fellow,dressed
>
> well but not over,stopped
> me by 'could you spare three cents please'
> —why guesswho nearly leaped
> out of muchtheworseforwear shoes

'fair friend' we enlightened this stranger
'some people have all the luck;
since our hero is quite without change,you're
going to get one whole buck'

not a word this stranger replied—
but as one whole buck became his
(believe it or don't)by god
down this stranger went on both knees"

green turns red(the roar
of traffic collapses:through
west ninth slowly cars pour
into sixth avenue)

"then" my voice marvels "what happened"
as everywhere red goes green
—groping blank sky with a blind
stare,he whispers "i ran"

One day recently—it was winter—I walked to Washington Square. When I arrived I thought: "Snow transforms the present into the past." The little park, usually crowded and littered, stretched white and empty from Waverly Place to West 4th Street, transformed into what it was when I first came to live in Greenwich Village, an illusion heightened by the few low buildings that remained. It was impossible not to think of Cummings, for he used to go there to feed the pigeons, knowing that most people despised them. In my mind I saw him again, standing in the snow, a knitted watch-cap on his head, scattering bread from a paper bag with his ungloved hand.

Index